MARY DOUGLAS

MARY DOUGLAS

Understanding Social Thought and Conflict

Perri 6 and Paul Richards

berghahn
NEW YORK · OXFORD
www.berghahnbooks.com

Published in 2017 by

Berghahn Books

www.berghahnbooks.com

© 2017 Perri 6 and Paul Richards

Library of Congress Cataloging-in-Publication Data

A C.I.P. cataloging record is available from the Library of Congress

British Library Cataloguing in Publication Data

A catalogue record for this book is available from the British Library

Printed on acid-free paper

ISBN 978-1-78533-422-1 (hardback)
ISBN 978-1-78533-561-7 (paperback)
ISBN 978-1-78533-423-8 (ebook)

Contents

Figures

ॐ Preface

Mary Douglas was one of the most important theorists working in the social sciences in the twentieth century. Her writings are now increasingly widely cited. Her commitment to anthropology as a disciplinary home remained important to her. Yet when she turned to the politics of risk and to the history of religion, she engaged respectively with political science, sociology, institutional economics and psychology, and biblical studies and literary criticism. From the 1980s, the titles of her books and articles indicated her determination to address the social sciences generally, yet in her late work she sought to renew her anthropological commitment to deep ethnographic engagement, albeit using secondary sources. Her work was always philosophically rigorous and she engaged repeatedly in debates with analytical philosophy about meaning.

Her most important contributions were to our understanding of what institutions are and how they work, to explaining styles of human thought, and to understanding the fundamental basis of social conflict and its containment. The theory she developed is quite unlike any other major tradition of social science explanation, such as Weberian sociology, rational choice theory, structural-functionalism, Marxism, poststructuralism, historical institutionalism or ethnomethodology. Drawing from Émile Durkheim's legacy, while avoiding many of the difficulties in Durkheim's own work, she developed an innovative account of the extent to which, in their most elementary forms, human social institutions can vary. She set out a novel account of how this variation can result in clashes and conflict, and of how these can be modulated so that social organization can be viably sustained. Her theory provided a powerful and very distinctive set of microfoundations for understanding causation, and therefore a rich set of resources for social science generally. No student of anthropology, economics, political science, sociology, development studies, religious studies or philosophy of social science can claim to understand the basics of their domain without some familiarity with the issues she addressed.

Yet, today, even in disciplines to which Douglas made her major contributions, surprisingly few scholars know her work in detail or of why it continues to matter for the future of the social sciences. There is only one major book-length study of her work (Fardon, 1999). Her name rarely appears in the chapter headings in standard student guides to the great theorists of institutions, social organization, culture, human thought, consumption or conflict. Even commentaries mentioning her work tend to cite just a small part of it, without recognizing the larger design. The overall scope and importance of her work has been missed, we argue, because arguments that seem puzzling when considered on their own only convey their full weight when seen in the context of her lifelong project. It is our aim in this book to bring out that overarching programme. We show that although Douglas ranged widely over regions such as Africa, North America, Europe and ancient Israel, and over topics as varied as consumption, violence, poverty, environmental dangers and religious belief, her entire oeuvre forms a single arch.

Our book offers a key to tracing out the spiralling rather than linear trajectory of Douglas' intellectual ambitions. We show that her arguments constitute a novel and sophisticated understanding of the dynamics of the amplification and the attenuation of dissension among and between human groups. How and why people generate dissension and work to reduce it is a theme present at the very beginning of her work, and it is to be found in her last public utterances. Social conflict was the most abiding of her abiding concerns. Our aim, therefore, is to bring out the as yet only imperfectly understood scope of Douglas' work as a major theorist of human conflict.

In each chapter's concluding section, we bring out the significance of the arguments examined in the chapter for understanding clashes between people, institutions, groups and ways of organizing. Each chapter develops the argument about how, in Douglas' explanation, people come to classify other people in hostile ways, whether by way of blame, ridicule or revulsion, how they sustain their own motivation to work together against those they classify as enemies, but also how people can then be reconciled, and how classification can accommodate acceptance and toleration. All these processes, Douglas came to argue, are the dynamic work of institutions. By institutions, she did not mean formal organizations such as the agencies of the United Nations. Nor did she mean the formal institutions that are the subject of much political science such as voting rules or legal powers and duties. Rather, Douglas argued that what really matter are the informal institutions of everyday social organization. (practice)

Rectifying the widespread lack of understanding of Douglas' project is not just a scholarly or antiquarian duty to provide a more complete history of theoretical ideas in social science. Something more fundamental is at stake. In many disciplines of the social sciences, approaches to explanation and interpretation have reached an impasse. Even the very idea of rigorous explanation of social phenomena is held, by some, to be in doubt. In this book we show that Douglas' arguments about the foundations of social science provide ways to overcome the impasse that should be taken seriously across all the disciplines that examine human affairs. As conflict – not least with regard to expressions of religious belief – proliferates in an ever more crowded world, Douglas' arguments matter because they point to a very distinctive and potentially highly fruitful way beyond this evident explanatory road block.

Both authors knew Douglas and benefited greatly from her advice. We have both sought to examine hypotheses derived from her theory in our own empirical work. In very different ways, therefore, we have each developed empirical operationalizations for concepts that are central to her theory. Briefly in Chapter 2, but in a little more detail in Chapter 5 below, we use some of our own studies to illustrate some of the ways in which her theory can be developed and applied in empirical research, and to show how the approach has influenced a variety of disciplines. Both of us initially grew interested in Douglas' work because it offered fresh understanding of the empirical puzzles that preoccupied us. We both found the well-known frameworks of, for example, rational choice, Weberian theory, historical institutionalism and poststructuralism unconvincing in their explanations of deep intransigence and of eventual reconciliation, of contrasts between those with very long and those with foreshortened memories and future time horizons in their decision making, and of why people's beliefs and preferences emerge, change and persist or wither at the particular moments that they do. Looking for more satisfying approaches, we came to Douglas' arguments in different ways. Richards was already persuaded of the relevance of Durkheimian notions, but was looking for a way to overcome the limitations of Durkheim's own arguments. By contrast, like many non-anthropologists who have used Douglas' work, 6 was initially attracted by Douglas' typology and only later came to appreciate the greater power of the Durkheimian causal engine that underpinned it.

For 6, those puzzles were initially ones of domestic public policy in the UK and later of public administration, although more recently his work has focused on the processes by which distinct styles of political judgement are cultivated in different periods in governments, and his work has increasingly examined decision making in governments on matters of foreign policy and international relations. In a large-scale study with Bellamy, Raab, Warren and Heeney, for example, he developed designs for examining the implications of Douglas' arguments about the ways in which informal organization in contrasting interprofessional relations in public services cultivates quite different ways of thinking about dilemmas between imperatives to protect client confidentiality on the one hand and to share data on the other (6 et al, 2007; Bellamy et al, 2008). Turning from public administration to policy decision making in the heart of governments and using archival sources, he challenged one of the classics of the study of decision making, Allison's (1971; Allison and Zelikow 1999 [1971]) *Essence of Decision*, by showing that Douglas' theory could be operationalized to code for contrasts in social organization and in styles of judgement between the Kennedy administration, and Khrushchev's and Castro's regimes in October 1962 in ways that would offer fresh and more powerful explanations than mainstream approaches. Because that study examined only a particular moment, he went on to examine whether Douglas' theory could explain change in political judgement over time, again using detailed archival sources from several postwar British governments. His work showed that Douglas' theory provided more satisfying explanations of differences in process within cabinets (6, 2016a), in trajectories of change in the life of each government (6, 2015b), for which Douglas' machinery can provide precise statements of causal mechanisms (6, 2015c) in vulnerability to unintended consequences (6, 2014b) and in degrees and types of opportunism (6, 2016b). He has also argued that Douglas' distinctive concept of hierarchy can help us to challenge the conventional wisdoms on how the organization of welfare states has changed over recent decades (6, 2015a).

Richards first encountered Douglas' work when he acquired a copy of her (1966) *Purity and Danger* while undertaking field work in western Nigeria in 1968. Like many other readers, he took it that Douglas was reiterating the argument familiar among anthropologists that society is a product of its culture. Only many years later (on reading *How Institutions Think*) did he fully grasp that her argument was almost entirely the reverse. Douglas was arguing for an institutional theory of culture, not a cultural theory of institutions. What people believed or expressed was the product of the dynamics of institutional ordering. Culture was the dependent variable. Modes of organization were the cause.

This argument struck like a lightning flash, when Richards was then struggling to explain the motivations of a violent group of insurgents in the civil war in Sierra Leone thought by many to be 'rebels without a cause' (Richards 1996). Their mode of organization was that of a sect.

They had been forced into this institutional ordering by their enemies in mainstream society, who were too strong to be overrun, but too weak or too afraid to fight the insurgents to a conclusion. An enclave culture of isolation and difference had grown up in rebel camps almost entirely cut off in the tropical forest from the larger society. The answer to the war was not to argue with the rebel fighters about their strange beliefs, which were a vague form of Marxism, but to change the dynamics of their institutional ordering. They needed, urgently, to be brought back into the social mainstream where a range of institutional arrangements, and associated beliefs, were to be found. Eventually, this was done by offering skills training to ex-combatants, as a tool for social reintegration via employment, and by ignoring rebel political beliefs and cultural preferences.

Douglas has been equally inspirational for Richards' most recent work on the Ebola virus disease (Richards 2016). Here the international response was dominated by large-scale and hierarchically ordered Ebola Treatment Units, generating many local myths about their true purpose, such as vampirism and organ harvesting. Douglas provided a theoretical backbone for a campaign to bring Ebola treatment to patients who were otherwise prone to flee into the countryside and spread infection. These much smaller and locally staffed centres were very controversial. One view among some medical professionals was that they were a recipe for further spreading the disease. But the much greater risk (as Douglas doubtless would have argued) was posed by fear and blame. Here the institution was talking, and in negative terms. It began to talk the message of Ebola control only when the institutional scaling was appropriate to the mode of thinking of enclaved villagers. Community Care Centres were recognized by villagers as something belonging, institutionally, to their world, and Ebola victims started to report early enough to cut infection chains and offer scope for palliative care. The epidemic thus turned a corner. Recent data have confirmed that this low-grid intervention undoubtedly saved lives (Pronyk et al, 2016). So Douglas' work is not just an abstract theory, but a tool for intervention in wars and epidemics.

Our short book provides an accessible introduction to her principal arguments and to some of the work that continues her legacy. It is intended for advanced students of social sciences, embarking on their own research activities. It will be of especial use to those who are keen to introduce systematic theory into qualitative analysis. It is not a guide to methods, though we do point to possible implications for research, especially in the last chapter. It is primarily a guide the main features of Douglas' theory, and its structure and implications. We endeavour to show the development of her thought, and to bring out its strengths and some of its limitations.

The book consists of five chapters, together with an unnumbered introduction and a references section. The introduction serves as an overview of the following chapters. The first four numbered chapters are organized thematically, but in a sequence corresponding to the development of the main arguments in Douglas' oeuvre. The fifth chapter offers a summation of her theory as it stood in the final decades of her life, incorporating significant contributions made by her collaborators. This chapter also pays attention to some of her critics and considers how they can be answered.

This more or less chronological approach is a deliberate choice. Douglas herself once wondered whether she should not have begun with *How Institutions Think*, the book from 1986 that first captured the full scope of her theory. An insightful reader of one of our drafts wondered if it would be better for us to do the same. But there are good reasons for beginning with ethnography. Although she presented arguments with implications for all the social sciences, Douglas was an anthropologist. If anthropology has any distinctiveness as a social science it is that it works from the particular to the general, even when research is designed to examine hypotheses, which was the approach for which Douglas came to argue. The fieldworker, confronted by deep cultural, social and organizational difference, is compelled to think comparatively. Douglas never lost her belief that ethnography – meaning a deep exposure to human communities whose ways of working and thinking challenge the analyst's own social assumptions – was at the very core of her discipline. Nor did she ever cease to identify herself as an anthropologist, even though the esteem in which her later work was held was perhaps greater outside her own profession. Thus, her theory only becomes fully compelling when the reader understands how it grew out of her earliest ethnographic experiences and concerns, and was revitalized by her later ethnography of the Hebrew Bible. In order to make these empirical moorings of her theory adequately clear, we have felt compelled to follow a broadly chronological life-and-works approach.

Acknowledgements

We began writing this book some five years after the death of Professor Dame Mary Douglas. Both authors had conversations with Douglas in the last two decades of her life, as well as many written exchanges with her about the substance of her writings. We each drew upon her work in our own research during her lifetime, when we benefited from her direct guidance. After her death, we have continued to engage profitably with her extensive oeuvre.

We are also especially grateful to Richard Fardon, Al Baumgarten (whose as yet unpublished work on Douglas' late writings has significantly influenced us: Baumgarten, in preparation), Mike McGovern, Ramon Sarró, Daniel B. Cohen, Aaron Michka, Warren Thompson and Mike Degani, and also to several anonymous reviewers for their many comments and suggestions on several drafts.

We are very grateful to Marion Berghahn for agreeing to publish this book and to her team, Duncan Ranslem, Sasha Puchalski, Caroline Kuhtz, Burke Gerstenschlager and Jon Lloyd for the care and attention they have given our book and for the commitment they have shown to the project.

We are very grateful to John Wiley and Sons Ltd for permission to use Figure 3.1 in Chapter Three, which is taken from 6, 2014a, at p. 93 of that article, and in particular to Kelly Hoff of John Wiley and Sons Ltd for her assistance in this matter.

Perri 6's work on the book was supported by the Leverhulme Trust (grant number F01374I).

Introduction

This introduction provides brief biographical information and a short description of Mary Douglas' influence, before discussing the significance of her contributions to both explanatory and interpretive theory across the social sciences. We show how her work engages with some major traditions of social theory. We also introduce the main theoretical puzzles and research questions to which her work sought to develop answers, and the main concepts and themes she developed in order to answer them. These topics are addressed in greater depth in subsequent chapters.

Douglas' Life

Douglas was born Mary Tew in 1921, to a father who was a district commissioner in the Indian Civil Service and a mother from an Irish family. After her mother's death and her father's retirement, she became a boarder at the Sacred Heart Convent, a Catholic school for girls in Roehampton in 1933. In her later writings, the school would become an occasional point of reference in her accounts of hierarchy – one style of social organization that she regarded as of general importance, though quite incorrectly understood by many of the social sciences.

After a short spell in Paris to take a diploma consolidating her already fluent French, in which she conducted exchanges over many years with leading French intellectuals, she was admitted to Oxford in 1939 to read philosophy, politics and economics.

On leaving the university, she joined the Colonial Office, where her interest in anthropology was quickened. In 1947, she applied to Oxford again to read anthropology, which she studied under Edward Evans-Pritchard, and felt the last embers of influence of the outgoing éminence grise, A.R. Radcliffe-Brown. Evans-Pritchard exercised a profound influence upon her. Decades later, she would publish a short account of his work (Douglas, 1980). That book also remains invaluable for explaining the origins of many of her own intellectual concerns.

This return to her teacher's thought undoubtedly sharpened her own theoretical focus. Her fieldwork for her D.Phil. was conducted in the Belgian Congo (now the Democratic Republic of the Congo) in 1949–50, among the Lele, a people living along the Kasai River. She visited the Lele again in 1953 to finalize her ethnographic monograph for publication, but thereafter returned only once in the 1980s. This was a short visit with momentous consequences for her thinking, as will be explained below.

In 1951, she married James Douglas, and they set up home in Highgate, where, apart from their sojourns in the United States in the 1970s and 1980s, they lived until the last years of her life. James Douglas was an economist and a former civil servant who at that time had just been appointed to the Conservative Research Department. In 1970, he became its director. He played important roles in providing policy advice to the centrist 'modernizers' of that party under Harold Macmillan and Edward Heath, resigning in the mid 1970s when Margaret Thatcher became party leader. After that, he made significant contributions to the academic study of voluntary organizations.

In the same year (1951), Mary Douglas moved to University College London, where she remained until the late 1970s. Her work in the 1950s was dominated by her African ethnography. During the 1960s, she began to write extensively for some of the weekly general readership journals influential in Britain in that decade, such as *The Listener*. Those outlets enabled her not only to present her arguments to a wider public, but also to use a series of short pieces about ritual to develop arguments for subsequent book-length publication.

In the 1960s, she consolidated her move to comparative and theoretical work, toward which she had aspired from the late 1940s when she first studied anthropology. This was the decade in which she began to develop a particular and distinctive Durkheimian approach, building upon Evans-Pritchard's own idiosyncratic developments of Durkheim's insights, which freed them from the straitjacket of Radcliffe-Brown's static conception of discrete societies.

This phase of her work culminated in her 1966 book of comparative analysis, *Purity and Danger*. It remains her best-known, most cited, most quoted and most frequently excerpted work. The book is widely remembered, not only among anthropologists, for five things. Its slogan – 'as a social animal, man is a ritual animal' (Douglas, 1966,

63) – is well-known, although its significance is often insufficiently appreciated. Second, the book's examination of the idea of dirt is widely cited, using an ancient common definition of it variously attributed to Lord Chesterfield, Lord Palmerston and William James, yet often wrongly ascribed to Douglas herself (Fardon, 2013c) as 'matter out of place', which made dirt into a case of anomaly. Third, the book is recalled erroneously for having offered a theory of disgust. Douglas hardly refers to that word and she never thought of *Purity and Danger* as an account of emotions. Fourth, the work introduced many readers to a scaly tropical mammal, the pangolin, via Douglas' reanalysis of the Lele cult of the animal, which she explained as a solution to a problem about anomalies in classification. Finally, the book is remembered for its explanation of the abominations of the biblical book of Leviticus as ways in which things deemed anomalous in the classification systems of the people of ancient Israel were prevented by prohibitions from threatening the social organization and social distinctiveness of the Jewish tribes. Yet *Purity and Danger*'s larger argument about the relationship between social structure and ritual is rarely recalled. Likewise, many readers failed to appreciate its methodological argument that if we are to see how social organization works, and notably how social organization cultivates particular ways of thinking, we need to track how anomalies are managed in specific social settings.

In 1970, she first presented her fourfold typology of elementary forms of social organization. The styles of thought cultivated in each of these forms would be basis of her method of comparative analysis. She continued to refine this typology over the next thirty-five years. The book *Natural Symbols*, in which the taxonomy was first set out, used some examples drawn from the ritual life of Irish Catholic communities living in Britain. Unfortunately, this led some readers to ignore the theoretical advance and to direct their fire at the case study material. She was disappointed that the theory of variation in elementary forms of social organization attracted little interest in anthropology itself. Although she worked diligently to produce her rigorous methodological template for its application in comparative anthropology, 'Cultural Bias' (1982a [1978]), her discipline responded with a shrug. By the 1980s, she began to use this scheme to present her arguments to other disciplines, and to address empirical problems of political conflict and religious sectarianism.

Political turmoil in the Congo and the demands of her own growing family ruled out further fieldwork among the Lele. Anthropologists sometimes look askance at those among their number who are no longer active in fieldwork, but take up comparative generalization in its place. Yet the decline in the appeal of her writings to her fellow anthropologists in Britain after 1970 was not due only to the lack of fresh ethnographic observation. The intellectual fashions in the anthropology of the period circled variously around Lévi-Strauss' structural analysis of myth, historical theories inspired by Karl Marx, or a dense ethnographic particularism shunning comparison or ambitious general explanation. With none of these approaches did Douglas have much sympathy, and by the mid 1970s she was beginning to be bored by debating them in the discipline's journals. The publication of her (1975a) collection of ethnographic essays under the title *Implicit Meanings* marked a kind of summation of what to date had been a conventional anthropologist's career path and intellectual focus.

In the late 1970s, her attention shifted away from Africa. Building on her ethnographic work earlier in the 1970s on meals and on drinking behaviour, her 1979 book with an economist, Baron Isherwood, examined the social organization of consumption of both private and public goods in Britain and other developed economies, thus consolidating her growing commitment to straddling boundaries between anthropology and other social sciences. By the 1980s, she was engaging very directly with major normative political topics concerning environmental and technological risks. British anthropologists at that time paid rather little attention to these writings. By contrast, the growing cross-disciplinary community of researchers working on risk came by the mid 1980s to regard her as a major figure. Her treatment of risk as a political concept led to her work being taken seriously among psychologists studying risk perception and by political scientists too. What was not so obvious to these other disciplines was that her arguments were still grounded in her Durkheimian theory, which she now synthesized in a wholly fresh manner.

During the second half of the 1970s and the early 1980s, there gathered around her a small cluster of people who would take her ideas into fields and disciplines far from her own interests. Some were her Ph.D. students, while others were established scholars simply attracted by her theories. Of those who continued to develop her legacy, four of those who worked with her in these years were especially important. Richard Fardon, who would later become her intellectual biographer (1999) and literary executor, continued to develop her Africanist anthropological concerns. In particular, in his work on societies formed from the fragments of nineteenth-century dislocation south of Lake Chad (today territory infiltrated by the Nigerian Islamist group Boko Haram), Fardon elaborated Douglas' Durkheimian concerns with ritual agency as a tool for composing peace. Steve Rayner used her theory for his doctoral research on extreme political sects in Britain. He showed how her arguments could be used to understand why people working in different kinds of social organization would think very differently about the past and the future. Later, he became internationally renowned as an influential scholar of environmental risk, using Douglas' theory to explain the polarization of debates about climate change and threats from a wide range of technologies. Michael Thompson, perhaps the most ambitious theorist among the group of scholars attracted to her, supplied much of the dynamic theory of institutional change underpinning her theory of institutional cultivation of thought style and classification. Gerald Mars applied her arguments in industrial anthropology and in particular to the study of dishonesty and crime in the workplace, as well as extending and deepening her interest in meals, drinking and consumption.

Douglas was awarded a personal chair in anthropology at University College London in the 1970s, but in 1975–76, her husband, James, resigned from the Conservative Party Research Department ahead of the change in party policy and organization led by the then new leader, Margaret Thatcher, with which he disagreed. With their children now adults, the Douglases were free to look abroad for new intellectual challenges. Like many British academics at the time, they were attracted to the United States. During a sabbatical as a visiting scholar at the Russell Sage Foundation in New York in 1977–78, she had encountered the influential American political scientist Aaron Wildavsky, who had become the Foundation's president. He secured her appointment there as Director of Research on Culture. Unfortunately, Wildavsky himself was soon demoted by the trustees and lost influence over the Foundation's work, later resuming his academic career at the University of California at Berkeley. Douglas continued to work with him, and in 1982 they produced what would become the greatest scandal of her career, the 1982 book *Risk and Culture* (see below). Wildavsky went on to make great use of Douglas' theory and to work with Michael Thompson, even though the Wildavskian rendering of her concerns with practices of social organization often appeared to become a theory of worldviews and ideologies.

In 1981, she left the Foundation and accepted the Avalon chair in the humanities at Northwestern University on the lakeside outskirts of Chicago. Her role there was to work on comparative religion. Although her writings about religion in the United States from the 1980s are not usually counted among her major writings, these papers

laid the basis for the turn she made in the 1990s, in retirement, to applying her anthropological theory and method to the understanding
of ancient Israel, as presented in the books of the Hebrew Bible. In
the 1980s, she challenged leading figures in the sociology of religion
such as Peter Berger, whose theory of secularization she regarded as
ill-founded. Equally importantly, her work in that decade began to
return to following Durkheim's own methodological argument that
religion provides not only a central case for understanding social organization and human thought more generally, but that its institutions also provide people with models of how to organize and think,
that are replicated in secular and everyday settings.

There then appeared what was perhaps her most important single book, *How Institutions Think* (Douglas, 1986). Although it was
written immediately before retirement, with the appearance of a final major statement, she commented that it might have been better
had she written it many years before her other books, for then her
whole oeuvre might have been better understood. The monograph
laid out the general theoretical basis of her Durkheimian account of
social causation. At the time, few people in her now scattered and
disconnected readerships – in anthropology, risk research, political
science and the sociology of religion – understood its significance.
Perhaps she compounded the problem of the work's reception by addressing a new potential audience as yet unfamiliar with her work,
seeking connections for her own neo-Durkheimian theoretical framework among the sociologists and historians of science, Ludwig Fleck,
Robert Merton and Thomas Kuhn.

Soon after her retirement from Northwestern University in 1985,
she returned to Britain, and to recognition in her former department
at University College London as professor emerita. Her final twen-
ty-two years, freed from academic routine, were perhaps her most
productive.

One strand of her work was to develop the theory underlying the
fourfold typology of basic forms of institutions and thought styles
that had preoccupied her since 1970 and that had organized her arguments about risk, danger and blame. She cultivated scholars across
several countries to make use of her approach, but their diverse interests, methods, disciplinary roots and geographical locations made it
very difficult for them to form a coherent Douglasian school.

Douglas remained at heart an anthropologist and was wont to
say her theories would amount to nothing unless they passed ethnographic scrutiny. This may have been a recognition of a blow landed
upon her in the late 1960s by one of the most influential critics of *Purity*

and Danger, Melford Spiro. Reviewing the book in 1968 for a leading journal, the *American Anthropologist*, Spiro had taken her to task on two counts. First, he had suggested that she had not grounded her analysis in a sufficiently thoroughgoing theory of symbolism. Second, he criticized her for failing to provide sufficient empirical justification for her claims.

The first criticism surely left her unmoved. Spiro was interested in psychoanalysis and symbolic archetypes. Her own concerns were closer to those of the philosopher Ludwig Wittgenstein, who sought to understand meanings through appreciation of the contexts within which words are used, and whose arguments she anthologized in her book of readings for use in teaching anthropologists, *Rules and Meanings* (Douglas, 1973a). What mattered to her was how rituals are to be understood in the shared contexts in which they are performed and through the shared understandings they cultivate. Spiro's other criticism of lack of empirical grounding would have seemed more damaging, because it implied that her ethnography was insufficient. Her account of the workings of the Lele pangolin cult was, in effect, judged to be too skimpy.

What was to be done? Further work in Central Africa was impractical. But a brief visit to the Lele immediately after her retirement in 1987 helped open up a new avenue of empirical enquiry. Most unexpectedly, and in ominous anticipation of the later killings in Rwanda, she encountered the Lele consumed by a witch-finding purge led by two Catholic priests. This, she saw, was a collectively effervescent reaction to years of civil war and economic immiseration. But how could priests – who might be expected to have some expertise in the ritual composition of social understanding – have come to the point of leading such a violent purge? Sympathetic colleagues in religious studies, intrigued by her earlier speculations in *Purity and Danger* on the Book of Leviticus, pointed her towards an era of history when priests had been similarly involved in responding to passionate political excess, but in a very different manner from that which she had observed on her return to the Lele. This was the period of the Second Temple in Jerusalem, around 500 years BCE. Now an empirical opportunity beckoned, if only by proxy. Wryly aware that she no longer had to endure the privations of life in a raffia palm hut, she worried that she might be considered to be no more than an anthropologist on holiday in the bible (Douglas, 1999b, v). But aided by several distinguished scholarly mentors, she accepted the challenge to develop the scholarly skills appropriate to a new kind of ethnographic analysis with astonishing vigour and seriousness.

This new ethnographically grounded study focused on the theme of social conflict and reconciliation. She used several books of the Hebrew Bible as sources of data about ritual and priestly politics among the people of ancient Israel. The series of books she produced during the 1990s and the early 2000s did much more than apply the theory that she had already developed to biblical history. More importantly, she returned to her debates with the structuralists of the 1960s who analysed myth and language and literature, and especially to the work of Roman Jakobson. This involved her in examining the structure of the composition of the Books of Numbers, and Leviticus, examining what work their distinctive literary forms might perform. She showed that the form was indeed the message. Literary form, and the compositional challenges it set, modelled dilemmas of social conflict. Relating this to her interest in social explanation, she used her understanding of relations between priesthood, sect, sacrifice and purification in ancient Israel to present an argument about the social uses of ritual invention, and the peculiar contribution of hierarchy to conflict containment and resolution.

This body of work brought her new readers in biblical studies, whose links with other sections of her readership across the social sciences were even more tenuous than those linking risk researchers with sociologists of religion. It was hardly surprising, then, that only a few scholars had a sufficient range of interest to appreciate the tightly integrated character of her thought, as it ranged across her apparently disparate studies on witchcraft, taboo, classification, consumption, eating and drinking, risk, blame, institutions, 'culture', religion, ring composition and the roles of priests.

By the 1990s, poststructuralist ideas were dominant in much of anthropology. Douglas' critiques of Geertz and Clifford and other advocates of such approaches made little headway, although *Purity and Danger* continued to be cited. Ironically, it was even taken up in a strangely recast form by the poststructuralist Julia Kristeva (1982 [1980]), whose arguments were in many other respects entirely antithetical to Douglas' own commitment to comparison across history and geography and to causal explanation. By the time of Douglas' death, researchers using her theoretical approach were to be found mainly among political scientists and others interested in political or organizational culture, or in the so-called 'new institutionalism'. For these researchers, the fourfold typology of elementary forms offered clear analytical appeal. Scholars in the field of religious studies found her arguments about ancient Israel highly stimulating, but were less interested in the theory of elementary forms of organization that she claimed underpinned them. The rather sudden arrival of her discipline, anthropology, in the emergent and expansive field of peace and conflict studies then seemed to herald a new outlet, something she herself anticipated in her penultimate book, *Jacob's Tears* (2004b), a collection of essays ostensibly about the Bible, but implying a subtext of concern with the infamous pogroms in Rwanda and the African civil wars of the 1990s.

In the last months of her life, the efforts of a few of her friends resulted in Mary Douglas finally being made a Dame, the equivalent for women of a knighthood in the British system of state honours. The French newspaper *Le Figaro* wondered at the tardy public recognition of this great anthropologist in her own country. By now, she was already terminally ill. She died in May 2007, shortly after giving an interview to the British political weekly *The Spectator*, which was keenest to ask her what her theory had to say about ways to mitigate the threat of international terrorism. The answer she gave was 'listen to your enemies', which was immediately misunderstood as a call for negotiation. She meant to urge people to comprehend Islamic terrorism as ritual performance.

Why Douglas' Work Matters Today

Some readers may be wondering why, if these were Douglas' empirical interests, and they themselves have quite other ones, they need to pay any attention to her work. After all, to many social scientists, African agricultural peoples of the Congo and their taboos, meals and consumption, ancient Israel and biblical studies, ring composition and perhaps even the concept of risk itself may have seemed both ill-assorted and unrelated, and also at times too recondite to be of much general or practical interest. Why struggle with these curiosities when urgent public policy concerns or even matters of business relevance seem more pressing?

Our answer to this question is both large and blunt. We will show that Douglas was using these topics to develop a tightly integrated and yet constantly developing body of theoretical argument centrally focused on grappling with the nature of political conflict, the dynamics of religious radicalism and terrorism, the challenges of environmental and ecological security, and basic issues of human dignity.

Moreover, her work provides very distinctive answers to some of the most basic questions to be addressed in every piece of research in social science. Why do people think in the way that they do? What does it mean to claim that someone is acting 'rationally'? Just what is an institution, and how great is the power of institutions relative to human agency?

First, she sought to provide a set of what might be called micro-foundations for a social science capable of explaining the full range of human social organization and thought styles. The required microfoundations would be found in rethinking the core concepts of twentieth-century social theory, such as institutions, cognition, ritual and rationality. For this, she drew upon arguments and concepts first developed in Durkheim's writings. Yet she found that Durkheim's materials would have to be synthesized afresh if some of the problems and limitations to be found in his work were to be overcome. Her central Durkheimian argument was that the institutional forms of social organization and of disorganization shape and therefore causally explain 'thought styles', meaning the manners in which people classify, remember and feel. Thought style describes not what people believe, but the way in which they think with whatever they believe. For example, it captures such things as how rigidly people treat their classifications, how flexibly they accommodate fallback options, how far they are prepared to contemplate compromise, how they conceive of the past and future, how they deal with things that appear anomalous within their implicit schemes for classifying problems and opportunities, and what emotions they attach to their beliefs. Her major statement of her account of the ways in which different elementary forms of institutions cultivate contrasting thought styles appeared only relatively late in her career, in the book *How Institutions Think* (1986).

The causal mechanism by which social organization cultivates thought style, she argued, works through ritual. Like the sociologist Erving Goffman (1967a) and the ethnomethodologist Harold Garfinkel (1967), Douglas did not just have in mind the grand, formal public ceremonies in which one group of performers presents and another larger group participates only as an audience. Like Goffman, she regarded the small-scale performative rituals of everyday conversation and writing, etiquette, the conduct of meetings, the layout of rooms, etc. as being critical. Her argument is similar to but not precisely the same as that to be found in Durkheim's *Elementary Forms of Religious Life* (1995 [1912]), or in the short monograph by Durkheim and Mauss, *Primitive Classification* (1963 [1902–3]). But Douglas' theory of ritual processes by which social organization inscribes itself upon the style of thought is a clear descendent of Durkheim's argument that basic categories are fixed through social ceremonial. However, what is

distinctive is Douglas' demonstration that social organization is replicated in the ways that people *use* the categories with which they
classify their problems, resources and relationships with other people.

Second, Douglas' project was to provide a theory of available variation in human social organization, which would in turn yield a general
method for social science. She argued that the elementary forms of institutional social organization exhibit only limited variation in all human contexts. She cross-tabulated the two dimensions of institutional
variation in social organization that Durkheim had distinguished in
Suicide (1951 [1897]) – namely, social regulation and social integration
or, as she called them 'grid and 'group'. Moreover, whereas in *Suicide*,
Durkheim attended to the apices of the dimensions, Douglas directed
attention to the forms produced in the resulting four cells, thus making central to her recasting of his theory the hybrids that Durkheim
considered too briefly and only secondarily. The four elementary
forms derived deductively are hierarchy (strong regulation and integration), individualism (weak regulation and integration), enclave
(weak regulation and strong integration) and isolate ordering (strong
regulation and weak integration). Contrary to the conventional wis-
dom (Alexander et al, 1987), she sees no 'micro-macro problem' in
social theory, for she argued consistently that the same elementary
forms organize people in the large and small scales alike. For example, she would have agreed with a significant part of Collins' (2004)
argument that micro-interaction rituals perform social organization
into being. But she rejected his (1986, 1999) claim that social scientists
should turn to Weber when explaining larger-scale problems of, for
example, state crisis or revolution. In the same vein, she argued that
these basic forms specify organization and thought style in any setting, irrespective of technological sophistication or field of endeavour.
Finally, she argued that in any social context, there will be mixing,
weighting, hybridization, settlement or conflict among these four elementary forms, and these relations will shape how people think.

These two aims required her to conduct, throughout her life, debates and exchanges with philosophy of a kind that had been central
to British mid century anthropology. In particular, she engaged with
problems in the philosophy of knowledge, language, meaning and rationality which made up much of what was, in the twentieth-century
analytical philosophical tradition that she knew best, defined as epistemology. For many philosophers in the British tradition, arguments
that social context explained how people thought were not simply
regarded neutrally (as Douglas herself thought of her explanations)
as ways of explaining human bias. Rather, many philosophers feared

that this kind of explanation raised the spectre of relativism – the doctrine that we cannot have good reasons to suppose that any of our
beliefs are reliable. For if social organization affects the very basis of
our thought, then perhaps everything we believe – and here 'we' includes social scientists themselves, not just people studied by social
scientists – is so systematically biased that the results of all human
inquiry, including scientific research, merely reproduces the biases we
bring to undertaking it.

Douglas had to debate several times with philosophers who supposed her to be guilty of relativism. Her strategy in answering them
was subtle. She never sought to claim for social science any greater
firmness or security in knowledge, other than that to which any other
human inquiry could aspire. As Durkheim (1995 [1912], 439–40) had
written, the categories of science have to accommodate themselves
to the categories of wider opinion, but the purpose of social science
is to explain opinion and to make it 'more conscious of itself'. Like
Durkheim (Jones, 1999), Douglas was a 'realist' about social institutions; that is to say, she regarded institutions as substantial constraints
and imperatives, not simply as artefacts of perceptions. Institutions
cultivate distinct kinds of bias in all of us. She freely admitted that
social scientists also ought to worry that biases from their own social
organization might well affect their findings or their interpretation
of those findings. There are no guarantees against systematic error.
On the other hand, again developing Durkheim's point, the aim of
her theory of the limited variety of basic styles of thought, and of the
ways of social living that sustained them, was to provide both a diagnostic tool by which social scientists, as much as anyone else, could
check each other's arguments for signs of bias and also a means of
using the different kinds of bias to offset each other. The final stage in
her reply to the philosophers was a very distinctively anthropological
one. It was also a move that was consistent with her whole approach
to explanation. She pointed out that both falling prey to relativism
and worrying about it in other people's arguments are phenomena
that wax and wane over time, but these trends can be *explained*, not
simply documented. Evidence of both rising scepticism and of panics
about relativism could be found in the historical record as far back
as postexilic ancient Israel and more recently in sixteenth- and sev-
enteenth-century France in the writings of Montaigne and Pascal.
Postmodernism, she thought, is a phenomenon that has welled up
and sunk away many times before. The thought style which relativism exhibits is something that itself requires explanation by reference
to the social organization in which both sceptics and those in a panic

about scepticism are sustained. The converse, she argued, is also true. Great certainty about the status of our knowledge rises and falls over history. Its booms and busts should likewise be explained by reference to the kinds of social organization that bias people toward thought styles of great and insistent certainty (this argument was later developed by Fuchs (2001)).

Although her principal goal was positively to build her own social theory, these first two aims also involved critique of dominant theories and approaches across the social sciences. On the one hand, in her 1979 work with Isherwood on household consumption and elsewhere, she argued against monolithic theories, such as the narrow and economistic forms of rational choice in which there is only one form of human rationality, with interests more or less determined by objective payoffs and optimized under constraint. She showed throughout her work that there are too many situations in which people, entirely reasonably and explicably, forego opportunities to advance their wellbeing for such theories to be adequate. On the other hand, she argued strongly against the postmodern, poststructuralist relativism of the 1970s and 1980s. These schools of thought supposed, first, that thought can float free of grounding in situation, constraint or organization, second, that there is an unlimited range of possible variations in human thought styles and, third, all that social science can do, therefore, is to document how people appear to think via an endless series of supposedly unique cases, without offering generalizing explanations for any of them. These three propositions, she regarded, respectively, as preposterous, lazy and lacking in intellectual curiosity and purpose. To the cohorts trained during these decades in sociology, political studies, business and management studies, anthropology, cultural studies and development studies to believe that the only options were a supposedly 'hard-headed' utilitarianism from economics or a supposedly 'humanistic' poststructural approach, her firm rejection of both in favour of a refurbished and resynthesized Durkheimian institutionalism seemed paradoxical – at once exotic and old-fashioned. In the years since her death, it has begun to be apparent to many social scientists that her approach might indeed offer a promising way forward beyond the impasses left by the prevailing traditions.

From the mid 1970s, when she published the first edition of her collection of ethnographic pieces, *Implicit Meanings*, Douglas developed a set of normative ambitions for her project, which had not been apparent in her work in the 1950s and 1960s. These later normative concerns have by and large not been well understood, either by her professional colleagues in anthropology or in the social sciences more widely. Almost certainly this is because she at first only revealed aspects of her normative argument in a piecemeal fashion, and then not always clearly or adroitly. Never did she show their full scale and character in a single key work. Her most important normative concern, it became clearer during the 1990s, was that social science should have something constructive to say about how institutions could be ritually composed, so that conflict might be attenuated through arresting the process by which each of the basic ways of organizing tended to exaggerate itself over time and become more extreme. This understanding might then provide an institutional basis for reconciliation among conflicted ways of organizing and living.

She once told one of us that at the time she toyed with the idea of confronting the arguments of John Burton, a major pioneer of peace studies, who was briefly her colleague at University College London. Burton (1990; cf. Dunn 2004) advocated a 'bargaining' approach to conflict resolution based on the notion of a universal hierarchy of human needs. But instead of writing a book overtly about the theory of conflict management, Douglas chose to use her ethnographic examination of several books of the Hebrew Bible to develop her account of what kinds of institutional capabilities might sustain the thought styles required for peace making and social reintegration, and for calming the frenzied and runaway processes of hostile classification such as stigmatizing people and demonizing groups.

Unfortunately, some of her critics were suspicious that she was smuggling into her social theory a set of normative concerns derived exclusively from her own Catholic faith. She admitted to a 'feeling for hierarchy' (Douglas, 2005; reprinted in Fardon, 2013b) that disquieted those who assumed she used the term in the way her critics did – to mean a coercive system of command and humiliation of subalterns. In fact, she meant something quite different by the word. Indeed, in some respects, she had in mind an opposite of what they understood it to mean. Inspired in part by the French historical anthropologist and scholar of Hindu practices and her Oxford contemporary, Louis Dumont (1980 [1966]), she developed an understanding of hierarchy as an institutional ordering that distributed powers across linked but separated spheres and that then tended to provide mutual checks and balances, for example, between church and state in the Holy Roman Empire.

Collaboration with Aaron Wildavsky in the 1980s, whose politics appeared to veer between libertarian individualist and U.S. conservative, and who could be ferociously hostile to environmentalists, did not help her normative concerns to be understood. Their jointly written book, *Risk and Culture* (1982), proved an uneasy compromise between their respective and distinct normative interests. Moreover, some of her most central concerns were submerged in the text. Wildavsky wanted the book to fight a contemporary political battle, whereas she wanted it to analyse more generally the dangers of social disorganization resultant upon fighting all kinds of battles so ferociously that complete breakdown threatens.

Her relationship with contemporary politics was not quite the same as that of her husband James, but Mary and James Douglas were both, although for different reasons, deeply repelled by Thatcherite monetarism. He was a centrist postwar conservative, pro-European economist with qualified Keynesian views who had worked closely with Edward Heath's administration. She rejected the Thatcherite ideology of rugged individualism and feared for its consequences upon social institutions, whereas he, as an economist, was alarmed most by the Thatcherites' strategic use of high unemployment, and their commitment to growth through the expansion of a financial sector based on burgeoning claims against wealth and production rather than on productive capacity itself. By contrast, her anxieties about the outlook expressed in Thatcherism concerned the risks that individualistic social organization would undermine social cohesion (Douglas, 1997; reprinted in Fardon, 2013b).

When she retired in the mid 1980s, before her work was complete, many people who knew her earlier writings therefore misunderstood her as if she were a straightforward conservative with ultramontane Catholic leanings, and supposedly hostile to environmental concerns.

Yet this picture of her normative positioning was quite wrong. For example, although nowhere in *Purity and Danger* is fascism discussed explicitly, a fierce concern runs through that book about the consequences of cults of purity and of sects that insist on drawing boundaries around supposedly pure social or ethnic identities. The idea that anomaly is something to be lived with by intelligent accommodation has political as well as methodological implications. In the 1979 book with Isherwood about consumption, she made her concern about poverty very clear, not so much as a matter of class in the Marxist sense as of its tendency to undermine human dignity. She was often in sympathy with the writings on poverty of the economist Amartya Sen. A late piece (2004a) attacked, in language of a vitriolic fury uncharacteristic of her writing as a whole, the contemporary form of arguments about the supposed 'culture' of the poor that some people held to be responsible for the perpetuation of poverty.

In the writings from her final years, the true and quite general character of the normative concern was made clear; it had been latent in her previous work, but it was obscured in *Risk and Culture*. That normative aspiration was centrally to develop a social science capable of explaining how conflict might be attenuated, channelled and contained in the face of risks of polarization and deepening opposition. Her final works were not only about ancient Israel. Societal conflict in late twentieth-century Africa, and not least the predicament of the Lele in the war-torn Democratic Republic of the Congo, was also implicitly present in these studies, though often without being mentioned directly. Perhaps that silence was chosen in deference to the interests of a learned audience of biblical scholars upon whose territory and patience she felt at times to be a trespasser. It is also likely that she hoped that using ethnographic material from deep antiquity, but also of fascination to Jews, Christians and Muslims ever since, would more effectively make the case that she was offering an argument of universal relevance than a book offering only examination of contemporary cases might have done. For just as she argued that relativism and realism are problems to be tackled not only on the basis of philosophical argument, but also with an appreciation of social context, so she chose ancient Israel for her case studies in conflict and its attenuation to show that the forms of social organization that make peace and war are in eternal ritual tension.

Thus, Douglas made her argument obliquely, as she always had in each of the periods of her writing. Her style is often conversational and full of domestic and common-sense allusions, and this has misled some readers into assuming lack of substance; in effect, they confuse whimsy in expression for flimsiness in argument. In her later books, however, the depth and substance are readily apparent when read closely. The Israel of antiquity provided a case study and a canvas on which to paint a much larger argument about the dynamics of conflict, the process of using social institutions to rein in conflict, and the role of ritual composition as a tool to defuse resentments and diffuse concentrated bitterness. The anxiety in *Risk and Culture* about sectarian extremism was now finally displayed as just one special case of those processes of extreme self-reinforcement that led to irreconcilable conflict and disorganization in any of the four main varieties of social organization that her typological theory had identified.

Her work matters in the social sciences today for two broad reasons. The first is that she identified a way out of the difficulties attending both postmodernist and narrowly rationalist optimizing approaches. As we will show in the following chapters, her causal, explanatory, institutionalist approach based on a limited plurality of basic forms of rationality is as empirically powerful as it is intellectually fertile. She provided rigorous and distinctive microfoundations for one of the most promising theories of institutional dynamics available in the social sciences. By these means, she also demonstrated the essential unity of structures and causal processes across the whole gamut of the social sciences, from the institutional economics of consumer choice to the analysis of poverty in development studies, and from the sociology of terrorism to the political science of environmental governance. Second, she was able to use that approach to apply her arguments about institutional dynamics to a central task of understanding the possibilities, risks and mechanisms associated with the task of containing conflicts.

We should also add that the significance of her work in the humanities remains high. Although her earlier work – especially *Purity and Danger* – continues to be widely cited in the humanities and in branches of cultural anthropology influenced by the humanities, her late work has had significant impact on studies of the Hebrew Bible. It is from here that her posthumous impact on the much broader field of religious studies and other specialist fields of literary and historical scholarship has begun to radiate brightly once again.

§ 1

Social Organization in Microcosm
Anomalies and Ritual Concentrate Conflict

This chapter examines the development of Douglas' method and theory between the mid 1950s and 1970. It concentrates on her theoretical use of her own ethnographic work on the Lele of the Kasai.[1] Douglas laid the foundations for, but could not yet construct, the fully developed body of theory presented in the 1980s. Key concepts were forged in the microcosm of the ethnographic studies in the 1940s and 1950s. In the 1960s, she began to use these concepts in comparative analysis. What remained to be developed was a fully causal and dynamic theory. This chapter traces the development of her conceptual framework and, in particular, it examines the centrality of her concepts of classification, symbolization, meaning, ritual and anomaly. The notion of an anomaly became central both to her theory of conflict and to her analytic method for designing research.

Institutional Intricacy in Containing Conflict

For a social theorist, the point of ethnography is not just to gather data about a particular case, but also to use this case as a microcosm for a much more general and, by implication, comparative argument. Douglas used her detailed ethnographic work on the Lele, a people living in what is now the Democratic Republic of the Congo, to support her general arguments in later works. A book on the Lele was published in 1963, fully ten years after the first draft of the material had been submitted as her doctoral thesis at Oxford. The monograph was preceded by a series of articles and papers covering parts of the same ground. Here, we consider these writings together.

In 1949, the Lele constituted a group of about thirty thousand people, inhabiting a small part of the southern edge of the African equatorial forest on the left bank of the Kasai River. Villages were small, averaging about two hundred inhabitants. Population density was low, at about two people per square kilometre. The men cleared small patches of land for women to farm, but spent most of their time hunting and weaving raffia cloth. Elders settled blood debts and administered a complex system of marriage transactions.

The Lele lived according to 'standards of suavely controlled behaviour' (Douglas, 1977 [1963], 7). Yet they were also beset by problems of accident, sickness and sudden death. Fears of sorcery, the presumed cause of these problems, gripped their imaginations, and from time to time convulsed the smooth surface of daily life.

Douglas focused first on the Lele economy. She contrasted the Lele with their linguistically related neighbours, the Bushong (Douglas, 1962; 1977 [1963], 1, 18–23, 41–51). The Bushong had well-organized chiefdoms, a strong work ethic and a great desire to acquire wealth. The Lele were less tightly ordered, worked less hard and lacked markets or money. Prestige based on virility and respect for age counted for more among Lele male elders than economic achievement.

One area where the Lele outshone the Bushong was in the production of raffia cloth (Douglas, 1958). This was of high quality and the main medium for payment of marriage fees, fines, and cult dues, as well as for bartering against outside necessities. When not engaged in planning wars and abductions, at least prior to prohibitions enforced by the Belgian colonial rulers after 1925, or in hunting and matchmaking, Lele men were primarily engaged in weaving the raffia cloth they needed for barter and social exchange. The accumulation of cloth from cult and marriage fees supported the senior men, leading Douglas to wonder whether Lele society had saddled itself with a pension scheme it could ill afford. Certainly, demand for cloth made it hard for Lele men to marry young. This explained the emergence of a form of polyandry known as the 'village wife', by which young men who were unable to acquire a wife by other means could be provided with quasi-marital support. This institution was the subject of her first major academic paper (Douglas, 1951).

In the field of marriage, the transactional complexity of Lele society became fully apparent. In Douglas' account, it proved to be an intricate marvel. A key reason for her examining the Lele, urged upon her by her supervisors and colleagues, was that in 1950 little research had been done on matrilineal communities. Matrilineal kinship in a male-dominated society posed certain challenges of group cohesion. In contributing a solution to the so-called 'matrilineal puzzle', Douglas (1969) suggested that matriliny had some advantages over patriliny. Notably, it achieved wider distribution of men, who constituted a key productive asset, and also of food, the principal consumption asset. The matrilineal clans of the Lele offered a man the option of remaining with his father in his place of birth or of moving to the village of his mother's clan, of which he was a member. He might be fed by the wife his father had helped him acquire or he might move to seek help from his matrikin, thus serving the cause of flexible adjustment in an impoverished forest-edge environment.

Superimposed on this system of flexible matrilineal connections was a patron-client system of mind-bending complexity. Douglas called these patrons 'lords'. A Lele lord was an elder from a matriclan with some kind of claim to precedence, such as first-comer rights to land. But a lord exercised little power beyond the capacity to assign marriage rights in young women born to his clients. This capacity was used to attract young men to a community. Clients, or 'pawns' in the terminology that Douglas later came to favour (1964), are described as being of semi-servile status. Yet Lele clients were routinely able to extract so many benefits from their lords that it is unclear who was more deeply bound to whom. Although in the 1950s and 1960s, Douglas was still years away from developing her concept of hierarchy, in retrospect her account of lordship and pawnship seems to exhibit some of its features, notably the combination of strong social integration and strong social regulation of the upper and lower ranks within Lele social organization. Clearly, the pawns were subaltern, but it is interesting to note the extent to which the pre-eminence of the lords was also subject to detailed prescription. On the other hand, strains of domination are also present in her account, with the relationship between the ranks apparently exhibiting hybridity with some isolate and despotic forms. Nonetheless, at least in the 1950s, the dangers of incipient isolate and despotic ordering were carefully contained by offsetting institutions of other forms.

The clientship system, as Douglas encountered it, reflected local exigencies. People became clients when a lord saved them from war, sickness or famine. But in other cases, clients had caused a death by accident or sorcery. To the Lele, almost every death was the result of human agency, whether overt or occult. Someone was to blame. In precolonial times, the Lele poison ordeal revealed the true cause and also administered the sentence. Some suspects merely vomited, which constituted proof of innocence. Others collapsed and died, which provided proof of their sorcery. The ordeal was an ingenious biophysical device reducing the blame game to a lottery. The decision brooked no argument; it was 'God's medicine' (Douglas, 1977 [1963], 241). Douglas failed to identify the plant involved, but Jan Vansina, a fellow anthropologist who worked among the neighbouring Bushong, suggested (although he too had few authoritative sources) that it may well have been either *Strychnos icaja* or *Erythrophleum guineense* (Vansina, 1979 [1969]; 1990, 300). *E. guineense* provides the poison for the sasswood ordeal known widely throughout the African forest margins as far as the Upper Guinea coast.

Because by the time of her fieldwork the colonial authorities had banned the ordeal, along with slavery (Douglas, 1960), Douglas had no observation-based data on how it was administered. Her brief account is based on a key informant, Makaka, a village leader who had twice taken the ordeal and survived (Douglas, 1977 [1963], 242). Its loss had severe consequences for Lele ideas of justice because, without it, responsibility for unexplained misfortune was now much harder to assign. Henceforth, lengthy forensic procedures based on divination were needed to judge guilt. Condemned people paid off their debt to Lele society by becoming clients. But the system was so much more complicated and time-consuming than it had previously been. Arguments about whether a person was truly a witch could drag on because detecting sorcery depended on divination, and Lele diviners were also suspected of being sorcerers, so they tended to deliver less clear-cut verdicts than the ordeal had done.

As was common in many western African forest-edge societies, the Lele also had important cults or sodalities linking elites and commoners. Lele cult rituals ensured health, fertility and success in hunting. The cults of the begetters and the pangolin, a mammal distinctively covered in reptilian scales, celebrated virility. The father of a first child would seek initiation into the begetters cult. Having acquired both male and female children, a father could seek to join the pangolin cult (see below). Parents of twins belonged to the twins cult. Diviners (sixteen of forty men in one small Lele village) might receive their vocation in a dream. Older diviners were frequently suspected of sorcery, a testimony to the fragility of their grip on power. From time to time, witch-finding cults directed against sorcerers threatened to convulse Lele society.

The monograph on the Lele introduced many of the themes of Douglas' later work. She paid close attention to the intricate ways in which respect for elders was prevented from becoming oppressive through the licensing of special cult opportunities for young men. This relationship formed part of the conception that she would later develop of hierarchical relations as reciprocal but asymmetrically ordered systems of social integration, and not merely and certainly not fundamentally based on orders issuing from a chain of command.

The study also opened up the examination of blame, and the problem of how to manage and contain blame, to prevent it giving rise to corrosive conflict, mistrust and fear, leading in turn to violence. Although in the early 1960s Douglas had no general theory of blame, her analysis of the problem of control of sorcery accusations stated the theoretical issue clearly enough. Accusations proliferated in situations in which tensions erupted among groups in Lele society subject to quite different accountabilities. The poison oracle provided a forensic procedure by which adjudication of accusations could be undertaken with the appearance of independence from any of the conflicting parties and indeed with the appearance of independence from human institutions altogether. The link between the danger that sorcery represented, the institution of blame and accusation, and the centrality of a forensic procedure was established in Douglas' 1960s account of Lele life, and was ready and waiting to be recast nearly thirty years later in the light of her subsequent work on risk more generally.

Moreover, Douglas showed that individual blame is incipient general political conflict, where people lack or are deprived of the institutional means through which to exercise care and thus to prevent misfortune. With the poison oracle unavailable to defuse such accusations, a runaway process led, during the 1950s, to fervent, emotional anti-sorcery movements sweeping through Lele communities with violent consequences (Douglas, 1977 [1963], 257). Blame, sectarianism and conflict were already linked by the dynamics of what she would later learn, from the cybernetic tradition of analysis, to call 'positive feedback'. She had also encountered the idea in Durkheim's passages on what he termed 'sacred contagion', though at first she was rather reluctant to adopt Durkheim's formulation (see, for example, her preface to the first edition of *Implicit Meanings*, where she imposed an inappropriate interpretation of Durkheim's term related to notions of infection, an error she would correct in her last works). She returned to the problem of blame in the 1980s and 1990s. The ways in which cult rivalries can be attenuated and channelled became one of the main themes of her late work on ancient Israel.

The sheer intricacy of the mutually offsetting processes in Lele social organization fascinated Douglas. She was equally alive to their fragility. Even in the 1950s, delicate intricacy did not suffice to stave off the dangerous collective effervescence of anti-sorcery cults among Lele people. As she published her monograph in 1963, not yet having encountered the developments in cybernetic theory and its vocabulary of 'requisite variety' that reshaped social scientific understanding of control systems, and still reliant on her Oxford anthropological training in functional analysis, she lacked a theoretical explanation for these balancing yet not entirely stable relations other than the often rigid structural-functionalism of her anthropological forebears. In that approach, every discernible set of practices or beliefs was thought to further the maintenance and reproduction of specific social forms. Yet even if this could account for offsetting, it had no explanation for instability or its possible consequences. In particular, anthropological structural-functionalism was manifestly inadequate to handle the obvious deep conflicts that shaped and convulsively reshaped Lele society. Nonetheless, the monograph on the Lele provided her with a case on which she would reflect for decades concerning institutional hybridity, whereby a provisional settlement could emerge among several distinct and rival institutional imperatives and commitments, embodying informal norms and tacit practices. Nonetheless, the instability of these settlements had already presented her with a case on which to examine the problem of what Thompson and Wildavsky (her student and collaborator, respectively) would later call 'viability'. By this, they meant the set of relations among mutually cantankerous institutions that might somehow prevent complete breakdown. A key question is then posed in the final pages of her monograph (e.g. Douglas, 1977 [1963], 258) – whether there might be other coarser and more robust ways in which institutions in friction could develop viable accommodations or whether such outcomes might be worse than the gridlock they replaced.

At the end of her life, Douglas would implicitly compare the Lele, with their rich plethora of institutional imperatives around age, matriclan, chieftaincy, intervillage accounting, problems of witchcraft and demons, institutions of divination and oracular judicial procedure, with the appearance of institutional sparseness and simplicity found in ancient Israel. It was a comparison she had already encountered in the work of her teacher, Evans-Pritchard, in the contrast implied by his ethnographies of the agricultural Azande and pastoral Nuer. Her purpose was to ask what subterranean and visible institutions would be both possible and necessary if an appearance of institutional austerity were to be sustained.

In particular, the Lele provided her with a series of examples of ways in which institutional rules were adapted to provide for special exceptions, in order to deal with what would otherwise be difficult contradictions, tensions or threats of conflict from rival, latent claims. The monograph on the Lele documented these with respect to what she would later in the 1960s call 'anomalies' in marriage, in relations between age groups and in the role of the poison oracle in defusing blame and accusation. The ways in which such anomalies could be generated by institutions, and managed (or not) by further institutions, would increasingly become central to her method and thus to her general theory of social conflict and of change.

Anomalies, Rituals and Dangerous Solidarities

After completing her work on the Lele material, Douglas pursued comparative studies with the purpose of building social theory. However, she continued to draw upon her African ethnography either directly or indirectly for the rest of her life.

Purity and Danger (1966) was the first major fruit of her comparative theorizing. It is still her best-known work. Sections and chapters from the book were widely anthologized, especially material from Chapters 3 and 10 on the abominations of Leviticus and on the Lele pangolin cult. She eventually placed a moratorium on further reprinting of excerpts because the practice tore these arguments from the context of the book's argument as a whole (Fardon, 1999, 83–99).

The core of the book was a reworking of several explanations first developed by Durkheim. Here, Douglas drew almost exclusively on Durkheim's (1995 [1912]) *Elementary Forms* and with occasional reference to the distinction Durkheim makes in *Division* (1984 [1893]) between mechanical solidarity, based on similarity, which might be enforced if found necessary, and organic solidarity, based on accommodation of difference. Her account of religion, ritual, symbol and classification in *Purity and Danger* argues, following Durkheim's arguments, that people ritually enact their social organization and develop classifications collectively to represent, in transposed form, aspects of the structure of that organization. Too often Douglas' book is misremembered as if it had proposed that symbolism explains action, when her point was exactly the reverse.

Purity and Danger began with an attack upon the unjustified distinction between 'primitive' and 'modern' thinking, which social science had been given by nineteenth-century thinkers. That distinction had become entrenched by Weber's thesis of 'rationalization' and the 'disenchantment' of a supposedly purely secular and ritual-free world achieved between the Renaissance and the Enlightenment in Europe (Weber, 1978; Schluchter, 1981 [1979]). Douglas argued that, on the contrary, all ways of apprehending the world depend, as Kant had claimed, on the deployment of prior categories. However, in considering the nature of these categories, she followed Durkheim's suggestion that they are moulded and sustained by social forces of ritual action in which symbols are deployed.

She then made her first foray into biblical studies, later to be an important ethnographic domain more accessible to her than the Congo. For the third chapter of *Purity and Danger* offered an interpretation of Jewish dietary laws – for instance, the ban on pork or certain kinds of seafood, or certain combinations of foods – as set out in the Book of Leviticus. She argued that these laws should be understood as a symbolic *aide-memoire* for the way in which society is organized, and not a reflection on the inherent or literal uncleanness of pigs. Each of the unclean animals is really anomalous. But anomaly only makes sense within a system of classification. In turn, those systems of classification reflect the system of societal organization, if not directly, then as transposed into an ideal form that the religion defends. Classifications inevitably face anomalies, meaning things that are classified in two or more rival ways or that cannot clearly be classified at all. Recognition of such things as salient will be driven by conflicts in social organization. People could, in principle, manage entities that appear anomalous in various ways; they might celebrate them, exploit them, prohibit or expunge them, suppress and debar them as dangerous or evil, or develop special institutions to treat them as exceptions to be controlled in reserved institutional locales. In *Purity and Danger*, Douglas' focus was principally on the contrast between the latter two. Her argument in 1966 seemed to regard debarring anomalies by prohibition as the signature of mechanical solidarity, and special accommodation as the hallmark of organic solidarity. The 'abomination' pronounced by Leviticus is the debarring of anomaly by prohibiting dissimilar things from coming into contact.

The reason why this chapter was so widely anthologized was that it set out for the first time Douglas' Durkheimian argument that social organization, not biology, explained cognition). What was not much commented upon at the time was that it also presented her methodological programme in miniature. Her argument here is that we understand correctly the kind of social organization driving the tribes of Israel only when we do what today would be called 'causal process tracing' – to develop and then test against data rival hypotheses about causal mechanisms at work, first in producing anomalies in classification and then in leading people to adopt particular strategies for dealing with those anomalies. If the Lele could at least sometimes proliferate special rules to handle exceptions (and she acknowledged that they sometimes engaged in seeking to suppress anomalies or to forbid or obliterate them from memory), Leviticus adopts a different strategy. The book instead specifies prohibitions in which anomalous things are eschewed as marks of the distinctiveness of the Jewish people. In her later works, she would extend this method by treating risks in technologically developed settings as anomalous things, for which the very same repertoire of basic strategies for managing them would be available, and the strategy selected would depend on the prevailing form of social organization. This would be true, she was to argue, as much for 1980s U.S. citizens worrying about nuclear energy or the future of the environment as for Israelites in the time of Leviticus and as for the Lele at the end of the colonial period, bereft of their poison ordeal.

Purity and Danger developed the implications of this insight by examining the causal mechanism by which social organization produces social classification and by which management capabilities anomalies are then cultivated – namely, ritual. For, as with religion, so it is with society. Rules and ritual are the inescapable external form: 'As a social animal, man is a ritual animal' (Douglas, 1966, 63). Ritual has real effects, both in terms of cognition and social learning. Ritual is a condensed set of practices that serve to fix modes of discourse about social values. In these practices, people enact a whole way of life, but in microcosm. In ritual, people enact their social classifications, but the ritual process also brings about transformations. One of the ways in which ritual process does this is to provide a means of institutionalizing the management of anomaly. She took the argument from Durkheim that classification and the management of anomaly though practices of classification, in religion as in any activity, is part of the institutions of a community and ritually enacted. She went on to trace it back to the nineteenth-century theologian and historian of ancient Semitic thought, Robertson Smith, although she rejected his use of the distinction between 'primitive' and 'modern' ways of dealing with anomaly.

But this immediately raises the question of what kind of ritual it is that can sustain classification and the management of anomaly, whether through taboo or any other style of thought. Here, Robertson Smith was no help. At this stage in her career, Douglas could not yet find the appropriate resources within Durkheim's writings to solve the problem. In *Purity and Danger*, she glancingly referred to

Goffman's (1959) work on the dramaturgy of ritual, though in fact his (1967b [1956]) argument that important ritual action is often commonplace interaction rather than grand public ceremonial would perhaps have been of more use. Her whole notion of how ritual sustains and manages problems in classification rests on an assumption of this sort. Only in her later ethnographic writings, which we discuss in the next section, did she fully work out just how ritual works to sustain classification.

The next chapter of *Purity and Danger* then reintroduced difference between 'us' and 'them' by way of a reworking of Durkheim's distinction between mechanical and organic solidarity. Mechanical solidarity demands similarity. Belief is totalizing. Organic solidarity recognizes complementarity. Belief is grounded in social organization, and when social organization is complementary and open, belief is more likely to be open to reflective development and revision.

Purity, then, is itself a key danger. Douglas' argument in her 1966 book is often remembered, especially among scholars of purity and purification in religious studies, for the argument that demands for purity and beliefs in pollution arise as ways of marking boundaries among people and of providing those boundaries with justifications (e.g. Frevel and Nihan, 2013, 8). This is not completely mistaken, but it misses an important nuance in Douglas' (1966) argument, later to be developed in her work on the dynamics of boundary reinforcement within enclaves. Her point was that people reach for claims of purity and pollution precisely when boundaries appear most insecure. Far from it being surprising that purity and pollution claims are used to further what Freud (1917) famously called the 'narcissism of small differences', this is precisely what Douglas' argument here recognized. In 1966, Douglas lacked a dynamic theory by which purity and pollution claims might reinforce small differences until they turned into fully mechanical solidarity, but she had provided some of the materials with which she would later build that theory, working alongside Michael Thompson (see Chapter 5 below).

Later chapters of *Purity and Danger* explored the range of possible belief systems in mechanical solidarity. This analysis included an important discussion of the accreditation and distribution of power. Douglas suggested that well-articulated parts of the authority system are accredited with explicit powers, but that where the system is less well articulated, we should expect people occupying ambiguous roles to be credited with uncontrolled, psychic powers. Among the Lele, such people were likely to be suspected of being witches. Ambiguity is, like contradiction, another case of anomaly in a system of classification. The incompletely classified are as challenging to as-similate as those who are classified in two or more conflicting ways. We can think of the embattled Lele male elder, in a weakly articu-lated sector of his society, caught in the ambiguities of treating women both as people and as a marriageable commodity. The more powerful the matchmaking elder became, the more distrust of him increased. Social breakdown loomed. Pollution talk, Douglas suggested, was one means of coping with such threats, because it embodied the idea that social organization is always something bigger than the sum of the manipulations to which its agents resorted.

'Cultural materialists' such as Harris (2001 [1979]) sought to criti-cize Douglas on the grounds that her explanation of purity and pol-lution claims was too abstract and that it failed to acknowledge the ecological context within which ritual practices emerge; the same sug-gestion is still made today (Frevel and Nihan, 2013, 7). Yet her use of her ethnographic fieldwork on the Lele and her detailed location of the pangolin cult in relations among generations, sexes and the ma-terial economy of hunting and exchange showed that this criticism was quite misplaced. The analysis of purity and anomalous impure things in *Purity and Danger* was entirely consistent with Douglas' own arguments throughout her career that symbols and beliefs must be understood in the context of social relations, including the ways in which available material goods are used, made and exchanged.

Yet it is true that the book's conclusion to this argument was unsat-isfactory. Lele men – caught in a web of their own devising – joined the pangolin cult, promising to ensure fertility and a good return to the hunt. Her own data showed that the pangolin often failed to de-liver and the elders of the cult were threatened with being unmasked as sorcerers. Members of the cult encompassed their difficulties in an act of atonement. They ingested the anomaly of anomalies. The pan-golin symbolizes the self-sacrificing function of those who mediate disputes by authoritatively spanning Lele classifications. In a 1972 paper entitled 'Self-Evidence' reprinted in the 1975 collection *Implicit Meanings*, Douglas emphasized the pangolin as embodying position of Lele sons-in-law in mediating interdynastic disputes within the kinship structure. She invoked the Eucharist to explain this. It made a neat ending, but there was something missing.

There is no better statement of the problem than the author's own critique in *Risk and Blame* that 'with much regret I left [*Purity and Danger*] without making any link between taboo-thinking, which uses natural dangers to uphold community values, and our modern ap-proach [based on science]. So a gulf was left unbridged' (Douglas,

1992a, 4). Douglas realized she had not carried through her programme. She had not accounted for what it was about Lele social organization that they did not simply treat the anomalous pangolin as
a straightforward taboo, which was prohibited and debarred. As she
wrote many years later in the introduction to the Hebrew edition of
Purity and Danger: 'I still think [the account of taboo as a debarring response to anomaly] holds good, but only within cultures which have
a strong classificatory bent, an obsession with classificatory completeness' (Douglas, 2010). She admitted in the book itself that the cor-
relation between social organization and forms of thought was not
worked out, especially for forms of social organization that would not
cultivate obsession with "classificatory completeness". She later inverted her understanding of Leviticus, making its programme one of
reconciliation through careful avoidance and through collective purification, not debarment (see Chapter 4 below). Only in subsequent
years did she develop a theory of institutional variation to explain
why some people debar and others celebrate selected anomalies.

To bridge the gulf required new empirical materials. This would
involve Douglas in studying the ways in which people dealt with supposedly 'modern' technological risks. But first there was unfinished
business. She had arguments to complete both with fellow anthropologists and with philosophers about classification and the taxonomic
basis of human thought.

Unfinished Struggles with Theories of Meanings

In 1975, under the title, *Implicit Meanings* (1975a), Douglas published
a volume of articles that had appeared in journals since the mid 1950s.
A second edition released in 1999 (Douglas, 1999a) added a few more
recent items and removed a few papers that seemed minor or, in one
case, embarrassing. Carlos Castaneda, an anthropologist shaped by
the California 'new age', was the subject of one essay; after he was accused of inventing data, Douglas removed this item from the new edition. Some of the collection was, in effect, an appendix to her previous
ethnographic work. For instance, it reprints two of her ethnographic
papers (Douglas, 1955; 1957) and a further version of her comparison between Lele and Bushong styles of organization and thought.
However, the collection's true significance was that it brought together her theoretical achievements with her ethnographic work.

The publication date of 1975 was significant, for it marked the end
of a quarter century in which Douglas had pursued what might be

considered a conventional British anthropological career, beginning with a major ethnographic study and followed by comparative work contributing to the theory of ritual, religion and symbolization, supported by debate invoking other leading theories of the day on these topics. Her colleagues thought of her mainly as an Africanist, in an era in which this was a prestigious calling for a British social anthropologist. But already by 1970, she had struck out to address debates about her own society and more generally about life in developed, industrialized countries, borrowing from and adapting sociological theories. After 1975, not only would she continue much further along this path, but she would also begin to direct the theoretical resources she had developed in the 1960s about classification, anomaly, risk and danger, and the proper structure and role of functional explanations in social science, toward the analysis of issues of large-scale political conflict. The 1975 collection can thus be considered a climacteric to her earlier career.

Several chapters also situated her arguments in relation to anthropological theories and debates of the 1960s and early 1970s. In these she addressed a number of important anthropologists of the day – Louis Dumont, Victor Turner, Claude Lévi-Strauss and members of the Griaule school of francophone West African ethnography. Several of these arguments aimed to show how and why, even though structural-functionalism had clearly failed, it was still important to understand the structure of social organization. Developed strongly in anthropology by Radcliffe-Brown and Malinowski, but articulated in elaborate theoretical detail by the sociologist Talcott Parsons, structural-functionalism was the theory that the institutions and common activities found in any society or setting were best explained by showing how they served the goal of stability of the society that was taken to form a single unitary and harmonious system. While individuals might kick against societal 'norms' and 'roles', for structural functionalists, this was simply incompleteness or 'noise' in the system, not evidence of any basic incoherence. The theory therefore could not explain, or even precisely describe conflicts, ambiguities and dynamisms, except as temporary but functional processes of creativity. Douglas rejected the approach, but she also recognized that no satisfactory account of conflict or dynamism was possible without considering the causal impact of social structure. She therefore remained committed to a structural conception of social organization. Moreover, if institutions of social structure do, as she argued, shape people's thought even when structures collide, then the process must be explained by way of a causal feedback loop, which is in effect a functional explanation. But in the papers from the 1950s, 1960s and 1970s reprinted in *Implicit Meanings*, she was still struggling to find a way to reject functionalism while still making appropriate use of functional explanation to understand how institutions themselves organize conflict. Not yet fully satisfactorily framed, these papers do nevertheless chart the path to the rigorous resolution she eventually found in the mid 1980s (see Chapter 3 below) and therefore they still repay reading.

Douglas demonstrated that even though functionalism was hopeless, because 'society' was not a well-formed unit, and even though it was nonsense to speak of society having 'needs', let alone of activities spontaneously springing up to 'fill' them, it was impossible to dispense with particular functional explanations if social science was ever to explain the very conflicts and complexities concerning the units of social organization that functionalism itself had so clearly failed to understand.

In the anthropology of the 1960s, many prevailing structuralist theories were, however, less functionalist in tone than they were ideational. In other words, they focused on structures of ideas rather than social consequences of institutions. In anthropology, these approaches documented and analysed formal relations among ideas encapsulated in myths. The theorist who developed this method more comprehensively than most was Claude Lévi-Strauss. In a paper entitled 'The Meaning of Myth', Douglas argued that either Lévi-Strauss was not enough of a structuralist or else he was a structuralist about the wrong things. Lévi-Strauss' vast cycle of works analysing myths, especially from Central and South America, had been devoted to making the case that distinctions that he found within the myths could be treated as 'oppositions' from which inferences could be drawn about a supposedly essentially dualistic ordering in human thought quite generally. Despite Lévi-Strauss' insistent denial, Douglas argued that his semantic analysis of the formal structures in stories was basically literary. As such, his account was useless for social science without an account of the institutional positioning of those who listen to them and the ritual contexts in which myth-telling takes place. Simply documenting and tabulating variations on common themes in stories tells us nothing if we have no idea who tells these tales to whom or why, or what is at stake for a community, for example, in *not* telling or knowing a particular story. For Douglas, the whole strategy of drawing inferences from abstract themes identified in stories, or any other product of thought, back to what the context must have been was fundamentally flawed. Rather, social science should start with context and then look at what use people make of the particular ideas they use: 'in order to analyse particular structures, [the anthropologist] must know [the studied] culture well first' (Douglas, 1999a [1975], 143).

Ironically, as we shall see in the next section, Douglas was attacked for precisely the sin she accused Lévi-Strauss of committing. In a 1972 paper on 'Self-Evidence (see below), she politely confessed her mistake and responded to what she had learnt from her critics by forming a more consistently Durkheimian argument that ideas do not drive social organization and that we can only understand such ideas by showing the causal work done by their social context.

This brought Douglas to draw upon Victor Turner's ideas about ritual dynamics, contrasting them with Radcliffe-Brown's structural-functionalism. Typically for her work, she addressed this problem with a case study in ethnographic microcosm. She reprinted a paper on jokes. Ironically, the paper began its life as a tribute to Radcliffe-Brown and his identification of the category of the 'joking relationship'. Joking relationships express social structure. Among the Bemba of northern Zambia, members of the crocodile clan joked that crocodiles eat fish, and members of the fish clan responded that this meant that crocodiles are dependent on fish, thus emphasizing clan complementarity. But she also upbraided Radcliffe-Brown for his 'dessicated perspective' and emphasized instead Freud's notion that jokes represented an eruption of the subconscious into consciousness. Spontaneity challenges ritual informality and formality alike. Two principles were now in play – structure and what Durkheim (1995 [1912]) called 'collective effervescence', or the process by which, when social institutions go into self-reinforcement and radicalization, they cultivate great extremes of ferocious emotion, whether of rage or hilarity and ribaldry. In this respect, her account appeared to resemble Turner's (1969) distinction between structure and 'anti-structure' or the experience of 'liminal' community. Part of her point was that they are not fully reconciled in either structure or function. Yet somehow this point was not brought out very clearly in the paper; the issue was not fully clarified until after she had embraced Michael Thompson's dynamic models. She dubbed the joke the 'anti-rite', stressing that a joke punctures solemnity. Thus far, at least, she borrowed from Turner, but without making use of Turner's dynamics of how anti-rites are reinforced in collective effervescence. Obscenity, on the other hand, she argued, is that which is classified as overstepping the mark. It threatens the social order and becomes an abomination. Some anomalies, it appeared, are so extreme that they provoke the kind of angry collective effervescence involved in suppression. The paper then moved towards a formalistic conclusion, with jokes serving as markers of institutional logic. It is as if Radcliffe-Brown has been quietly re-admitted. Unfortunately, where *Purity and Danger* might have led us to hope that ritual dynamics would now be used to provide foundations for the explanation, this issue was effectively put on hold. The great rituals, she implied, are only about the assertion of hierarchy and order. At this stage, she could see clearly what was wrong with functionalism, but she was not yet able to show an adequate way forward that still made use of the basic logic of functional explanation.

The ethnographic papers in *Implicit Meanings* were curiously hesitant about addressing the fact that ritual is performance. In her anthology of readings for students entitled *Rules and Meanings* (Douglas, 1973a), both the ethnomethodologist Harold Garfinkel and avant-garde composer John Cage, who later in his career used chance procedures to generate his works, such as the 1951 *Music of Changes*, make cameo appearances. Yet the role and significance of performance – and specifically bodily performance – as a means to generate and order social fields was not really explored in *Implicit Meanings*.

This was all of a piece with a somewhat unexpected critique of Durkheim in the Preface to *Implicit Meanings*. Here she castigated the great sociologist for allegedly imposing an 'us and them' categorization on primitive religion.

Douglas seems not to have fully grasped, at this stage, what Durkheim meant by 'sacred contagion'. To Douglas at this stage in her career, contagion implied pollution resulting from disrespect for sacred things. In fact, Durkheim was outlining a notion of positive feedback in the social domain, closely associated with the idea of collective effervescence, as applicable to the kind of enclaved institutions developed in the French National Assembly in 1790 as to the native Australian ceremonies he had analysed in greater detail. Douglas had not yet found a way to approach collective effervescence, or the conflict it both reflected and amplified, and was not to do so until her later work, when she returned once more to the concept of sacred contagion in the context of renewed work on Leviticus (Douglas, 1996a). Nor had she yet thought through what collective effervescence might be in institutional forms *other than* the enclave.

Nevertheless, the short paper on laughter entitled 'Do Dogs Laugh? A Cross-cultural Approach to Body Symbolism' did represent something new and important in her output. Surely, this reflected the growing influence on her work of colleagues in biological anthropology at University College London (a leading scholar of primate and human evolution, Robert Martin, is acknowledged in a footnote). First published in the *Journal of Psychosomatic Research* in 1971, and therefore postdating the paper on jokes by four years, the paper on laughter announced the assumption 'that there is a universal, cross-cultural language of bodily interruptions ... [and that] laughter is a unique bodily eruption [because it] is always taken to be a communication' (Douglas, 1973, 86). Effervescence was back on the agenda. Deployment of 'the full bodily range of expression for grief and joy' might also be transformative as well as reflective of social order (ibid., 88). Thus, a path was opened to the possibility of incorporating a theory of ritual dynamics in her later work on institutions and thus to an eventual rapprochement with the effervescent strand in Durkheim's work.

The second edition, published in 1999 (Douglas, 1999a), concludes with an important chapter from a volume on classification she edited with the philosopher of science David Hull (Douglas and Hull, 1992) devoted to exploring applications in social science of arguments made by the philosopher Nelson Goodman (e.g. Goodman, 1970, 1978). Douglas' piece, entitled 'Rightness of Categories' (1992b), develops an anthropological version of Goodman's philosophical thesis about similarity. The argument is that people apply categories appropriately, ably following rules about what is counted as being similar to what, and both learn to do so and teach by using exemplars. In his famous work *Word and Object* (1960), the analytical philosopher Willard Van Orman Quine had criticised this approach. Quine argued that when an informant points to a rabbit and addresses the anthropologist or local child with the word 'gavagai', the anthropologist or child cannot know whether what is meant is 'rabbit' or 'white tail' or 'running' or 'lame' or 'lunch'. Ostension, or identifying something by pointing at it, Quine infers, cannot explain meanings. Implicitly (writing for anthropologists, she avoided citing philosophers), Douglas answers Quine by saying that when ostension is repeated and carried out in its context of everyday interaction ritual, it can be part of a disambiguating performance. When the anthropologist or child has developed enough understanding of the ritual institutions in which ostension is practised, disambiguation can be achieved, meanings can be fixed and similarity can be rendered stable. When someone occupying what their interlocutor understands to be a teaching role points to something as an exemplar, or when ostension as ritual is successful, understanding is achieved because the roles of teacher and learner are already sufficiently established. This means that it is possible for the learner, whether a child from a community or a visiting anthropologist, to draw appropriate inferences from a set of cues about what would count as the simplest teaching example and what kinds of class is being exemplified. For example, drawing appropriate inferences from the use of mime as tuition rests on the prior and implicit ritual fixing of conventions between teacher and learner about what counts as a mime, so that the reference can be fixed. The ritual involved in fixing such conventions is not grand formal public ceremonial, but quotidian ritual interaction – namely, the routine etiquette and demeanour through which people literally act out the prevailing social organization (Goffman, 1967a). Quotidian ritual interaction order is exhibited in such things as the manner by which people greet each other and closing conversations, the conduct of meetings and the layout of meeting rooms, practices of pointing or not pointing at things or people, acceptable and unacceptable forms of speech, and the available genres of rhetoric used in everyday conversation. By these means, elementary institutional forms of social organization are performed and sustained and, conversely, the forms come to specify the ways in which poor and good performance are sanctioned. It is only when we refer to a set of prevailing social institutions exhibited in these quotidian interaction orders, including 'thin' ones linking neophytes and established members, that we understand how people practically overcome Quine's dilemma about meaning. It is repeated ritual interaction in *general* socialization that enables people to use ostension to disambiguate each *particular* term.

Having argued this point, Douglas then goes on to revisit her argument about Lele animal classification, showing that the relevant exemplars to which people point are not the animals, but those of social organization itself. Among the Lele, the features of social organization that most importantly shaped classification included territory, overlordship and enmity. Animals provide a notation, but the social ordering is the model, not the animals. The exemplars may not provide detailed explicit instructions about what exactly an animal exemplifies or symbolizes, or what ritual performance is appropriate to dealings with an animal in hunting, farming or divination, for detail often remains implicit in ritual interaction. However, the whole system of animals as symbols provides the Lele with a schema against the background of which they can continually test, investigate, check and examine the fit between their own performances and the degree to which the classification system continues to exhibit stability. In this respect, Douglas likens the system of animal symbolism to a pressure gauge or a medical diagnosis. Lele reflect on the results of ostension, of hunting ritual, etc., because it enables them to sustain their ritual puzzling over the general state of their own relations with their background theory. From Goodman, Douglas borrows the argument that the relationship between the exemplars and the theory they exemplify is indeed circular. Yet the circle is neither unintelligent nor logically vicious. This is because the ritual process of constant testing leads to continual mutual adjustment of exemplars and the definitions of the (e.g. animal) classes they are supposed to exemplify or of the ritual practices that are intended to sustain learning. To Goodman, she brings the anthropological argument that the learning process in both the individual acquiring the language and in the community conducting its constant investigation of its categories is achieved by everyday ritual interaction.

This paper, although published in 1992, draws heavily on Douglas' African ethnographic work, and her decision to include it in the second edition of *Implicit Meanings* showed that she thought it deserved consideration alongside her early work. The argument had great significance for her thought generally. A quarter of a century after *Purity and Danger* appeared, 'Rightness of Categories' provides the causal mechanism missing from her most famous book's argument about just how social organization manages anomalies. Her argument in this paper itself serves to exemplify her approach to problems about meaning quite generally. She regarded these philosophical puzzles as ones that had to be tackled anthropologically, because meaning something is a practice that is only sustained under particular institutions. For the article used her ethnography of Lele animal symbolism to build some of the microfoundations for the central thesis of her entire published oeuvre – that social organization is ritually enacted and that ritual enactment is what sustains classification as a practice. Most importantly, she argued that ritual sustains whatever degree of consistency people's style of thought achieves, both for appropriate inference and for damagingly unfortunate cases of inference from exemplar to class, such as those involved (as we shall see in later chapters) in the uncontrolled conflict-fanning blame and accusation associated with the witch-finding crusade or ethnic pogrom. For in uncontrolled blame, the self-reinforcing loop between institutions, people's own investigations and categories may be all too tight; rightness of categories may then become the problem. The circle is not logically vicious, but it can all too readily become morally so.

The Reception of Douglas' Ethnographic Work

Douglas' (1963) book on the Lele appeared at a time when anthropologists were reconsidering the role of structure, history and regional dynamics in their approach to ethnographic writing. Her study was recognized as the product of perceptive fieldwork, though her time in the field was considered short by prevailing standards. Moreover, her focus was a single, rather small group sampled at an evident moment of flux, without much in the way of an historical or regional frame of reference. The book was rarely adopted as a teaching text (Fardon, 1999), but for the author, it remained a deep well from which she continued to draw throughout the rest of her career.

Douglas subsequently sought to align her ethnography with some of the main theoretical debates of the day among Africanist anthropologists. She contributed to debates about kinship theory through developing her own solution to the persistence of matriliny (Douglas, 1969) and tried to bring some order to anthropological analysis of sorcery and witch-finding crusades (Douglas, 1970b; 1999c). This brought the central issue of blame to the fore in her work.

Critical reaction to her ethnography was limited. Nonetheless, her comparison of Lele and Bushong modes of production (Douglas, 1962) attracted the attention of a rising star of U.S. anthropology, Marshall Sahlins. In his influential reworking of economic anthropology, *Stone Age Economics* (2003 [1972]), parts of which were written in Paris in 1968 against the background of the student uprising and were fashionably Marxist in tone, Sahlins claimed that Douglas' 'brilliant comparison' shared common ground with his own arguments about the domestic mode of production. He was attracted by her suggestion that the key to the difference between Lele and Bushong lay in political organization. He assumed that chieftaincy coerced the Bushong to work harder. But this was not Douglas' argument; rather, she suggested, hierarchical political organization freed the Bushong from some of the burdens of dispute settlement. In the preface to the second edition of *The Lele of the Kasai* (1977 [1963], xi) Douglas saw through Sahlins' milk-and-water Marxism. 'His writing often seems to criticize those who fail to exploit fully their economic potential ... [and] he seems to think it better to live and work in a society where there are rewards to strive for and a high level of incentive for individual effort.' However, it is only fair to add that Douglas herself was on fairly shaky ground in her comparison of Lele and Bushong. She recognized that the Lele had poorer environmental endowments than the Bushong, and this implied that material outcomes could not be judged without careful measurement of factor endowments and labour productivities. Subsequent quantitative studies of African hoe cultivators have shown repeatedly that groups short of land worked more intensively for less return per unit of labour. This inverse relationship between population density and effort appears to be borne out irrespective of the mode of political organization (for data and cases, see Netting, 1993).

If the critical reception of her ethnography had initially been sparse, those arguments that she presented afresh in *Purity and Danger* attracted a large and mostly admiring critical response (Fardon, 1999). This book was widely adopted in teaching, in part because anthropologists saw it as a synthesis of an emergent focus in the discipline on structuralism and symbolic classification. It has remained in print since it was first published and has reached a wide readership in many fields beyond anthropology, perhaps especially in the humanities. In an iconographic age it seemed – despite Douglas' critique of Lévi-Strauss – to encapsulate the public perception of the anthropologist as a decoder of symbols, notwithstanding Spiro's (1968) reservations about the weakness of her theoretical underpinnings in this regard (see above).

Some reactions to *Purity and Danger* alerted Douglas to an important difficulty with her argument. Two anthropologist colleagues, in particular, argued that, in focusing on symbols and rituals, Douglas herself had neglected the larger sociological context. Bulmer (1967) and Tambiah (1969) both argued that 'anomalous' animals (the cassowary in highland New Guinea and the otter in northeast Thailand) had ambiguous taxonomic status because they reflected societal tensions and organizational challenges. In effect, animal taboos could be 'decoded' only by being placed within a broader societal and cosmological context. The issue was not what the pangolin signified to cultists, but what societal problems the cult was used to address.

Bulmer (1967) described how Karam hoe cultivators of highland New Guinea face dilemmas in their relations with their in-laws. On the one hand, they relied on affines to help them work and protect their land. On the other hand, these affines could establish their own claims on scarce land. The cassowary was associated with the problem because it behaved more like an in-law than an outright enemy, and was found in distant forests where the help of in-laws was most needed and the land was least easily protected. In short, the creature was an anomaly because it symbolized an acute social dilemma.

Douglas did more than simply concede the point. She incorporated Bulmer's and Tambiah's arguments into her own increasingly Durkheimian scheme. Indeed, she republished their studies in her 1973 pedagogical collection of readings, *Rules and Meanings* (Douglas, 1973a). In the Myers lecture published in 1972 and reprinted in *Implicit Meanings*, entitled 'Self-Evidence', Douglas (1975a, Chapter 17) revisited her ethnographic materials to show how the Lele and

Leviticus could be fitted within a sociological scheme that also embraced Thailand and the Karam. Now there was support from the ethnographic work of others to support her claim that social organization is the key to understanding taxonomies of nature.

She later received a challenge from Lewis (1991), who drew attention to the way different but related animal species perform different symbolic or taxonomic tasks in closely related societies. The pangolin is often sacred in central Africa, but there are two species, and not all societies choose the same species. The Lele only made cult of the smaller, less impressive tree pangolin (*Manis tricuspis*). This appeared to puzzle her critic.

Ohnuki-Tiernay (1981) took a different tack. Two approaches in anthropology were to be differentiated in understanding the classification of the natural world – cognitive anthropology (otherwise termed 'ethnoscience') and symbolic classification. Previously regarded as opposed, Ohnuki-Tiernay suggested that both approaches are valid, but that they each address different phases in the processes of perception, conception and symbolization. Cognitive anthropologists, she suggested, focus on the earlier phases, being interested in what she terms 'memory codes'. What kinds of cues or clues are needed to recall the kind of entity addressed? Is it a fish? Can it be eaten? Those interested in symbolic classification address 'analogy codes'. What does this fish signify? Is it an omen?

Ohnuki-Tiernay proceeded to outline the history of the emergence of the catfish in Japan as an instance of analogy-code making. The symbol has a specific history. The 1855 earthquake was thought by many peasants to herald the expected fall of the feudal regime. In that moment of excitement, the catfish became a portent for and icon of social change. Ohnuki-Tiernay's criticism of *Purity and Danger* was that the analogy code of the pangolin among the Lele is insufficiently specified. Douglas cited evidence only that the Lele were fascinated and vaguely threatened by the creature because it did not fit into a scheme of classification. She did not explain whether, how or under what circumstances it became an analogical code.

Douglas' response to her critics varied. Although she embraced Bulmer and Tambiah, Lewis was politely but briskly dismissed. Zoology had got nothing to do with it. The symbolic affordances of various animals were selected by different social problems. There was no answer to Ohnuki-Tiernay, perhaps because her criticism of Douglas is incidental rather than the main focus of the paper.

Douglas (2000) expressed the warmest admiration for Valeri's last (2000) work and sought largely to co-opt his argument, as she had done with Bulmer's and Tambiah's, despite the fact that Valeri had developed severe criticisms of her arguments in *Purity and Danger*, and even her later revised (1999b) views on food rules in Leviticus. Among Valeri's key criticisms of her 1966 book is his argument that its strengths are better thought of as lying in its theory of anomaly than in its claim exhaustively to have explained all taboos as responses to those anomalies. He did, though, recognize that Douglas had by then modified her theory considerably to recognize both the greater diversity in ways in which people can deal with things they find anomalous, in addition to taboo, and also to acknowledge a greater diversity of practices falling under the concept of taboo than the dirt- and pollution-related ones she had examined in *Purity and Danger*.

Valeri also criticized Douglas' (1966) account for violating her own methodological precept of considering taboos only as part of complete systems (including permissions as well as prohibitions, and also in some cases practices of neglect of things considered problematic). Conversely, Valeri noted that many taboos are applied to things that are not *logically* anomalous in a scheme of classification, a criticism Douglas later (2005b) acknowledged and sought to remedy in her work on ancient Israel.

However, Douglas' (2000) review of Valeri's book gently insists that for the special condition of those settings where social organization *does* cultivate a commitment to classificatory completeness and suppression of anomaly, treatment of dirt and pollution is the consequence. Implicitly, therefore, she reasserts the *institutional* basis of her theory, an aspect that Valeri hardly recognizes because he criticizes her for offering an explanation of anomaly as a *logical* feature of any classification scheme.

As we shall see below, much of her argument in her 1986 *How Institutions Think* – which Valeri fails to cite, even though he cited her subsequent writings dependent on it – was devoted to showing that what is counted as anomalous in the first place is itself the work of institutions, not of the cognitive or logical working out of concepts taken to be basic drivers of thought. Nevertheless, she freely admitted (2005b) that *Purity and Danger* had failed to make this nearly clear enough. Ironically, Valeri's own account of taboo based on a strategy of distance and proximity management turned out, as Douglas recognized, to be more closely akin to her own mature project than he recognized.

One puzzle remains about the critical reception of Douglas' ethnographic project. Can grand theory be successfully raised on fairly narrow empirical foundations? Fardon (1999) notes that, despite a warm anthropological response to *Purity and Danger*, Douglas was conscious of the muted reception of the ethnographic body of material on which it rested. Spiro (1968) had openly voiced the charge. Did the lukewarm reception for her Lele monograph prove him right?

Douglas herself tried to explain away the problem as a product of her decision to write in English about a people located in a francophone African country, as well as on the then eminent 'Manchester school' of Africanist anthropologists, of which Max Gluckman was a leading figure, and whose regard for her work was unfortunately scant. But response was also muted among scholars of the Congo. *The Lele of the Kasai* merited only three mentions (in a book of 428 pages) in the grand ethnohistorical synthesis of Equatorial Africa by Douglas' close associate, the Belgian historian and anthropologist Jan Vansina (1990). A more recent book by an anthropologist of western equatorial Africa (Guyer, 2004) gives Douglas a higher profile, but this is mainly for the use Guyer makes of her theoretical arguments.

Thus, an impression persists that while Douglas herself regularly reverted to the Lele for theoretical inspiration, her professional colleagues rated her ethnography less highly than her theoretical work. A few, quite unfairly, muttered behind her back about 'anthropology of the verandah', as if she had done more observation and interviewing than participation in the Kasai. Some may have felt her work was too much in debt to key informants, or even perhaps to the enquiries of Catholic missionary priests.

All ethnographies are indelibly marked by their mode of research support, so it is unfair to single Douglas out for criticism in this respect. But she remained touchy about the issue, as suggested by her prickly response to Van Beek (1992), in a paper tracing the element of co-production linking ethnographer and key informant in the writings of Griaule and Dieterlin on the Dogon of Mali (Douglas, 1992c). She did later acknowledge the Catholic missionary dimension of her fieldwork (Douglas, 1999d) and toward the end of her life, she also collaborated with a number of expatriate Lele scholars on a study of material culture, though the results were not published before her death. Nevertheless, some dissatisfaction on her own part with her fieldwork seems to be implied in the remark that: 'If I could go back to the Lele, I would try to learn their language more thoroughly' (Douglas, 1977, xiii).

What needs to be firmly dispelled, however, is the notion that Douglas as a theorist cared little about evidence. It has to be admitted that some of her middle period work is illustrated by examples for which her empirical evidence lacks the rich ethnographic depth of her work on Lele, and some of these could be deemed by hostile critics to be opportunist, or even whimsical. For example, some might make these criticisms of her discussion of the taxonomy of vintage wine in *How Institutions Think*. But Douglas herself was in no doubt that her theoretical arguments were only of value if they could withstand testing against a wide body of empirical materials. The seriousness with which she took the challenge of evidence in her later work on the Hebrew Bible shows how far she was prepared to go to apply the principle that social theory requires the most thorough of ethnographic groundings.

Conflict as Blame, Tension and Collective Effervescence

By the mid 1970s, Douglas was working her way stepwise to developing the materials for her understanding of the mechanisms by which social conflict was generated, but still had yet to develop them into a fully specified theory, or an account of the relationship between conflict amplification and attenuation. Nonetheless, the basic concepts had been identified in her writings from her first quarter of a century of research.

Building on Evans-Pritchard's insights on witchcraft accusations Douglas (1970b, 1980) took the centrality of blame and accusation as a ritual act conducted as an attribution of responsibility in circumstances of adversity, fear or loss. Although she had earlier argued that ritual is central to classification and to social organization, she had not hitherto fully extended that analysis to blame itself. Durkheim (1995 [1912]) had defined blame as an example of a 'negative rite', although rather oddly – at least from Douglas' point of view – he had taken it to be the mildest form of such rites. Douglas (e.g. 1970b, 1973b) recognized, as few anthropologists had done, that occult belief in witches depends for its continuation in the public domain on the existence of prior accepted or enforced modes of settlement of disputes in order to control the dangers of fission in communities that might already be small either in number or weak in terms of control of land. For the Lele, the diviners and the poison ordeal served that function, but when the Belgian authorities forbade the ordeal, the diviners lost authority. Lele life was disordered and violent enthusiasm and moral panic became difficult to restrain, without the emergence of other modes of settlement.

Douglas' approach implies the need for two kinds of evidence – evidence of witchcraft beliefs, and evidence that these beliefs are sustained by effective methods to settle cases. Recent work (Grijspaarde et al., 2013) using a sociometric approach shows that the number of witchcraft accusations in 182 communities on the margins of the Gola forest in Sierra Leone varies systematically with size and accessibility of settlements. The distribution is an inverted 'U'. Larger settlements closer to main roads and cities and smaller more isolated forest-edge villages are less likely to generate witchcraft disputes than medium-sized settlements with a moderate degree of isolation. This is because in smaller forest-edge villages, there are fewer protracted land disputes to provoke witchcraft accusations in the first place, but in larger, accessible villages, 'big men' can more readily hire a witchfinder to defuse disputes, allocate blame and arbitrate settlement of damages. In the Mende-speaking communities of the Gola forest margins, villagers believe in witches to the extent they find it worth maintaining institutions to prosecute and arbitrate cases. In short, there is no expression of witchcraft accusation without the means to diagnose and punish it. It is not that a 'cosmology' or ideology already exists and then institutions settle around it; rather, institutions generate cosmology, which is the central point of all of Douglas' work.

Douglas' analysis of blame in the writings of the 1960s rested for the most part at the level of the blaming of individuals, as in witchcraft accusation. *Purity and Danger* had hinted at the possibility of extending the analysis to the blaming and stigmatizing of whole groups, and the institutionalizing of classification systems to provide the appearance of justification for systems of social organization based on systematic mistreatment. But the crucial step was not yet taken.

In her work on the Lele, Douglas had considered the use of forensic procedures such as the poison oracle as ways of defusing confrontations and perhaps even also of diffusing blame. In the absence of law with consent, even the poison ordeal might serve to contain conflict, provided that it were seen by the accused and their accusers as being performed in a tolerably objective and reliable manner. It was a feature of African poison ordeals that, so general was confidence in their efficacy and objectivity, those accused of witchcraft at times volunteered to take the test. In some communities, once the poison had been taken and vomited, the person was immune for life from further witchcraft accusations. Douglas saw a similar logic at work in the description by the historian Keith Thomas of the role of integrative religious institutions of confession, exorcism and blessing, before their breakdown in Reformation Europe – a situation that seemed to mirror the logic of the situation prior to the 1925 Belgian decree outlawing the Lele poison oracle (Douglas, 1970b). In an introductory article (Douglas, 1970b) to an edited collection on witchcraft accusations and confessions she recognized that blame itself has its own forensics, which can reinforce and amplify conflict. But this recognition would only be more fully developed into a theoretical argument about causation and dynamics in her work two or more decades later.

The recognition in the work on the Lele of the hugely disruptive role of violent collective effervescence in the periodic outbreaks of witchcraft cleansing cults was not yet followed up with a full understanding of the dynamics of ritual conflict. All that had been achieved in *Purity and Danger* was the appreciation that rival forms of social organization were at work between the institutions for suppressing anomalies or forbidding anomalous things and institutions for accommodating them by licensed exception. The analysis was still at this stage a static one, as if the burden of Radcliffe-Brown's structural-functionalism had not yet been fully shaken off.

To the materials for understanding conflict derived from Durkheim and Evans-Pritchard, Douglas had added some emphases of her own. The first was that the adversities, things feared and things classified as potential or actual sources of adversity would typically be those that were anomalous in classification. In effect, classification as a social practice is designed to emphasize and ritually bring about stability and institutional order in an unstable world. Yet it can never completely or adequately do so. Indeed, by an unintended consequence, some of the categories used to try to achieve that outcome would themselves only amplify disorder and conflict. Things that are perceived as likely to cause loss or even catastrophe would therefore be likely to be those that were either incompletely classified or that were subject to two or more rival classifications. Evans-Pritchard had worked hard to explain contradiction in classification, for example, in Zande thought about sorcery or Nuer claims about twins being birds. Douglas (1980, 108–15) criticized her teacher's explanation for explaining anomaly away by using translation strategies that produced too much coherence and that did not sufficiently follow through Evans-Pritchard's own (only partially acknowledged) Durkheimian methodological precept (Evans-Pritchard, 1965) of explaining social values by reference to social organization rather than to ideas. Conflict cannot be reconciled by theological or translational work on concepts alone.

Second, she also showed that particular categories used for anomalies typically coded for danger. The concept of danger was intimately linked with that of anomaly, and indeed as one universally thrown up in every kind of social organization throughout geography and history. Its role is to mark not only boundaries against physical loss but also social boundaries against threats to classification. The tendency for categories used for difficult, problematic, anomalous things gradually to become equivalent in meaning to the idea of 'danger' was one that would become central to her work on the idea of risk in later decades.

The third distinctive resource she brought to the understanding of conflict in the 1960s was her emphasis on the marking of classified boundaries around what she would later openly refer to as 'groups'. At this stage, the reinforcement and amplification of boundary-marking in moments of collective effervescence lacked a name and an account of its cybernetic dynamics. But the rigidity and purity-seeking of boundary-marking between groups in conflict provided her with a key part of a mechanism she could invoke to show just why groups organized according to Durkheim's mechanical solidarities might be so destructive when they collided, either with each other or with groups organized around principles of organic solidarity.

Also still missing at this stage was any way of developing Durkheim's careful acknowledgement, in both the discussion of the French Revolution in *Forms* and in his analysis of educational change (Durkheim, 1977 [1938]), that the destruction of collective effervescence might be as institutionally creative over the longer run as it was brutal in the short.

These arguments identified her peculiar strategy. Although she had not yet developed the machinery with which to demonstrate it, her 1960s work on the Lele already showed that both conflict and the delicate design of offsetting institutions by which conflict is at least partially and incompletely contained are processes that must be explained functionally. In a period when many anthropologists, sociologists and political scientists were coming to believe that the only way out of the dead end of structural-functionalism was to go back to methodological individualism, her strategy was distinctive. However, making the argument convincing required her to develop some new machinery for identifying, comparing and contrasting the basic forms of social organization. These forms, she was already arguing, cultivate the thought styles that either deepen conflict or contain it. It was to that task that she would devote much of the 1970s and 1980s.

Note

1. All cited works by Mary Douglas are listed in a separate section of the references entitled 'Cited Works by Mary Douglas'.

2

COMPARING ON A GRAND SCALE
Elementary Forms Do the Organizing

This chapter examines the major developments in theory made in Douglas' 'middle period' from 1970 through to the mid 1980s. It argues that even though in this period many people thought that she had abandoned her previous interests, adopted a new theory and started to work on quite different problems from the ethnographic issues of the 1950s and 1960s, the very converse was the case. She developed the typology of a limited number of elementary forms of social organization precisely to solve the problems she had set for herself in those earlier years. This chapter examines that typology and shows how it was grounded in an underlying theory. It contrasts the different ways in which Douglas tried to present this theory. It also examines the transformation made in the 1980s of the central concept of anomaly developed by Douglas in the 1960s, once the concept was combined with a novel typology. Douglas' collaborators then proceeded to demonstrate that it was not only methodologically important, but also causally central to the theory of dynamics and change they provided for her theory. We examine her turn to the study of risk not as a change of subject, but as a way of deepening her theory of the manner in which organization cultivates thought, of the ways that anomalies can be managed and of the tendency for concepts used to characterize anomalies to collapse into codes for danger, especially when conflicts deepen and social organization begins to polarize. This chapter also examines the arguments made by critics of Douglas' typology, and summarizes some of the principal rejoinders made by her and her associates. We also briefly review two typologies offered by other scholars for purposes apparently similar to Douglas' own, but which we show to be differently based.

Douglas' work in the 1960s argued with increasingly force and clarity that social organization drives cognition, not the other way around. *Purity and Danger*, for example, had shown that ideas of the anomalous pangolin in Lele life, or ideas of prohibited prawns in Leviticus, neither reflected biological facts about scaly anteaters or crustaceans nor were myths developed in a theological vacuum around which people subsequently began to organize; rather, they formed parts of systems of rationalization for social boundaries and structures. Accountabilities among people and institutions, and boundaries between groups or tiers within a group will always be represented using some particular classifications or symbols. There is no necessity underpinning prohibitions on pork or prawns. These prohibitions are instances of exemplary classifications by which social boundaries are marked. Eschewed foods are commonly used for such a purpose since eating is a daily and often communal, routine yet ritually rich activity. In principle, Lele people could have used something other than the pangolin around which to represent and organize their complicated settlements among generations, sexes and roles. But the prevailing form of social organization seeks expression in classifications of things in people's immediate surroundings. If to many the animal seems exotic, it was familiar to the Lele hunters and doubtless was an everyday talking point.

Prohibitions, the manner in which symbolic exemplars were treated, and myths and justifications around them all resulted, Douglas argued, from intricate accommodations made between different strands and styles of social organization, by which conflict is both sustained but also managed and, when management works, is contained. In turn, the accommodations defined and specified available interests rather than being shaped by prior or given payoffs. Douglas showed that people enacted these aspects of organization ritually. The ritual forms directed attention and memory, fixed and reinforced categories, and could also bring about real change in social organization. She had shown that some things were generic social universals for which some particular categories would be found in any social context. These included boundaries, dangers and powers. But all this remained very schematic. Douglas' work would have remained a set of unredeemed theoretical promises if she had not developed three things: an account of the available variety of elementary forms of social organization ('elementary form' is Durkheim's 1995 [1912] coinage); a way of explaining and predicting the particular types of classification, rituals and ways of managing anomalies cultivated and sustained in each; and some dynamic theory of how self-reinforcements could disorganize themselves as well as clash with other forms (as Durkheim himself had shown for large-scale institutional arrangements, in the 1984 [1893] book *Division* and for the individual will to continue with life in the 1951 [1897] book *Suicide*).

It is important to appreciate just how great her ambition was. Implicitly, Douglas' argument in *Purity and Danger* was that humanity is one species subject to many of the same basic constraints everywhere, at every scale of organization and in every period of human history. Therefore, she concluded, variation in the basic ways in which people think must also be limited.

The development of her theory in the 1970s was premised on her next, deeply Durkheimian move in the argument – one that was decreasingly fashionable in anthropology at the time. She argued that the limitation in variety should be explained at the level of the most fundamental dimensions of the ordering of relations among people, rather than simply by locally contingent and case-specific features of context.

This was the reason that she needed to develop a typology of universally available elementary social forms. Organizing her theory around a small number of universally found dimensions of variation in social organization had major consequences for the relationship her approach could then have with other traditions of theory in the social sciences. It implied a commitment to two distinctions not widely accepted, even by other traditions emphasizing the importance of social organization and institutions. The first of these distinctions is that between the form of social institutions and their content. Consider two commonly used terms in social science: 'bureaucracy' and 'market'. In content, bureaucracy is concerned with the administrative work carried out in support of the activities of states. In content, markets provide the basis for the exchange of resources for goods and services, whether by means of money or barter. But there is no single institutional form that describes all bureaucracies or markets. Weber famously diagnosed hierarchy in bureaucracy, but was very careful to insist this was true only of his ideal type and made clear that the Prussian and German cases he knew best were very far from instances of that ideal type. Some are cases of 'club government' (Moran, 2003), which are, in Douglas' terms, enclaved. Accounts of highly individualistic bureaucracies are not uncommon. Michael Lipsky (1980) in effect identified the importance of both individualistic and isolate orderings among street-level bureaucrats. Others have identified despotic isolate forms in Nazi and Soviet bureaucracies (Fraenkel, 1941; Stern 1984 [1975]; Montefiore, 2003). Markets, too, can be individualistic, oligopolistic and enclaved, and also at times rather hierarchical when the structure of supply chains is taken into account, as studies such as Stinchcombe's (1990, 194–239) work have demonstrated, or indeed fragmented, ad hoc affairs marked by isolate ordering. Unlike for wheat, for example, there is no single centralized global exchange for the commodity rice (Latham, 1998, 1). Merchants and, indeed, rice-dependent countries strike deals where they can. Moreover, most bureaucracies and markets exhibit some mix of these forms, constantly changing subtly in the relative weight of hierarchy, individualism, and enclaved and isolate ordering. In this way, Douglas' argument provides a much richer conceptual framework for the building of explanatory theory than does the empirical 'markets, hierarchies and networks' trichotomy (e.g. Thompson et al, 1991) adopted by the 'new institutionalist' sociologists in the 1980s, and to which many still cleave (6, 2015a).

The second distinction to which this strategy committed Douglas was also a deeply Durkheimian one. Her argument distinguished between the empirical aspects of institutions and their underlying elementary forms. Although the loose trichotomy of 'markets, hierarchies and networks' appeared at first sight to identify underlying forms, as we have noted, it did not do so in a consistent and rigorous way. The distinction between the empirical and the elementary form levels of analysis is therefore a distinctive feature of Douglas' approach. It is not shared by most other institutional traditions. For example, historical institutionalist and rational choice institutionalist frameworks do not recognize it at all, and even many of the sociological institutionalist traditions do not use the loose trichotomy. For historical institutionalists, for example, the context that institutions furnish and that helps to explain people's decisions is a local, empirical affair and therefore varies widely in its empirical forms. From her early debates in Oxford, this use of 'context' had always seemed to Douglas to be ad hoc – indeed, to be little more than what she termed 'handwaving' – when what was required was clear, specified, parsimonious explanation. That required not simply giving up context and resorting to taking preferences as given, but also a theory of what a context is and what basic variety in context means for explanation. As the argument in the previous paragraph shows, the distinction between empirical and elementary forms has important theoretical advantages. But when, in the 1980s and 1990s, Douglas sought to present her theory in ways that might attract allies from among the followers of other institutionalist traditions, it was this Durkheimian distinction between the elementary and the empirical levels of analysis, as much as the particular typology of forms at the elementary level, that was to remain a point of divergence.

Durkheim's translator, Karen Fields (Durkheim, 1995, lx), glosses the French sociologist's concept of an elementary form as being the social equivalent of an elementary particle in physics, from which more complex forms are built, right up to those we can observe without complex instrumentation. Like elementary particles in physics, elementary forms of institutions for Durkheim (Fields suggests) 'have an underlying identity that persists despite increasing change and limitless diversity'. Like a physicist, therefore, Douglas needed a typology of elementary forms.

The typology she developed was to provide a method for comparative anthropology by diagnosing the presence and relative weighting of elementary forms in different contexts. It would also explain at a general level just which kinds of cognition and rituals could be expected to be cultivated in exactly which kinds of social organizations.

Typology and a Further Attempt to Explain Ritual

Natural Symbols, published in 1970, can be classified together with the first edition of *Implicit Meanings* as belonging to a period of transition in Douglas' thought. It was once again comparative anthropology. Nonetheless, its use of data from family memoir to illustrate some of her arguments offended the methodological sensitivities of some colleagues. Like *Purity and Danger*, the book was centrally concerned with questions about ritual and its relationship with belief. Although Douglas would later recant some of the argument, *Natural Symbols* was a hugely important milestone in the development of her theory. Several distinct arguments were pursued.

The book's most general argument was that symbols – such as those deployed in religious life – are selected, developed, cultivated and used not because they are somehow obvious or ready to hand, as a result of biological processes, or through being modelled on the body, but because they serve the imperatives created by particular forms of social organization and disorganization. As Durkheim and Mauss (1963 [1902–3], 11) had argued for classification in general in their monograph on 'primitive classification', 'the classification of things reproduces [the] classification of [people]'. In *Natural Symbols*,

Douglas shifted Durkheim's and Mauss' argument slightly to make the case that the ways in which symbols representing the human body are used replicate and effectively but indirectly symbolize forms of social organization. This argument had been latent in *Purity and Danger*, but now Douglas set it out using machinery from a part of Durkheim's argument that she had not used before. In 1970, when she wrote *Natural Symbols*, she had not yet formulated the concept of a thought style. A second transposition of Durkheim's and Mauss' argument – from explaining particular items, such as symbols or categories, in the overt content of thought to explaining styles of thinking – was one that she would make a decade and a half later in *How Institutions Think*.

However, Douglas began the main argument of *Natural Symbols* with the observation that some whole societies (however defined) and some contexts within them exhibit very strong commitment to formal, explicit, ceremonial ritual performance, and others exhibit very little. Writing in 1970, the immediate connection between symbol and ritual required little explanation. Douglas argued that none of the standard contextual claims about historical change – industrial production, advanced technology, urbanism, which are the usual historicist attempts to distinguish 'modern' from 'pre-modern' settings – will serve to pick out those settings where ritual is heavily articulated from those where it is not. Nor will differences in ideas or ideologies provide an explanation. As Durkheim had intuited, Douglas finds that variation of social organization is a more plausible explanation of ritual practice. In order to explain varieties of everyday ritual performance, a richer typology of basic forms of social organization was needed. In *Natural Symbols* (Douglas, 1970a) she worked with a fairly simple contrast between strong and weak articulation of ritual. At this point, she had no empirically specified set of general contrasts between styles or types of ritual, although her field materials were already strong enough to suggest ways of doing this. Nevertheless, the book paid much closer attention than *Purity and Danger* to what ritual does. It laid out her argument that ritual is not, as many 1960s radicals had claimed, a kind of sham or insincere keeping-up of appearances, nor just another aspect of symbolization, but a causal mechanism by which categories are fixed and social organization is sustained.

To develop her fourfold typology of forms of social organization, Douglas turned to the work of the educational theorist and sociolinguist Basil Bernstein. Bernstein tried to explain differences he believed he had observed between working and middle class households in the use of language, in a series of papers (e.g. Bernstein 1971, and subsequent volumes in the series) by distinguishing between a 'restricted code' and an 'elaborated code'. Bernstein himself (e.g. 1975 [1966], 54–66) emphasized the concept of ritual mainly in formal ceremonial in the household and school settings, partly under the influence of *Purity and Danger*. His theory was important for Douglas because she regarded his account of language use as a treatment that recognized the ritual aspects of speech, even – indeed, especially – in the everyday, secular, conversational settings in which socialization of thought style takes place. Restricted codes exhibited a narrow range of rigidly organized alternative formulations of speech, which were replicated in the body and were used to reinforce discipline and social control; intentions and reasons remained implicit. They were, he claimed, based on what he called a 'positional' system of family organization with ascribed role categories and permissions to speak and act on the basis of status. This, he thought, he observed in working-class households. By contrast, he thought he had found in middle-class households uses of language that selected from a wider and flexibly organized range of linguistic alternatives. Reasons were made explicit and intentions overtly stated. Social structure in the family was less disciplinarian. This he called a 'personal' family system. Interestingly, the famous U.S. political scientist and sociologist Robert Putnam has recently (2015) revived Bernstein's argument. Although Bernstein sought to avoid making explicit judgements concerning the superiority of either code, his account suggested he considered the elaborated code to be more civilized. Douglas rejected this view. For her, the interest in restricted code lay in the notion that it represented a style of ritual, grounded in a more disciplined form of social organization, and that this might explain the greater articulation of ritual in such settings. Whether Douglas persuaded Bernstein to separate the form of control from the type of code or whether he had in any case been moving in that direction, in *Natural Symbols,* Douglas cross-tabulated the two dimensions, and in some of his later papers, Bernstein did the same thing. In the cells of the cross-tabulation she identified four types of social organization.

In a later chapter, she reworked Bernstein's category of personal and positional control as the degree to which an individual is controlled by pressure from others and labelled this dimension 'group'. Then she recast the type of code as the degree to which classifications are shared openly or are private to the people involved in a given setting, labelling this dimension 'grid'. In so doing, she had worked her way back to Durkheim's (1951 [1897]) two dimensions of institutional variation – social integration and social regulation.

Defining social regulation or 'grid' by classification created some difficulties. For it is the case that classifications are ideas. They are supposed to be explained by social organization or be symptoms of it. They are not supposed to be the things doing the explaining. Only in later formulations did Douglas provide a definition characterized by tightly or weakly disciplined kinds of substantive social accountability in relations and organization describable independently of ideas. There is little point now in trying to map Bernstein's categories very precisely onto those that Douglas identified. She conceded later that the fit was less than precise. Bernstein provided a runway for take-off, not the aeroplane itself. In any case, there were several definitions in *Natural Symbols* of her own two dimensions, and the differences among them were not completely resolved, even in the second edition, where she revised the treatment of the typology. Obsessing about these difficulties should be avoided, since *Natural Symbols* proved to be only a first draft of a complex argument.

It is however, worth noting that only on one page (Douglas, 1970a, 59) did Douglas acknowledge that the ultimate source of the approach was Durkheim's distinction. Even in her later writings, she made only scant acknowledgement of these Durkheimian roots. Perhaps the earliest explicit discussion is by Ostrander (1982, 17) some twelve years after *Natural Symbols* was published, in a volume of essays edited by Douglas herself and devoted to applications of the scheme. Seemingly, this relative silence has a reason. Douglas did what Durkheim himself had failed to do, and so liberated the full potential of a less than fully worked scheme. She cross-tabulated the two dimensions in order to attend to the forms identified in the cells rather than those that are found at the apices, which is where attention is directed in Durkheim's account.

At this stage, Douglas only gave numerical identifiers to the four forms. However, they were clearly recognizable as what she would later call hierarchy, enclave, isolate ordering and individualism. She argued that these forms are permanent features of human life in both large- and small-scale organization and when using either simple or complicated technologies. Thus, she directly challenged Weber's claim that human history exhibits a progression towards more 'modern' forms that are novel, unique and rational. Schematically, she proposed that ritual would be strongly articulated in the world of strong social regulation or 'high grid'. However, in the world of weak regulation, she did not predict the complete absence of ritual practice. That she considered impossible, presumably on the Durkheimian argument that without some ritual practice, at least of an informal and quotidian kind in ritualized everyday interaction, people could not maintain even the categories necessary to negotiate in discretionary environments. Rather, she expected such settings to be characterized by waves of unstable fervent collective effervescence such as millennialism. Only in her later writings would she clarify that this is to be expected specifically in the combination of weak regulation with strong social integration in the enclave quadrant.

Given the preoccupations of mainstream anthropology at the time, not least with historical and Marxist debates, it is unsurprising that some were confused by or heartily disliked *Natural Symbols*. Some of Douglas' choices of illustration for her arguments led Edmund Leach to dismiss the book as Catholic propaganda. To an extent, she turned her back on these jibes. Determined to persist with her typological approach to structural theory meant that after the mid 1970s, she began to engage with a multidisciplinary field, in the hope of establishing her case more widely across the social sciences.

From Typology to Method

The rhetoric of *Natural Symbols* promised a 'dynamic' theory able to facilitate global comparisons among settings, societies and periods. A programme of that kind required the still schematic typology to be turned into a method, consisting in a set of indicators that could be used in fieldwork to code and locate cases, and that would be capable of being calibrated across cases both for consistency in comparison and to enable the measurement of the degree of change over time within cases. Having rounded off her African ethnographic work with the collection, *Implicit Meanings*, Douglas turned, in the second half of the 1970s, to this new task with energy and determination. Then, in the early 1980s, while working at Northwestern University, she began to draw upon colleagues and her former doctoral students back at UCL to develop the approach into a method.

Her first major systematic statement of the typology, prepared shortly before her move to the United States, took the form of her 1977 Frazer lecture published in 1978 by her hosts, the Royal Anthropological Institute as an Occasional Paper, under the title 'Cultural Bias' and subsequently reprinted in another collection of her papers four years later (Douglas, 1982a [1978]). Both the title and the framing of the argument were surprising. 'Culture' had not been a term of any great prominence in Douglas' previous writings, but occasional uses fully a decade before (e.g. Douglas, 1999a [1975], 106–15) had indicated that she defined the term as the set of ideas, myths, beliefs, values and goals found in a given social setting. Probably the change in terminology reflected the growing use of the term during the 1970s in theory in anthropology, political science and sociology (e.g. Almond and Verba, 1963; Bell, 1976; Geertz, 1973; Hebdige, 1979; Sahlins, 1976). In *Natural Symbols* and in *Purity and Danger*, she had laid out the programme for explaining beliefs, values, etc. by reference to the form of social organization, even if she had not worked out in those books a way of measuring organization independently of cognition. The monograph sharply rejects the view that culture requires no explanation (Douglas, 1982a [1978], 184–85). Yet, oddly for a study in method, she avoided a tight definition of her key term.

The short monograph on cultural bias presented the method under the title 'grid-group analysis'. The label would prove durable, at least as a reference to her method of static comparison, even if it was something of a millstone. Unfortunately for Douglas' larger ambitions, emphasis on the analytic method of coding and prediction of patterns came, for many readers, to obscure the underlying causal explanation that it was supposed to serve.

The causal explanation was that the form of social organization, now called 'the social context' rather than 'social structure', should, by ritual means, cultivate the patterns of cognition, which in this study were called 'cosmological values'. Two years after 'Cultural Bias', in her short book on the ideas of her teacher, Edward Evans-Pritchard (Douglas, 1980), she tried out another term, 'accountabilities', focusing on a concept of how social organization might manifest itself in relations among people and empirical institutions. This was not an entirely happy choice, for among non-anthropologists, accountability tends to be understood to mean quite straightforwardly the formal, explicit duty to provide some account of one's actions to a second party, as in financial accounting, or as in the role of the British Permanent Secretary as the 'accounting officer' for a government department. Being held to account is a formal and an episodic affair, once every year before the Public Accounts Committee or once a month before a review committee. Douglas' anthropological usage required no such conditions. Instead, it simply emphasized the continuous and often informal pressures and demands placed by institutions upon people, without any implication of a duty to supply retrospective description and self-justification. Now that she was trying to reach out to other disciplines, the usage was in fact a liability, and she used it more sparingly thereafter.

Douglas' theory in 'Cultural Bias' certainly takes what most scholars would call a structural view of what social organization is. The two dimensions of variation are aspects of what most people would call social structure, and likewise her description of those features of social context which do the explaining, structural factors. Yet in this instance she also largely avoided the term 'structure'. When she used it at all, it was to describe *strong* degrees of vertical separation in status between higher and lower positions, as in, for example, the case of hierarchical ordering. In this presentation of her theory, the phrase 'social structure' was reserved for special cases of what more generally might be referred to as social context. Nor did she at this stage write of 'social organization'. That would come later (see, for example, some of the late papers collected in Fardon (2013a)), after Thompson, Ellis and Wildavsky (1990) had provided her with a more dynamic account of how the elementary forms furnished 'ways of organizing'. In 'Cultural Bias', social context is addressed by static comparison. Only later did she come to her mature view that social structure is itself a dynamic force capable of and, indeed, constantly engaged in assertion, deepening and extension in each of its particular forms, and therefore a motor of conflict among those forms.

'Cultural Bias' set out measures for social organization by social regulation or 'grid' and social integration or 'group'. The former was measured by control, division and the deployment of instruments for conflict control. This was an altogether superior definition than the one given in *Natural Symbols*, for now the grid dimension was defined by social relations exclusively and not by ideational factors such as classifications, which are supposed to be what the whole structure explains. Social integration is operationalized by the porousness of boundaries, the scope for interaction across them, and degrees of individual autonomy (1982a [1978], 205–8). This, too, was much clearer than the somewhat loose term 'pressure' placed on an individual by other people, which Douglas had used in *Natural Symbols*. The 'cultural side' of the explanatory relation was measured by stances toward nature, time, space, health and justice. The result was a structured measurement system organized according to the study of both the 'independent variables' of social organization' and the 'dependent variables' of symbols and ideas. The argument was illustrated with examples from comparative anthropology, sociology and even art history.

'Cultural Bias' made clear that the derivation of the four forms, as represented by the cross-tabulation, was a deductive inference. In this respect, the ambition of the theory was to replicate the scheme of deductive inference (with its lemmas and theses derived from fundamental axioms) given the highest respect in the natural sciences.

However, by the late 1970s, deductive approaches had come under suspicion among anthropologists. The shift towards inductive designs for research, and toward reliance upon categories taken from the people being studied, was advocated by Clifford Geertz and others, and was beginning to be fashionable by the time Douglas published 'Cultural Bias'. Geertz himself (e.g. Geertz, 1973) had written of his method as being the decoding of 'cultural systems', and perhaps Douglas' choice of 'culture' for her terminology was made in part to open up a conversation with those who used Geertz's categories. But the gulf between them in terms of method and approach to theory building was unbridgeable. In the subsequent decades, under the influence of the anthropologist Maurice Leenhardt and later the historian of anthropology James Clifford, the turn towards inductive research and etic categories came to be allied with a thoroughgoing interpretivism, in which the aspiration for causal explanation was rejected (for a Douglas-inspired critique of this kind of interpretivism now spread across other social sciences, see 6 and Bellamy (2016)). Even as Douglas was adding rigour, clarity and measurement capability to her theory, the discipline of anthropology was moving in a different direction and was losing interest in the kind of explanatory approach she defended.

However, in 'Cultural Bias', Douglas' four forms of social organization were still not yet given the labels by which they would later become well known. Now the numbers used in *Natural Symbols* simply gave way to letter codes. For ease of reference, the following brief summary uses the names by which the four forms became better known from Douglas' later writings (especially Douglas, 1992a, 1996b).

The combination of strong social regulation or 'grid' with strong social integration or 'group' results in hierarchy, in the very particular anthropological sense that Douglas gave the term, consistent with the understanding propounded by Louis Dumont (1980 [1966]), even if (alas) this clashed rather sharply with common usage in sociology and political science, where often the term is used to mean command or even just inequality. Dumont (1980 [1966], 65) defined hierarchy as 'the principle by which elements of a whole are ranked in relation to the whole' (see Barnes (1985) for a discussion). In the same spirit, Herbert Simon (1996, 184–86) defined hierarchy as a 'system analysable into successive sets of subsystems', indicating clearly that the overarching system exhibited a significant degree of integration. For common membership provided by social integration meant that the regulation could not be simply coercive and required that even subalterns had their own proper status in the community, even though the system of rule-based authorizations would make those status discriminations asymmetrical ('a hierarchy has to have a first place, but the next place is not without honour': Douglas, 1993a, 181). Power follows authority and status, and ultimately rests with the whole integrated community. In reading Douglas on hierarchy, this specific usage must always be kept clearly in mind.

Weak integration and weak regulation yielded individual choice and discretion and therefore resulted in negotiated relations, which in Douglas (1982b) came to be called, clearly enough, individualism. Here status, if it has any independence at all, follows power, which is achieved by individual control of resources and through attracting followers with hope of rewards or advantages.

Weak social regulation – where, for example, authority is remote or local rules have been introduced by a community itself or where prescription is actively rejected – combined with strong integration yields a condition in which people can rely neither upon individually negotiated relations, for those would undermine integration, nor upon superior authority, for that would undermine the particular manner of their own integration. Therefore, to sustain such cohesion as is possible in these conditions, people resort to assertively insisted-upon beliefs and emotions attached to strong membership. It is here that the theory predicts that collective effervescence in the registers identified by Durkheim – sectarian fervour and even millennial or witchcraft-cleansing cults – will be unleashed.

In the presence of weak integration, strong regulation will lead people who cannot easily sustain collective action with others and who are subject to tight controls to evade or succumb to those controls. Unable to rely on others and at risk of arbitrary control, people will adopt short term, coping strategies (cf. 6, 2016b). Here, theory predicts manifestations of what has sometimes been termed 'isolate ordering', as perhaps manifest in secretive underclass rituals of subversion encountered in slavery-based societies.

In deriving these four forms, therefore, Douglas needs no separate or additional theory of power. Power is a vectored pattern of relations among the forms. Within each form, distinctive practices of powering are sustained. These are practices of authority in hierarchy, of the self-assertion of those who can broker their way to controlling resources and so secure support from followers by expectation of future reward in individualistic ordering, of collective assertion in enclaved settings and, where there is power at all in isolate ordering, of the practices of a despotic form of the passing on of constraints by imposition.

Although some of Douglas' later collaborators such as Wildavsky would not consistently follow her in this regard, she herself was consistent throughout her writings that her typology did not treat any of the forms as 'unmarked' or of limited application. All the forms will arise because people will reach for them in disappointment with any of the others. Nor, indeed, were the inequalities between senior and subaltern in hierarchy, between patron and client in individualistically ordered patronage systems (such as those found in the late Roman republic: Wallace-Hadrill, 1989), between prophet and acolytes in enclave ordering or between despot and serf in isolate ordering, to be treated simply as marked and unmarked pairs. Each depends on the others.

Are these four the only elementary forms of social organization and of bias? Douglas devoted several pages in 'Cultural Bias' to the argument that there may indeed be one other form, the possibility of which she had briefly acknowledged in *Natural Symbols*. In her subsequent writing, she never used it, although Michael Thompson (e.g. 1982b, 2008), who drew heavily upon her work, would later make the fifth form central to his reworking of her theory. The typology is a scheme of forms of social organization. But what of those few rare individuals who operate outside social organization, at least as far as and for as long as it is feasible to do so? In several parts of the world, people voluntarily withdraw to live the life of a recluse or hermit. Douglas (1982a [1978], 205) decided, given the form that she had given her diagram, that this possibility lay 'off the map'. Nevertheless, she sought to provide an extended characterization of the hermit's life (1982a [1978], 232–38). The reason that this lies 'off the map' is that while the hermit withdraws from social life, that withdrawal is not collective, as is the withdrawal of the enclaved sect, but individual. But nor is it enforced from without, as in the condition of the isolate pushed to the margins, confined but still within social organization. Like hierarchical life, hermit practice is usually one of ritualized discipline, often of a spiritual kind, yet entirely avoiding the social integration of hierarchy. Like individualistic ordering, individual choice is exercised, but the hermit withdraws from all transaction and brokering, and the discipline is incompatible with the day-to-day discretion afforded under individualistic institutions. Unfortunately, Douglas' examples in her discussion are less convincingly classified under that form than are her examples of the principal four kinds. She admits that Henry David Thoreau – an example she discussed at length – withdrew very partially (Emerson allowed him to live at Walden rent-free), only temporarily (his longest stay was just over a year) and with the project of writing for publication: 'The more that the hermit thinks it worthwhile speaking out and seeking for his voice to be heard abroad, the more he is edging onto the social map and becoming part of the throng to which he preaches. The most silent are the most authentic representatives of this cosmology' (Douglas, 1982a [1978], 235). Many historical hermits have not even sought to meet this condition. The stylite saints were fed by generous crowds of followers and preached at length; the so-called 'desert fathers' of early Christianity formed a kind of enclave. Some cave-dwelling hermits in the Buddhist tradition take withdrawal further. Yet even the celebrated Tibetan hermit Milarepa composed vast quantities of poetry intended to be read by others. Moreover, when he broke the pot in which he boiled his nettle leaves – his final dependency on other people – he died, presumably of starvation (Michael Thompson, personal communication, 2015), thus poignantly indicating limits to the feasibility of what Douglas described as the 'most authentic' practice of hermit life. Moreover, although Douglas – no hermit herself – praised the integrity of the eremitic vision in 'Cultural Bias', in fact, it has its own biases and carries no greater guarantee of clarity of vision, let alone of practical usability, than any other form. Milarepa's end describes what Durkheim might have called a form of suicide distinctive of an eremitic form of *a*social organization.

As Douglas admitted at the end of 'Cultural Bias', what was still missing was a clear account of causation, to redeem the promise in *Purity and Danger* of an account of just how ritual works to cultivate ideas from social organization. Causal explanations were given, but neither with emphasis nor formalization. However, she did make it clear that in the case of some of the 'cosmological values' – such as those of justice – beliefs are cultivated through *ex post facto* rationalization and justification of the form of social organization in order to defend it against potentially undermining anomalies. The four elementary forms are fragile islands of consistency, vulnerable to waves of anomaly crashing over their shores. Therefore, they require culture as a set of sea-defences against the possibility of anomalous overwhelming. In other cases, causation takes the negative form of blinkering. The constraints of 'social context' obscure from people in those settings the relevance or appeal of ideas other than those locally cultivated.

Although not fully acknowledged in 'Cultural Bias', the causal relation is a functional one, because 'cosmological values' concerning, for example, the foreshortening of planning horizons in isolate life, or the lengthening of collective memory in hierarchical ordering, are in fact solutions to organizational problems (specifically, the problem of how to sustain the form of organization) created by the combination of strong or weak regulation and integration. Just as reaching for fervent commitment to belief and principle provides a fragile and provisional solution to the difficulties of sustaining organization in the absence of authority, and the ability to negotiate or secure individual loyalty instrumentally, so in each of the elementary forms, the way of thinking about justice, time, etc. are cognitive resorts for dealing with difficulties and challenges created by institutional ordering, defined by the two dimensions of variation. On the other hand, analysis is not directed at some supposedly unitary 'society'. Rather, units can be specified at any scale or aggregation. This is because the whole point of the theory is to explain conflict among the elementary forms and to explain conflict within each form from data on breakdown, when established resorts fail to provide workable solutions to the organizational problems. In short, the functional explanations actually undermine functionalism. Douglas had now found a decisive way out of Radcliffe-Brown's and Talcott Parsons' functional*ism*, but without abandoning the centrality of functional explanation.

Even so, in 'Cultural Bias', the inflammatory word 'function' was eschewed. The defence of the functional explanations that underpinned her theory would have to wait until the mid 1980s. Nonetheless, Douglas paid a price for coyness about causation in 'Cultural Bias' and for postponing its analysis until her later writings. *Natural Symbols* appeared to make the extent and form of ritual part of what was to be explained – as if ritual were on the side of cognition along with the 'cosmological values'. Thus, the Durkheimian insight which had been much clearer in *Purity and Danger* was now partly submerged, namely, that ritual, in its everyday Goffmanesque (1967a) form, was in fact a causal mechanism. Its role was to explain *how* the two institutional orderings described in the two dimensions could work to cultivate and reinforce ideas, beliefs, symbols, cosmological values and 'culture'. As a result of this underspecification, her theory, in the minds of many readers, came to be seen as being no more than a typology, because the causal engine was only explained separately and rather later, and in the book *How Institutions Think*, which many found inaccessible.

Moreover, in this 1970s formulation, Douglas was unclear how she wished the reader to regard social regulation and social integration. Binary contrasts between strong and weak locations on her two dimensions were emphasized, but she also made it clear that, in principle at least, she regarded the two axes as continuously differentiable, and made occasional references to 'moderate' scores, locating some contexts more toward the centre than the periphery of what was thereby turned from a table of cells into a chart of scales. Indeed, as late as 1996, when she republished several papers using the typology in a volume entitled *Thought Styles*, she still maintained the interpretation of the dimensions as continuously differentiable.

Neither option is entirely happy on theoretical grounds. The binary interpretation preserves parsimony and captures well the underlying argument that the elementary forms of human social organization can only be plural to a limited extent. Yet it makes it difficult for the scheme to demonstrate the content of, and provide means of comparative scaling for, hybrids, messy settlements and mixed forms that are the common condition of most social agreements, at all but the tiniest of social magnitudes. Conversely, continuous differentiability undermines the notion, put most clearly by Thompson (1996, 2008) using terms from complexity theory, that the four forms are discrete 'attractors'. It also fails to do justice to Douglas' own argument, which would be stressed in her later writings on risk, that the four settlement types often face each other in adversarial confrontation and countervailing reaction rather than in contented alliance. While mathematically, there are ways of modifying both interpretations to allow for these things (Gross and Rayner, 1986), the modifications lose the clean lines of something intended to be elementary.

Four years later, in 1982, Douglas published an extensive and varied edited volume under rather anodyne title *Essays in the Sociology of Perception* (Douglas, 1982b). Dull as this seemed, it was a title that signalled clearly her intention to appeal to sociologists, just as her book of the same year with Aaron Wildavsky indicated her determination to direct her case to his discipline, political science. The use of the term 'perception', a term of art for philosophers and psychologists more than for sociologists, further signalled that she now wanted her theory to be understood as one that explained something much broader than those matters sociologists tended to consider as 'culture', for at that time, the word tended to be used in sociology much more narrowly than anthropologists used it. It was also intended to give greater precision, for sociologists then tended to consider social relations, institutions and 'context' as part of culture, whereas Douglas' central claim was that they explained the *cognition* that she defined as belonging within culture. Finally, it was intended to generate interest in the theory among those who studied 'risk perception', even though the *Essays* were not principally about risk.

The volume appeared in the same year as *Risk and Culture*, discussed below, which announced her new empirical focus. This collection displayed some of the first studies carried out using the method that she had laid out in 'Cultural Bias'. These ranged from theoretical development using Thompson's mathematical modelling, to a small survey of industrial scientists, to historical works on ancient China, to her former Ph.D. student Steve Rayner's participant observation studies on revolutionary sects in late 1970s south London.

As well as Ostrander's attempt to ground the typology in a wider field of social theory, Douglas now gave labels to the four forms. In her introduction, she offered 'atomised subordination' for the weakly integrated but strongly regulated condition she would later call 'isolate' ordering. The term left unanswered the question of whether it was not also possible to find such a context among people who were not subordinates. A constitutional monarch, strongly bound by duty and limited in its range of social relationships, is as likely an instance of a person bound by this form of ordering as a slave. Hierarchy was at this stage qualified as 'ascribed' in order to contrast it with the achievement-orientation of individualism. The qualification was later dropped, doubtless because the distinctions of status reflected authorizations granted to positions rather than, in the usual sense, ascribed characteristics of individuals. Finally, enclave was known at this stage as 'factionalism'.

Of particular importance for the development of the theory were the two papers in the collection contributed by Michael Thompson (1982a, 1982b), which for the first time supplied a dynamic theory of change between forms to what had hitherto been a typological theory of variation designed for cross-sectional comparative analysis. Thompson at this stage drew upon catastrophe theory models of sudden change, but he would later draw on cybernetic systems theory, thus explaining less drastic forms of change using combinations of feedback processes.

Another important innovation was contributed by the philosopher and historian of science David Bloor, who recognized the centrality to Douglas' method of the analysis of things that are anomalous in classification. His paper showed that the treatment of things found anomalous in each of the four forms could be mapped directly onto the typology of such treatments developed by the philosopher of science Imre Lakatos for dealing with anomalies in evidence for scientific theories. This led to the wholesale adoption by many of those who used Douglas' theoretical arguments of Lakatos' typology of 'monster exploitation', 'adjustment', 'barring' and 'acceptance' as thought styles for handling anomalies.

Douglas' postdoctoral fellow, the psychologist James Hampton, set out the first use of the method for attitudinal survey design, developing what was then intended to be a basis for a validated set of standard questions and scales. These would later provide Dake and Wildavsky (1990) with the starting point for their approach to designing survey instrumentation to test Douglas' theory, an approach that continues to be used (cf. Kahan et al, 2011, discussed below).

Also significant for future developments was Rayner's derivation from the theory of predictions about perceptions of time and space in enclaved settings that he then tested. This study would be influential not only in subsequent work by Douglasians on time in organizations (e.g. Peck and 6, 2006, 50–77), but also in shaping Douglas' own thinking about sects and enclaves (see e.g. Douglas and Mars, 2003, discussed below in relation to Douglas and Wildavsky, 1982). Rayner's (1982) study filled out the argument of 'Cultural Bias', for it laid out, much more clearly than Douglas herself had done, a functional explanation of both collective memory and shared notions of the future, for example, in planning horizon. Thus, in enclaved institutions, we expect the planning horizon to be foreshortened because this will sustain the urgency of principled collective action. Glorious redemption will soon be possible if only everyone cleaves firmly to the principles. Failure to do so will bring about cataclysmic catastrophe. Meanwhile, the group to be held together by its shared principles (recall that by definition, the enclave lacks capacity to offer incentive or authority) will require a long collective memory of the past to sustain its social integration. However, because the enclaved group must sustain itself by heavily marking off the moral or spiritual worth of members from nonmembers, that past will be the subject of a Manichaean division into noble heroines and villainous traitors. This stance toward time serves to maintain the organizational form of enclaved ordering by buttressing members against challenges to its cohesion.

The work on method begun in 'Cultural Bias' on mathematical modelling by Thompson and on attitudinal scaling by Hampton was extended a few years later by Rayner and the then Columbia-based mathematician Jonathan Gross in their methods manual for Douglas' theory, entitled *Measuring Culture* (Gross and Rayner, 1986). Gross and Rayner's book is important because it is the only full-length statement of method and methodology for empirical operationalization intended to test particular theories derived from the general theoretical framework that Douglas had devised. The book worked with the version of the theory treating the two dimensions as continuously differentiable rather than as binary. A central methodological proposal was that researchers should measure and code on the dimensions of variation rather than on the four forms, because this would, the authors argued, achieve greater validity and reliability. Developing Douglas' argument in 'Cultural Bias', Gross and Rayner argued that the dimensions should be regarded as polythetic, by which they meant that multiple alternative operationalizations are possible. No single measure is necessary and several may be sufficient. After describing a very demanding strategy for data collection involving large-scale survey work, ethnographic observation and qualitative interviewing, the book presented a mathematical procedure for quantification and aggregation, and even a program to generate software to implement it. There are, as far as we are aware, no empirical studies to date fully and exactly following Gross and Rayner's method, though various aspects of what they proposed have been implemented. A major difficulty has been that a full implementation would be very expensive because it requires data collections on a very large scale.

At this point, it may be helpful to pause to consider just what Douglas had achieved by the early 1980s by way of reorganising, re-synthesizing and sorting out the fragmentary materials that Durkheim had left behind for social science, and how she had done so in ways that avoided some of Durkheim's own most obvious blunders. From *Forms*, she took the concept of multiple elementary forms of organization potentially present in every human setting from the materially simplest to the most complicated. The monograph on *Primitive Classification* provided the core causal arrow – that social organization cultivates classification in its own image. This is then applied to both the local world of problems and resources, and also to other people who are organized differently but with whom it is necessary to deal. From *Forms*, she also took the argument that ritual provided a causal mechanism through which classification could be fixed, but in a different register in each of her four elementary forms. *Suicide* and the lectures on *Moral Education* provided her – even if she needed to travel via Bernstein's work to find them – with the two most basic dimensions along which human institutions could vary, and how far they feasibly could vary. By cross-tabulating the basic dimensions, she achieved a deductive rigour that Durkheim's own account lacked, even though many anthropologists in the 1970s and 1980s no longer used deductive rigour. Ditching the misbegotten notion of a unitary 'society' and focusing on the multiplicity of conflicted institutions through which people must navigate, she was able to avoid Durkheim's late (and somewhat bizarre) metaphysics in which he posited a 'homo duplex', split by ego and society, interior collective and self. Perhaps most interestingly, she peeled away from Durkheim's corpus the dull, cracked veneer of Parsons' and Radcliffe-Brown's structural functionalism to reveal a hitherto obscured theory of conflict, diversity and instability that Durkheim had bequeathed in his finest works (e.g. 1977 [1938]). Fardon (1987) described Douglas as a 'faithful disciple' of Durkheim. This was a view shared by recognized Durkheimians such as Robert Bellah (see Bellah, 2005). Yet her fidelity to the underlying project was one that allowed it to be recast in ways showing the tight theoretical integration of Durkheim's programme and the scale of its enduring relevance long after the loosening of the straitjacket into which Parsons had forced the great French sociologist.

Using the Typology to Explain How Conflicts Amplify

If the typology and the method were to convince a wider set of social science disciplines, then Douglas needed to use them in a major study to show their explanatory power. At the time she formed the plan for a first full-dress empirical application, her strategy seemed sensible enough. She would write a book applying her ideas in a technologically advanced Western society for the first time. In Aaron Wildavsky, she had found a collaborator who was keen to apply the theory to a study in the United States, in what could be considered the heartland of social science. Moreover, he was already a political scientist of distinction at the height of his reputation, following the publication of books on the British civil service (Heclo and Wildavsky, 1974), public budgeting (Wildavsky, 1964), and relationships between policy analysts and politicians (Wildavsky, 1979). The weighty, detailed and closely empirically analysed tomes Wildavsky had produced in the 1970s suggested their collaboration would now yield a similarly data-rich monograph of impressive authority. Even Wildavsky's setback at the Russell Sage Foundation (see the Introduction above) was offset by his return to Berkeley, where his disciplinary prestige was not greatly diminished by the events that took place in New York. The choice of environmental politics as a topic offered Douglas the chance to show that the moral and social pollution anxieties she had examined in *Purity and Danger* among people using simple technologies were continuous with those of people using complicated equipment and machinery, and worried about pollution emanating from technological sources. It was also important for her to use her theory to explain deep societal disagreements (in this case regarding the uses of nuclear power) to allay any lingering suspicions that her invocation of social structure still hid remnants of structural-functionalism, according to which supposedly viable polities generally selected well-adapted technological outcomes.

Yet the resulting book was a disappointment. In fact, worse than this, it was a major scandal in the communities of scholars working on risk, to whom it was mainly pitched. In some respects, it was also an embarrassment to those around Douglas who had helped develop her approach, since it appeared to compromise the integrity of her own theory.

The concept of risk had originally been developed in the context of gambling and had at first meant only the probability of an outcome, whether welcome or unwelcome (Bernstein, 1996). It was a calculable factor, and something with which engineers and economists, as well as statisticians, felt well able to cope, and therefore contrasted with uncertainty (Knight, 1921). Yet even at the start of her career, Douglas saw from her fieldwork that risk was often understood in a social rather than a technical light, as a concept applicable to something uncertain, and therefore ambiguous or anomalous in classification. In effect, the Lele, and others among her informants, saw risk as something that coded for danger or likely harm. Her point was not simply a semantic one about the use of the word 'risk' in English. Rather, she argued that the social effort and the investment made in institutions with which to manage both probabilities and uncertainties are ones that render Knight's logical distinction of limited use in understanding social behaviour, such as the relationship between either of these terms and the management of conflict.

Because political debates about environmental and technological risks in the 1980s tended to emphasize the supposed novelty of the issues, as if these were both substantive surprises and also the product of entirely 'modern' social processes, Douglas was keen to intervene in order to show how her theory could be used to challenge both these misconceptions. She also wanted to show that her theory of anomaly management could predict and explain why people in some settings exploited some kinds of risks, while in others accommodated, allowed or just accepted them. All life was accompanied by risks. It was thus banal to reflect on risks in general. What was interesting, from the perspective of the social sciences, Douglas thought, was why certain risks were emphasized and others were downplayed. Why was it often thought more risky to live next to a nuclear power station than to drive a car, for example? Risk assessment, she understood tended to vary according to social setting.

Wildavsky's interest in the topic, by contrast, was unambiguously partisan. He wanted to use theory to argue that the political views of radical environmentalists and opponents of certain technologies, such as civil nuclear energy, were really part of, and perhaps cover for, a larger politics about how people should live – a politics he rejected. Some of the more partisan, right-wing remarks made in the course of the book also provoked some readers. Douglas' biographer Richard Fardon (2010, 143) concludes from examining her papers in the Northwestern University Archives that these almost certainly came from Wildavsky's pen. Whereas for Douglas the method and the typology had been designed to provide a degree of political detachment, and to treat all the elementary forms as inescapable, universal features of community life, if present in different proportions in different empirical settings, Wildavsky seems to have wanted to argue that one elementary form – the weakly integrated, weakly regulated, individualistic mode of social organization – was the most desirable. (In later writings he came to recognize that this was not at all that Douglas' theory implied; see the discussion below of Wildavsky (1998).)

Risk and Culture was not a detailed analysis of a structured empirical dataset, but more an assertion of an argument with strong normative overtones. The argument restated much of Douglas' theoretical position, but the book did not provide the compellingly detailed empirical vindication that would have been helpful at this point. The authors argued that the perception and selection of the severity of risks in the fields of environmental policy and technological development, and even the selection of risks to which to attend or to bear, reflect the differing social organizational contexts of those making the conflicting claims. Failing to anticipate the rapid professionalization of 'green' campaigning movements, the book presented their organizations as inherently voluntary and largely 'sectarian', and implacably opposed to values and judgements about risks of nuclear power emanating from 'professionals' embedded perhaps too securely within government hierarchies. The well-honed argument that 'risk' had become a synonym for 'danger' and attached in particular to things found anomalous in rival forms of classification is wrapped around a somewhat cursory characterization of the U.S. nuclear energy debate. This was clearly derived from the argument in *Purity and Danger* that anomaly tended to be reduced to codes for danger, and the refinement of that thesis in *Natural Symbols*, in which it was proposed that this tendency was most likely to be amplified in strongly integrated settings and especially in enclaved orderings. 'Cultural Bias' had been careful to argue that the aspects of cognition explained by the theory were biases in respect of the time, space and formal aspects of justice. Now Douglas had extended the list of 'dependent variables' to include the severity and probability of risks. *Risk and Culture* in this regard was perhaps little more than a restatement of earlier positions, from which Wildavsky could launch his partisan assault.

Using the verb 'to select' about risks proved to be a distinct liability. To some unsympathetic readers (Boholm (1996) is one), it appeared to suggest a tactical process of conscious and deliberate choosing, to the advantage of particular interests, whether vested and otherwise. By contrast, it is apparent from the larger context that Douglas meant it to imply the attention-directing, biasing, culture-cultivating capabilities of locally prevailing forms of social organization. Douglas and Wildavsky decided to conclude their argument with a chapter entitled 'Risk is a Collective Construct'. This also proved a minefield. For Douglas, perhaps innocently, 'construct' was simply a noun derived from the verb 'to construe', as she later tried to explain (Douglas, 1992a). Yet even at this date, the word was already being used by poststructuralist analysts to refer to cultural 'constructions', by which those scholars meant to imply the autonomy of ideas floating free of social structure, a notion that Douglas firmly rejected. To many trained in the engineering and statistical analysis of the environmental and technological risks discussed in the book, the word implied that 'constructed' risks were somehow 'contrived', 'imaginary' or 'unreal', something she was again later forced to deny (Douglas, 1992a). Even the unambiguous rejection of relativism in that very chapter was not enough to convince the book's critics that it was not part of her agenda. Others did understand the argument, but were scandalized by what they regarded as the 'reductionism' of treating the perception of risk as 'nothing but' expressions of preference generated by social organization, as if this implied she thought the issues (environmental pollution, for example) unworthy of serious intellectual consideration in their own right.

Methodologically, the book also compromised something important in Douglas' argument. It assimilated the hierarchical and individualistic forms of organization to 'the centre' of supposedly established, mainstream life in the United States and, by implication, other advanced Western polities. Thus, the argument positioned enclave forms as a 'periphery' of marginal opposition and treated isolate life as little more than passive ballast. Quite why hierarchy and individualism were now to be given such theoretical privilege was never made clear. Subsequent work by, for example, Hood (1998), has shown clearly that there are plenty of cases of enclave and isolate ordering in government and other large and important organizations (see also 6, 2011, 2015b). Nor was it clear just what the notion of the mainstream really meant in this context, other than to imply that heterodox ideas must be perverse.

Indeed, the book made some even more fundamental compromises in Douglas' own theory. *Risk and Culture* presented the four elementary forms as 'cultures', characterizing these as if they were worldviews or ideologies, and then went on to label them with such terms as 'egalitarianism' (for enclave ordering) and 'fatalism' (for isolate ordering). In doing so, the book appeared to abandon the inner structure of explanatory argument that that had been the long and careful labour of Douglas' previous three decades of work, namely that it was social organization that functionally, and by ritual mechanisms, created organizational problems and challenges to which ideas were provisional and fallible solutions. It is true that Durkheim (1961 1925], 1973) faced the same problem when he tried to explain that he used 'individualism' – which, for Douglas, is the weakly socially integrated, weakly regulated form – to mean a form of quite general institutional ordering that sustains a cult of the individual person, not a nineteenth-century set of political beliefs associated with, for example, Herbert Spencer and Samuel Smiles. Nonetheless, Durkheim had sought to explain his usage carefully to make clear the structure of his explanation. Wildavsky, by contrast, was especially determined, as in other publications of his from this period, to argue that ideologies demanding protection for the physical or natural environment were inherently committed to egalitarianism in the socialist sense of that term. Whether or not the more conservative and hierarchical strands of environmental ideology (e.g. those advocated by Scruton, 2012) are as incoherent as Wildavsky's argument implied matters less than that they are indeed ideologies. After all, all ideologies both generate anomalies internally and have them imposed from without. The treatment in *Risk and Culture* of 'culture' as ideology left it very difficult to understand the different aspects of political cognition at work in, for example, conservative, hierarchical and radical socialist variants of environmentalism. Because Wildavsky had pressed for the definition of enclave as 'egalitarian', it became very difficult to diagnose correctly all the enclaved institutions, including those lacking left-wing or 'green' agenda, vulnerable to the same millennial forms and emotional excesses that resulted in collective effervescence. The fact that enclaves emphasize inequality on the boundary between members and nonmembers became hard to reconcile with what *Risk and Culture* claimed was their defining worldview.

Obscuring the distinction between organization and cognition on the one hand and identifying culture with ideology on the other led to shallow explanation that only reinforced the suspicions of Douglas' critics that her entire typology was little more than a party trick. For at its worst, *Risk and Culture* appeared to suggest no more than that big

ideas explained little ideas, meaning that people worried about particular risks because they had grand ideological beliefs into which their
particular worries fitted. All of Douglas' careful functional explanations about grand ideas being *ex post facto* rationalizations of particular
styles of thought cultivated in forms of social organization seemed to
be abandoned. Only in subsequent years, when Douglas introduced the
concept of a thought 'style' to contrast with the term ideology, was the
content of the theory clarified again.

Worse still, and again probably under Wildavsky's influence,
Douglas now appeared to be referring to individual persons as 'individualists' or as 'egalitarians', thereby turning what had been a theory
of context into a theory of individual dispositions. Rayner (1992, 106–
8) defended the logic of Douglas' earlier argument in 'Cultural Bias'
by distinguishing between the 'mobility hypothesis' in which people
are shaped by their context, to the extent that the same individual will
exhibit quite different cognitive styles when social relations and structure change, from a 'stability' hypothesis – apparently Wildavsky's
view – that people seek to order their lives in such a way that they
remain within a context where one of the elementary forms is dominant and with which they are comfortable, having been acculturated
or socialized into it early in life. Rayner's argument was that evidence
for the stability hypothesis had never been produced.

In all these respects, the book must be deemed something of a disaster. Although Douglas never published any direct recantation, one way
to understand some of the arguments made in her later works is to see
her repairing the damage step by step, but without obvious disrespect
to her influential US mentor. Her 1985 book *Risk Acceptability According
to the Social Sciences* used an extensive review of literatures from psychology and organization studies to provide a platform for restating
her central arguments about the shaping of individuals' assessment
of risk by institutional factors, but carefully avoided reasserting propositions about a weakened 'centre' proposed in the 1982 work. It also
avoided the kinds of remarks about environmental risks and organizations that had been so provocative in her writing with Wildavsky. In
Risk and Blame (1992a), she worked hard to show nothing in her argument implied that dangers or risks were in any sense imaginary. In *How
Institutions Think*, she restored, deepened and clarified the underlying
logic of explanation compromised by *Risk and Culture*. The relabelling
of the four forms in *Risk and Blame* and in *Thought Styles* would restore
their definitions on the basis that the institutions of social organization
are the 'independent variables' in Douglas' explanation. A late paper
on 'traditional culture' would completely bury any hint or appearance

left in the minds of some readers of *Risk and Culture* that some cultures, especially among the developmentally disadvantaged, were somehow morally more suspect than cultures of materially wealthier societies. And a final series of works about conflict mitigation, channelling and containment would slough off any impression she followed the pugnacious Wildavsky's preference for simply combating and defeating a particular 'culture' regarded as more dangerous than the others. One by one, over the subsequent quarter of a century, the blunders of *Risk and Culture* would be undone. Unfortunately, many of those who read *Risk and Culture* were sufficiently put off that they left her later works to one side; even today, for many, her reputation remains damaged by this 1982 book.

Nevertheless, despite all these weaknesses, the book was important in several ways. Centrally, the argument showed why and how the conflict between business, government and environmental movements had deepened, polarized and amplified in the United States. Although as yet Douglas was not ready fully to adopt Michael Thompson's cybernetic theory of positive feedback in each of the four forms, the book clearly documents exactly the kinds of self-reinforcing radicalization to be expected if those mechanisms operated. The book also opened up a major new terrain of research and argument for Douglas, both regionally in North America, and in disciplinary terms in political science and sociology, and in the multidisciplinary study of risk. Her arguments were fiercely controversial in these fields, but attracted some students and supporters. These two disciplines still provide the most extensive citation and discussion of her typological theory.

Wildavsky would go on to work with a psychologist, Karl Dake, to develop survey instrumentation for measuring risk perception in ways that were designed to test how far individuals' awareness of and anxiety about particular technological and environmental risks showed patterns predicted by the theory (Dake and Wildavsky, 1990). This study provoked protracted debate among quantitative survey researchers studying risk perceptions (see below) and in turn helped significantly to raise the interdisciplinary profile of her arguments.

Later Typological Studies

After *Risk and Culture*, Douglas continued to use the fourfold typology and, indeed, to use it much more consistently in relation to her underlying theoretical project than she had done in her 1982 collaboration with Wildavsky. Much of her time in the 1980s and 1990s was taken up with using the typology to examine issues around risk and also consumption choices. Then, in 1998, in collaboration with the policy scientist Steven Ney, she published a fresh theoretical statement of its basis in a book entitled *Missing Persons*. This was not, however, an empirical study. After 1998, the fourfold typology would not again be the principal burden of argument in any of her subsequent book-length studies, though it continued to be discussed in several of her articles.

In the field of the study of risk, after *Risk and Culture*, there followed an altogether more scholarly and less polemical (1985) study entitled *Risk Acceptability According to the Social Sciences*. This was based on an extensive review of literature and concluded with a cautious critique rather than a partisan flourish.

During the next few years, there followed a series of articles developing the argument and collected as a volume entitled *Risk and Blame*. The collection includes papers on risk in the field of health, including HIV and AIDS, as well as articles returning to Douglas' earlier African interests. A chapter on leprosy provides an important connection between her earlier concerns with African witchcraft accusation and her more recent understanding that notions of risk are dependent variables determined by social organization. In the medieval European world, leprosy was less a disease than an accusation. It could be applied to a variety of conditions, but with the common result that the sufferer was subject to social stigma and separation. Douglas reviewed historical evidence that the arrow of accusation fluctuated according to the organizational context. In the eleventh and twelfth centuries, leprosy was a diagnosis applied to socially elevated members of church and state. It indicated, she suggests, something amiss in hierarchical relations of governance. Perhaps it was a sign from God that the esteemed had erred? But as market relations spread from, roughly, the late twelfth and thirteenth centuries onwards, the arrow of blame pointed in a diametrically opposite direction. Lepers were now found among a footloose labouring underclass. Here was a symptom of a new kind of institutional sickness, affecting labour mobilization arrangements prone to periodic market failures. Leprosaria, she detects, were an early form of dole. In short, the disease and the stigma it was given were associated not with potential causal agents of disease, but with changes in political economy. The diagnosis was the effect and disorganization the cause.

It was in the mid 1980s that Douglas' theory acquired a new name. 'Cultural Bias' had referred to her approach as a method of 'analysis', and calling it 'grid-group analysis' merely identified the method by the dimensions. 'Culture' was treated there as the 'cosmological' aspect of thought that was to be explained. At various points in *Risk and Culture*, Douglas and Wildavsky had referred to the approach as 'a cultural theory' of the selection and construction of risks. But the phrase remained in the lower case and it was not yet exactly a firm proper name. Wildavsky's article with Michael Thompson on 1986 on information rejection and his 1987 chapter on responsibility in public management were among the first pieces to announce the name as 'cultural theory' without a definite article. It would not be long before capital letters would be granted. The decision to adopt the new name probably seemed adroit in that decade when fascination with the concept of culture had reached its apogee in disciplines beyond anthropology itself.

Yet it had severe costs. It appeared to suggest that culture did the explaining when the whole point of her argument (and the 1978 'Cultural Bias' was very clear about this) was that institutions explained culture or, rather, institutions of social organization explained those cognitive aspects of 'culture' that could be described as thought style. But by the 1980s, under the influence of figures such as Geertz, the sharp distinction between culture as ideas and social organization was eroded in the minds of many anthropologists, sociologists and political scientists. The label 'cultural theory' now appeared to suggest an argument either: (a) that, as *Risk and Culture* had suggested, big ideas such as worldviews or principles explained little ideas about risks, about crime, about religion or whatever the researcher examined on the ground; or (b) that explanation need consist in little more than pointing out that some phenomenon or other had an elective affinity with one of four undifferentiated general syndromes, each of which was 'a culture'. The first of these was the very reverse of Douglas' own intentions, although it may have reflected Wildavsky's views in the 1980s. The second was a travesty, lacking any clear explanatory mechanism. Yet, given the new label, it proved difficult to shake off these connotations.

The situation worsened by the 1990s when there emerged a field of 'cultural studies', which consisted mostly in inductive studies of a kind that took ideas and symbols to be fundamental, and that was often interpretivist in approach. This new field, in which theoretical argument was often described as 'cultural theory', quickly became better known than Douglas' approach. The result was confusion, in which those who disliked much of what was done in 'cultural studies', for reasons Douglas could readily share, were discouraged from undertaking a close examination of her writings.

Perhaps because in the 1980s she had remained committed to the terms 'grid' and 'group', Douglas herself was somewhat slower than her students and followers to adopt the new name. For example, her major statement in 1986, *How Institutions Think*, not only eschewed the title, it positively avoided the word 'culture' altogether. However, the 1992 collection loosely united by her interests in risks did carry the subtitle 'Essays in Cultural Theory'. By then, Thompson, Ellis and Wildavsky (1990) had popularized the name in the title of their book, *Cultural Theory*, and associated that name more firmly with the four forms than with the two dimensions from which Douglas had derived them. More importantly, Thompson had used *Cultural Theory* to lay out his theory of dynamics, which enabled the authors to claim that the change of name reflected the move from the static comparative analysis in 'Cultural Bias' to the new cybernetic framework focusing on feedback processes. After their book appeared, the name 'cultural theory' became widely accepted for the remainder of the decade as a growing number of researchers began to apply the typology (and, rather more rarely, the dynamics) to ever more contemporary problems. It was only from 2000 or so that scholarly attention among those who drew upon Douglas' arguments returned to her account of causal mechanisms by which institutions cultivate styles of thought, leading one of the present authors to suggest in 2001 for the first time in print that the theory should be more accurately be described as a neo-Durkheimian institutional framework and therefore should also in future be developed in that direction.

Douglas' own empirical interests, though, remained focused on the issue of danger. Once again exploring the causal process by which forms of social organization might cultivate particular ideas and the uses to which these ideas might be put, Douglas now turned back to the concept of blame, and the results were brought together in the 1992 collection. In her ethnographic work before 1975, she had examined individual blame for particular outcomes, unambiguously accepted by all as adversities. She now allowed the concept to cover attacks by collectivities upon other collectivities, where the focus was less on the responsibility attributed than in the extent to which there was ideological argument about whether the outcome was genuinely harmful. These later debates about blame were as much about stigma, conflicts over distributional fairness in corporate decision making, or the varying weights to be attached to environmental loss or damage as they were about the accusations of individual occult responsibility for injuries and disasters around which her work on blame in the 1960s had focused. She now showed that blame is much more than moral condemnation of those deemed to have caused harm. Whereas in *Purity and Danger* she had focused on the strand in blame and stigma that relates to classification and anomaly, her studies on blame in the 1980s reproduced in the collection *Risk and Blame* (Douglas, 1992a) brought out more clearly than in 1966 (when she lacked the theoretical resources) that blame and stigma are the products of processes of institutional change. The nub of the blame game, she argued, rests upon the institutionalization of information rejection, upon an unwillingness to consider certain kinds of information that might exculpate or upon 'muffled ears' to particular kinds of information – an argument collaborators developed further (Thompson and Wildavsky, 1986; 6, 2004: see Chapter 5 below).

In the papers in *Risk and Blame*, Douglas clarified the argument in *Risk and Culture* that the risks that give rise to the greatest anxiety, like other anomalous elements in any form of classification, are those that most threaten the social organization in which they are anomalous. In response, people use notions of danger to blame people they hold responsible for the injustice of creating anomalies (defined differently in each elementary form of organization), thus consolidating their own organization, and hence, she argued, the tendency in contemporary politics to equate risk with danger.

When, in an influential article from 1990 reprinted in *Risk and Blame*, Douglas called risk a 'forensic' concept, she almost turned the concept of forensics inside out. No doubt she was thinking of the poison oracle, but the article was overtly about Europe and North America. She argued that risks are invoked as part of a process of investigating putative guilt or innocence. Of course, in a court, most 'forensic' evidence is collected and analysed to investigate causation, and only a small part of it bears directly on the guilt or innocence of a particular individual for a particular act, presumed for the sake of argument to be a crime. But Douglas' use of the word was chosen to emphasize the person-directed aspects rather than the issue-directed ones. Her point was that when we declare something risky, we mean first that it is dangerous and not simply that it is a chancy affair that may be calculable with probabilities, and, second, we only bother to declare something a risk if doing so serves the purpose of making an argument about fault for that danger. What actually we do when we use risk, she argued, drawing upon and extending Thompson's and Wildavsky's (1986) argument about information rejection in companies and bureaucracies, is to engage in blame by suppressing information inconvenient to prevailing institutions. In the paper about leprosy in medieval Europe, she argued that the diagnosis constituted just such a form of information rejection because it provided an alternative to fixing broken labour markets. In addition, the concept of blame provided some of the functional causal machinery for the self-reinforcement of each elementary form of social organization – a necessary argument if the revived Durkheimian approach was not to fail in the way that structural-functionalism had done. This would reconnect the argument about risk with the cybernetic theory of dynamics and change, as supplied for her theory by Thompson.

Finally, the papers collected in *Risk and Blame* made a critical shift in Douglas' presentation of her theory. Picking up on the achievements of her 1986 book *How Institutions Think* (see Chapter 3 below), these papers treated elementary forms of social organization as congeries of institutions, and explicitly linked her theory for the first time with neo-institutionalist trends in economics, economic history, sociology and political science that were influential from the mid 1980s onwards. After stumbling in *Risk and Culture*, she was once again treating her theory as an institutional explanation of culture, not a cultural explanation of institutions.

In the papers in *Risk and Blame*, Douglas had largely been content simply to apply the fourfold typology as she had developed it in 'Cultural Bias' in 1978, but her later work explored it in more interesting ways. In some of the essays collected in *Thought Styles* (1996b, esp. 45), Douglas suggested, as discussed more fully in the next chapter, that the 'negative diagonal' (top left to bottom right, linking isolate and enclaved organization) might be an institutionalizable relationship, in which enclaves recruited among isolates, and through which exhausted enclaves might release people into isolate social orders. Moreover, in both settings, future time was foreshortened, and people withdraw from power and status, although for different reasons. *Risk and Culture* had conjured up the 'centre', or a kind of strategic alliance of individualism and hierarchy on the 'positive diagonal'. Douglas then backtracked, thinking that the privileging of 'the centre' was misguided and that other bilateral relations might be institutionalized along the diagonals. By this stage, others were identifying vertical and horizontal bilateral relations that appeared capable of being institutionalized, much as she had identified diagonal ones (see, e.g. Coyle and Ellis (1994); and, subsequently, Thompson (2008) for a general classification). Quite how all this related to the underlying theory of institutional drivers was not always made sufficiently clear.

One further development was of significance at this time. Some of the papers collected in the 1996 volume *Thought Styles* showed Douglas now showing interest in isolate organization as something more obviously 'in the active voice' (Douglas, 1982c) than it had appeared in *Risk and Culture*. Indeed, she now speculated about a growing trend towards isolate organization in industrialized countries, almost as if she was seeking to resurrect the once-influential fears of social atomization set forth by David Riesman and his co-authors (1961) in *The Lonely Crowd* in the early 1960s. This contrasted with some hints in 'Cultural Bias' to the effect that 'advanced' countries were characterized by deepening individualism. If this suggested some uncertainty of aim, then the lack of sustained empirical testing of her theory was becoming increasingly problematic; doubtless some hostile readers switched off, suspecting her theory was little more than an intellectual game for initiates.

Applications of Douglas' Typology

In fact, serious efforts to test the theory were getting under way. A large body of empirical work has now been produced in the four decades and more since Douglas published *Natural Symbols*, examining hypotheses taken from her fourfold typological theory of variation announced in that book. Whether it tests the right things is a matter to which we will return in the last chapter, where it will be suggested that some of this work has at times failed to keep a clear distinction between the dependent and independent variables implicit in the theory. Adherence to the fourfold typology is not in itself a safeguard against trying to explain little ideas with big ideas. The operationalization of independent institutional variables poses a major methodological challenge, since the researcher has to go beyond the discourse of informants, whether in surveys or the in-depth interviewing often favoured by anthropologists. In order to gain a perspective on this empirical material, we need to consider applications of the fourfold typology. This in turn means introducing the group of scholars who gathered around Douglas hoping to help her in her empirical task.

If there has ever been a Douglasian group or school with a sense of collective endeavour equivalent, perhaps, to the Durkheimian school of social science at the beginning of the twentieth century, then it would consist in those who have made use of the theory of limited variation in elementary forms of organization and its fourfold typology. The typological strand in her work has been influential in political science, public administration, business and management studies, criminology, development studies, health services studies – indeed, almost everywhere save in her own disciplines of anthropology and sociology of religion. A two-volume set compiled by 6 and Mars (2008) collected some of the most important and influential article-length studies of this sort. Again we make no attempt to summarize that extensive body of material here, but offer a brief guide for those interested to read further and provide some brief evaluative points about the relationship to her underlying theory.

One important qualitative test case was Rayner's (1986a) study of hospital laboratory biosafety procedures and how these vary with organizational context. There were others. Price and Thompson (1997) set out to apply and test the theory in montagnard communities. Coyle and Ellis (1994) brought together an influential set of mainly qualitative and historical studies. In political science, Lockhart's papers (Coughlin and Lockhart, 1998; Lockhart, 1999) on political culture extended Wildavsky's use of the theory to make a significant contribution to that subfield.

Rayner (1988), focusing on sects and cults and radical communities, introduced the notion of 'rule sets', showing that the integration of these rule sets in sectarian life replicated strong social integration. He examined the apparent paradoxes that pursuit of simplicity within the enclaved community required great complexity in rule sets, and incurs high transaction costs in collective decision making. A key part of his argument was a distinction between *extensiveness* (the number of rules a solidarity or institutional system requires) and *intricacy* (the proportion of likely events covered by each rule). He showed empirically, if perhaps contrary to expectations, that enclave forms require very extensive rule sets, but could operate with moderate or low intricacy. Clearly, the approach could be extended to cover other institutional settings.

Quantitative work has been sparser. Early results seemed promising (Hampton, 1982), but due to the vagaries of social science research funding in Britain in the Thatcher years, these initiatives were never fully followed through. Grendstad (2000, 2001, 2003a, 2003b; Grendstad and Sundback, 2003) published a series of quantitative survey tests of predictions from the theory, using scales calibrated by Karl Dake and Aaron Wildavsky (1990). Marris et al. (1998) tested predictions from theory and were able to achieve quite strong goodness of fit using quantitative methods.

Mars' *Cheats at Work* (1982) is one of the most widely cited works using Douglas' theory, especially in sociology, criminology and management and organization studies. In the literature on the informal economy, it is regarded as a classic. Mars elegantly derives from the theory four predicted forms of workplace crime from the 'fiddling' of expenses to sabotage by way of cheating customers and managers to grand corruption, and a set of conditions of organization under which each is expected to emerge and be sustained, before examining ethnographic data on workplaces expected to meet those conditions. The book concludes with a brief consideration of the question of how far it is possible to reduce workplace crime overall if each of the elementary forms is likely to cultivate its peculiar malpractice, and with some thoughts on public policy concerns to manage the informal or alternative or illegal economy. Mars has since published a series of further studies on workplace crime and workplace accidents using the theory (many are collected in Mars, 2013).

The category of isolate ordering is unique to Douglas' approach. Even those who are sympathetic to Douglas' work have made little use of it, perhaps assuming with Thompson that isolates are not very 'active'. Others have seen the relevance of taking isolates seriously, but understandings of isolate ordering vary. In a major study applying Douglas' theory to public administration in government across history, Christopher Hood (1998) suggested that it could be understood as 'contrived randomness', where arbitrary outcomes are more or less deliberately induced in order to exercise control over subordinates.

In two chapters in an edited volume from 1994, Dennis Coyle (1984a, 1984b) argued that it was possible for people in high office also to be isolates. The category cannot be reserved, on theoretical grounds, only for people who are poor or downtrodden. He suggested that Durkheim's own category of despotism should be used for this case of isolate ordering. The implications of this insight for understanding how anomalies would be managed by those in structural isolate despotic positions were taken up in 6's (2011) study examining political judgement as thought style, using the case of the Khrushchev regime in the Soviet Union during the Cuban Missile Crisis. He argued that structural despots seek to pass on or impose upon others the constraints to which they are themselves subject. This produces something that initially looks like the stigmatization of monsters found in enclaves, but is much more brittle – for when the despot fails, there is nothing to fall back upon but to accept the anomaly as a loss or setback (6, 2014a, 2014b, 2015b, 2015c).

The single most influential and widely cited work developing the theory beyond Douglas' own account of the limited plurality of elementary forms was *Cultural Theory* by Thompson, Ellis and Wildavsky (1990). In fact, many political scientists interested in 'political culture' and management scholars interested in 'organizational culture' know the theory only from this source and not from Douglas' original writings.

Thompson, Ellis and Wildavsky introduced several innovations. They did not emphasize the distinction between social organization and culture in the sharp fashion that Douglas did in 'Cultural Bias' and *How Institutions Think*. Rather, for much of their book, they treated organization and culture as parts of one and the same manifold. They were interested in explaining conflicts and provisional settlements among the four elementary forms. In effect, the theory was re-presented as one focused on the 'sociocultural viability' of the forms – that is to say, on the conditions under which these forms can persist, and conversely how they tend to disorganize themselves. Making a transition from Michael Thompson's interest in mathematical catastrophe theory to a concern with systems theory more generally, the fifth chapter introduced an account of how events of different kinds will cause 'surprises' in each of the four forms, leading to shifts in organization among and between them (as opposed to shifts within them, based ability to resist recognizing surprises). For *Cultural Theory*, a surprise is a special case of anomaly. It refers to a situation in which the prevailing institutional form of social organization leads people to expect events that are consonant with their own ordering, whereas in fact it transpires that the world is more like the description given by one of the others. Surprises matter for the development of the theory because they are the only mechanism by which positive feedback can be interrupted and by which other organization forms might assert themselves, as people retreat from institutions that deliver disappointing surprises.

But can people in, say, enclaved or hierarchical institutions actually recognize an event as something indicating that the world is more individualistic than they had expected? Or will the blinkering of their own biases lead them to misrepresent the event in order to force it to fit their view of the world? Thompson and colleagues suggest that there is a particular stage in the positive feedback dynamic in any one elementary form, where self-reinforcement is not so far advanced that blinkering is complete. It is at this stage that surprises can be received and recognized for what they are, and this is the moment when they can have a disruptive effect on social organization by a process of social learning. Whereas Douglas would sometimes write of the four forms as being institutionalized in ways that might appear to suggested fixity and permanence, Thompson et al. used the theory dynamically to accommodate instability and flux.

Cultural Theory was and remains controversial. Among many, the shorthand use by Thompson et al. of the terms 'hierarchist', 'individualist', etc., caused discomfort, although the authors make clear that these are not intended as psychological types. Critics might then ask what are they intended to indicate? A good answer, we will show, requires arguments that Douglas developed specifically concerning the theorization of ritual and styles of thought.

The book brought to the wider social science community the particular readings of the four forms that Thompson and Wildavsky had been using in the 1980s. In particular, they treat the enclave form as 'egalitarianism' and the isolate form as 'fatalism', whereas other researchers influenced by Douglas' work are very cautious about such a characterization.

Thompson's biggest point of divergence from Douglas was over the importance of the two dimensions of social regulation and social integration or, in Douglas' terms, 'grid' and 'group'. He accepted the robustness of the four elementary forms, albeit using the terms 'egalitarianism' and 'fatalism' for what Douglas by the 1990s came to call enclaved and isolate institutions, but Thompson placed importance on a fifth form of hermit-like voluntary withdrawal from social engagement prefigured in passing by Douglas in 'Cultural Bias'. Douglas' writings suggested that she accepted Durkheim's arguments in *Suicide* and the lectures on *Moral Education* that social regulation and integration were the most basic dimensions of institutional variation. In her view, no other set of dimensions of variation in organization proposed in subsequent social science has proven so robustly general in its relevance and application, or in its explanatory power. The derivation of the elementary forms from the combined variation in strength of these two dimensions was not, for Douglas, merely a mathematical convenience, but reflected a real institutional grounding.

By contrast, Thompson (1996) and others argued that there are many ways to derive the four forms and that while social scientists ought to be realists about the forms, they need not be realists about the dimensions. In a recent book on democracy, for example, Hendriks (2010) was able to derive them by using standard political science measures of diversity in preference aggregation procedures. On one dimension, he distinguished between majoritarian or aggregative and non-majoritarian or integrative systems for treating votes. On the other, he used the distinction between indirect or representative ways of articulating people's preferences and direct, self-governing ones. This, he showed, produced four forms of democracy. He then proceeded to demonstrate that they each articulate in constitutional systems one of Douglas' elementary forms of social organization. Three decades earlier, Schmutzer and Bandler (1980) produced a well-worked-out mathematical derivation of the four forms quite independently of Douglas, which Thompson (2008, 72–78) argues is as good as Douglas' own. Schmutzer and Bandler posited as basic terms the concepts of transactions and ties, network closure and status. Using these categories alone, they derived the same four forms as Douglas had done using Durkheim's dimensions. However, although this was mathematically elegant, from Douglas' point of view, Schmutzer's and Bandler's argument would have to be regarded as theoretically questionable. Douglas' theory regarded status as something derived rather than foundational, and took the transaction to be the very reverse of a theoretically axiomatic concept. In her view, it takes heavy institutional work (namely, *weak* social integration) to cultivate such a category as a 'transaction'. Thompson (2008) restated his view that between the two derivations, there is only a presentational question concerning how best to persuade readers of the value of the typology. A different view would be that these two positions do indeed reflect a difference of theoretical substance concerning the most basic dimensions of institutions and of the means by which the limited plurality of elementary forms can be demonstrated.

Criticisms of the Typology and Responses

We turn now to the criticisms made of the typology. In 1970, critics of *Natural Symbols* were not especially interested in this aspect of that book. Within anthropology, the book was not received well and few mainstream anthropologists have ever thought to use the typology. Many thought it too simple, although ironically many of the distinctions in types of social organization then used by anthropologists were binary and so were even simpler. For example, Leach's celebrated (1954) distinction between *gumlao* or 'democratic egalitarian' and *gumsa* or 'ranked aristocratic' forms was only mildly complicated by recognizing a subtype of *gumsa* called *shan*, which was monarchical and feudal. Rayner (1982, 1986b) showed that Leach's account actually required something like Douglas' richer theory in order for it to work at all. Indeed, Leach's distinction really encompasses the vertical dimension of the degree of power distance and differentiation: it has no recognition at all of the importance of distinctions on any horizontal dimension.

When 'Cultural Bias' refined and restated the typology with greater rigour, this new version was paid scant regard by either anthropologists or sociologists. Indeed, to this day, it is a text more frequently read by political scientists and organization scholars. The typology began to attract more attention from critics, including anthropologists, when, in the 1980s, Douglas began to use it to try to explain patterns of risk perception among people living in contemporary North America and Europe.

Much of the opposition to the typology came from the field of risk perception studies. Interestingly, positions among the leading researchers in this field have softened in recent years. A pre-eminent figure in developing the psychometric approach to risk, Paul Slovic has recently done work that is much more compatible with Douglas' approach (Kahan et al., 2006). Drawing together criticisms made by risk scholars over a decade, Renn (1992) suggested that four elementary forms are too few to explain the full empirical variation we can observe. The same point had been made a decade earlier by Nelkin in her attack on *Risk and Culture*. In defending Douglas, Hood (1998) considered and answered the charge that the typology provides just 'nursery toys'. He pointed out, as we have done with respect to Leach in anthropology, that many theories for which supposedly greater complexity is claimed actually rely on *fewer* elementary forms.

Other traditions of research on institutions recognize two forms. Prospect theory (Kahneman and Tversky, 2000) uses just two basic structures – the domain of losses and the domain of gains. The institutional economist Oliver Williamson (1985) identified hierarchy and markets as fundamental, but no other forms. Some added clans (Ouchi, 1980) or sects or 'networks' (although that last category is especially vague and may well cover hierarchical and individualistic networks as well as enclaved ones: 6 et al., 2006; 6, 2015a). They all lack any recognition of the distinctive importance of isolate ordering or the importance of the 'negative diagonal' on Douglas' chart running from isolate to enclaved institutions that Douglas (1996) argued is key to understanding conflict dynamics and that Richards (1996) demonstrated empirically for the west African civil wars of the 1990s.

Ironically, Alexander and Smith (1996) made the opposite criticism from that of Renn and Nelkin, arguing that four is too many for the theory to be sufficiently parsimonious, and risks allowing ad hoc explanation. However, ad hoc explanation occurs only when the theory is misused – for example, if scholars mistakenly infer social organization from thought style rather than examining social organization, predicting thought style and then testing that prediction. It is by no means inherent in the theory.

Thus, Douglas can be absolved of the charge that her theory is oversimplified in comparison with its rivals. Furthermore, as already shown and as the next chapter demonstrates more fully, the theory is not (contrary to Bellaby, 1990) just a descriptive typology. Moreover, a degree of parsimony is a positive virtue in an explanatory theory.

The fiercest and most implacable critic of the typology in the study of risk perception has been the psychologist Lennart Sjöberg. Perhaps his most telling criticism was that the support provided by empirical studies for the theory tended to be that they found statistically significant results, but rather small effect sizes. Unfortunately, Sjöberg's (1997, 2003) charge was based on an assumption that led him to miss Douglas' central point. He claimed that because we do not observe pure cases of a single elementary form very often, the theory fails. First, at least as Thompson et al. (1990) resynthesized it, the theory itself predicts hybridity to be the common condition. Indeed, in *Risk and Culture*, Douglas and Wildavsky had allowed for hybridity between hierarchy and individualism, although it was never clear why this should be inherently more stable than any other hybrid of two, three or all four elementary forms. Although Douglas emphasized the 'adversarial' relationship among them, she also recognized both the possibility and the desirability of interaction, settlement, common ground, etc.

Second, Sjöberg objected to the use of distal (remote) factors such as social organization in explanation because he considered that a good explanation is one that prizes goodness of fit over all the other methodological virtues in explanation, such as causality, parsimony and generality. Douglas' (1986) argument, in effect, is that we have good reasons, if we want to avoid banal, shallow and unsatisfying explanations, to trade some goodness of fit for some of these other virtues.

As Przeworski and Teune (1970) pointed out in the very year that Douglas first published her typological theory of institutional variation, all explanations in social science must strike tradeoffs among at least four canonical virtues, which cannot be maximized simultaneously in one and the same piece of research. These are goodness of fit with the data, causality (or the capacity to capture the nature of causation), generality (or applicability to a definable set or class of cases such that structured comparisons can be drawn with other sets) and parsimony (the use of the smallest number of explanatory forces necessary to explain the outcomes) (6 and Bellamy, 2012). Just because we cannot, in any one piece of research, optimally satisfy all four, it does not follow that any tradeoff is acceptable. On the contrary, some are clearly better than others for particular research questions. Nor does it follow that research programmes should not be designed that can do reasonably well on all four virtues over a cumulative series of related studies. Parsimony, Douglas argued, should be pursued at the level of elementary forms, of which she found four. She presented the case for a programme ambitious with respect to each of these four, which has a very distinctive view of how each should best be achieved and in which relations among the four canonical virtues are tightly integrated.

A rather different kind of challenge has come from some sociologists over the two dimensions from which Douglas derived her four elementary forms. A well-formed typology should use dimensions that meet three criteria, namely that the dimensions are: (a) independent of each other (for example, one should not be a subset of the other); (b) of the same conceptual order as each other (for example, both should measure *explananda* or factors that need to be explained, or else both should measure *explanantes*, but a single typology should not combine measures of each type); and (c) capable of measuring variation in one and the same unit of social organization. Dimensions that do meet these standards cannot be said to be fully orthogonal to (i.e. independent of) each other. A few critics have raised doubt as to whether Durkheim's and Douglas' two dimensions of social regulation and integration meet all these standards, though most accept that they meet the third, for they are offered as being capable of measuring social organization at any scale.

Spickard (1989) and Fardon (1999, 213–25) discuss the fact that Douglas revised her formulation of the dimensions during the 1970s and perhaps even during the 1980s, not least between the first two editions of *Natural Symbols*. Some formulations presented the dimensions themselves as being about ideas and classification. However, by the time she wrote *How Institutions Think*, she had clearly come to regard this account as unsatisfactory. In some earlier formulations, the two dimensions appear as different kinds of 'pressures' (Douglas, 1982a [1978]) for accountability imposed by institutions upon people. After her 1980 book on Evans-Pritchard, she made much less use of the concept of accountability, probably because she needed a conception of the dimensions broader in scope than the notion of demanding retrospective accounts of behaviour from individuals or formal groups. Certainly, any formulation in which one dimension is defined as being about classification (a practice in the deployment of ideas) and the other defined as being about membership (a practice of social relations) will risk lacking orthogonality, since membership is a type of classification. Such a typology would fail the second of the three standards. However, none of Douglas' own formulations is guilty of this.

Spickard (1989) and Fardon (1999) raise the question of whether 'grid' is in fact the wider concept encompassing all forms of social regulation other than those arising from membership of a group.

However, it is not necessary to define the vertical dimension as a catch-all. Douglas (1989) offered a reply to Spickard, arguing, as she had in 'Cultural Bias' (1982a [1978], 202), that the strength or weakness of control by insulation was at the heart of the vertical dimension. This avoids leaving 'grid' defined merely as all forms of regulation other than those captured by membership. The particular kinds of discretion involved in weak regulation, for example, can be clearly derived from the core notion of insulation, independently of any assumptions concerning groups. But Douglas never fully followed up on this aspect of her theory. Concern for the dimensionality of elementary forms of social organization was downplayed in her late studies on ancient Israel by a focus on processes of ritual ordering and conflict settlement. Perhaps 'grid' and 'group' were not essential after all?

Despite all the work done by Douglas and colleagues, and the answers they have provided to critics, several key problems with the typology remain unresolved.

One concerns the relationship between the cross-tabulation of the two dimensions and the reality it is intended to capture. At issue is whether the dimensions should be treated as binary or as continuously differentiable. These interpretations yield different understandings of what the middle of the table shows. In binary interpretation, it is not of much significance. In Douglas' own continuously differentiable reading, it must, logically, represent a point of greatest mildness in each form where they might meet in idealized perfect organic solidarity. But that seems odd for a table of mechanical solidarities. A solution is to make the representation three-dimensional (6, 2003, corrected in 6, 2006). But then what is the 'zero' point on the dimensions? Is it at the centre, as Thompson (2008) insists, or at one of the corners? Largely, this is a technical matter of modelling rather than a fundamental theoretical issue. But the two views do represent different conceptions of the relative status of the forms and the dimensions.

Unfortunately, much of the literature using Douglas' typology tends to be descriptive in a 'bird spotting' vein rather than explanatory, simply using the typology for coding. In other words, too many scholars merely apply the typology in a purely diagnostic and descriptive fashion in order to identify the relative importance of the four fields of social solidarity as 'cultures'. Some of those who use the typology venture a little further to identify correlative strengths and weaknesses, abilities and debilities cultivated in each form. But there matters often rest. When used in isolation from the underlying theory and especially from the explanatory machinery discussed in the next chapter, the typology can become something of a snare. Indeed, some of these studies make a fetish of the notion of 'culture' in precisely the manner against which Douglas sought to argue in *How Institutions Think* and other writings. In much of the schematic use of her work, too little real explanation is achieved.

Related Typologies and Theories

There are some parallel and cognate theoretical traditions closely related to Douglas' work and where the practitioners have often taken cognisance of Douglas' achievements. We review two of them briefly here.

The social psychologist Alan Page Fiske was trained as an anthropologist. He went on to develop a typological theory of variation in what he explicitly calls the 'four elementary forms of sociality' (Fiske, 1991, 1992). Here, we discuss his theory as presented in his 1992 article (his 1991 book is an extended version). Fiske argues that most of social life is motivated and evaluated through social agents combining four basic psychological models: communal sharing (CS), authority ranking (AR), equality matching (EM) and market pricing (MP). In Fiske's account, communal sharing is defined as collective pooling of resources, in which people do not calculate individual entitlements and duties precisely on each occasion that pooling is done or maintained. By contrast, for him, equality matching requires the precise calculation of each individual's claims against each other person in ways that prevent unequal gains that might otherwise lead to resentments. Authority and market relations are understood in the conventional manner as being, respectively, situations where resources are collected and allocated by a central agency to which each person is accountable, and by the prices that resources can command in transactions only constrained by background rules on property rights.

The theory can be illustrated by an ethnographic example supplied in Fiske (1990). A gift of kola nuts is made to the bride's family in a Moose village marriage negotiation (Burkina Faso, West Africa). The nuts are bought in the market (MP) and shared among the bride's family according to age-based seniority (AR). Some are given to women and junior males, and these are subdivided into equal piles, from among which members of the group choose, with the divider taking his or her share last (EM). Finally, a single nut may be split and consumed by a group of friends with no thought as to who takes what portion (CS).

Whereas AR corresponds roughly to Douglas' 'hierarchy' and MP even more roughly to her 'individualism', Fiske's CS and EM emphasize different aspects of Douglas' 'enclave' ordering. Unlike Douglas, he has no way of explaining the significance of isolate ordering.

One argument Fiske makes for presupposing the universality of these four psychological models is that each embodies one of four basic measurement procedures: nominal (CS), ordinal (AR), interval (EM) and ratio (MP) scaling. But this means that the four models are incommensurable, unlike the four forms of solidarity in Douglas' theory, regulated by the axes of grid and group, and Fiske has no ready way of explaining when the different procedures will be invoked or how they will combine or clash.

In contrast with Fiske's account, much of Douglas' theory is driven by the realization that institutional viability flows from the ordering of practices in the interrelated domains of sacred and secular time. Fiske baulks at theorizing social dynamics. Noting correctly that Douglas' theory uses functional explanations, he wrongly takes it to be functionalist and goes on to associate her with what he terms 'obsolete theories of social evolution'. He then ducks the question of how his own theory might play out in a world of social dynamics, noting only that 'not much is known about the combinatorial syntax of the models' (Fiske, 1992, 711).

Since commensurability of the kind provided by Douglas' grid-group axes has been ruled out, Fiske is reduced to invoking culture as an exogenous variable, in order to tie the elementary social schemata together. 'A major problem is ... how people select a particular implementation of a specific model in any given context ... [but they] are probably guided primarily by cultural rules' (Fiske, 1992, 713). In conversation, Douglas often disdained this kind of argument as 'Bongo-Bongo-ism'. By this, she meant the tendency for anthropologists to reach, in difficulty, for cultural difference as a *deus ex machina* – 'yes, but not in *my* tribe' or 'yes, but not in the south'. It was the very defect her own theory was designed to overcome. Culture is a product of institutional choices, not its cause.

Fiske accepts that his own theory is Douglas' theory back-to-front. '[Here] I have been considering the various functional constraints on the use of the four models. The converse perspective concerns the effects and correlates of the use of each model' (Fiske, 1992, 715). He commends Thompson et al. (1990) for having shown a way forward. Culture is output, not input. But Fiske is also probably correct to imply that much more work is needed to fully identify the mechanisms shaping institutional viability.

At the end of his paper, Fiske casts his lot with the emergent field of evolutionary psychology. Darwinian selection is the missing mechanism. In later work, the cultural *deus ex machina* returns; Rai and Fiske (2011, 65), for example, argue that what is now termed 'relationship regulation theory' is driven 'by individuals and groups constituting different social relational models'. How and through whom this 'constituting' is done is unclear. Getting answers to questions about socially constitutive process is one of Douglas' central concerns. As we have shown, her later work returns to the neglected, performative aspect of the Durkheimian heritage, where she delves into the compositional practices of ritual inventiveness through which human groups elaborate viable new modes of cooperation and conflict settlement.

To distinguish it from Douglas' framework, Kahan describes his approach as 'cultural cognition theory'. Rooted in cognitive psychology, it offers to explain particular perceptions of risk by reference to general worldviews. He acknowledges that he and his colleagues are using a modified version of Douglas' typology of elementary forms. As one would expect, Kahan's two dimensions are of worldviews, not of social organization. One is scale from hierarchy to egalitarianism; although Kahan does not use the term, it might be thought of as a measure of power distance. The other runs from individualism to solidarism. The resulting four forms are therefore simply 'hierarchical individualism', 'hierarchical communitarianism', 'egalitarian individualism' and 'egalitarian communitarianism'. Kahan rejects Douglas' argument that isolate ordering is a distinct form at all and claims that there are no significant empirical examples of it. Appropriately for an ideational and a methodologically individualist theory, many of the measures of the independent variables used by Kahan et al. (2011) focus on worldviews rather than people's location in social organization. Like Dake's studies, their survey work uses attitudinal scales, along dimensions patterned on Douglas' dimensions of 'group' and 'grid' to measure the worldviews of a large sample of subjects, and a battery of scales for people's recognition of risks in such fields as climate change, gun control and pollution. In 'Cultural Cognition of Scientific Consensus', Kahan et al. found that subjects recognize a scientist with elite credentials as an 'expert' in a particular field much more readily when that expert's position conforms to, rather than contradicts, the risk perception dominant among people who share the subjects' own worldviews. As a result, individuals with opposing cultural worldviews end up with strongly divergent beliefs about the state of 'scientific consensus'. People hear what they want to hear, but this is influenced by cognitive commitments that may have a social basis. In other experiments, Kahan and colleagues have found that cultural outlooks similarly filter individuals' assessments of the strength of empirical evidence on various risk issues, and that individuals impute more credibility to risk experts they regard as sharing their own worldview than to those they understand as taking an opposing one. The result is both an intellectualist conception of conflict and also one in which forms are, if they have any significance at all beyond being commonly observed clusterings of views, psychological phenomena only contingently related to practices and ways of being organized and disorganized. This can readily provide one kind of account of why conflicts amplify, based on the straightforward thought that people fight because they disagree. But it offers no very convincing account of how it is possible for people come to live together despite disagreement. Yet this is perhaps the commonest basis for viable social organization throughout human history.

These limitations of ideational theories of 'cultural cognition' lead us directly to consider Douglas' development of her account of the dynamics of conflict as it stood in the early 1980s.

Elementary Forms and the Turn Toward Conflict Studies

For Douglas, the real importance of the four elementary forms was that they yielded a theory of conflict among and between them. Each elementary form developed its own 'cosmological values', its own claims of justice, its own conception of how to think about the past and the future, and the duties that each supposedly places upon people. Those conceptions could not avoid clashing.

With the resources of her account of institutional incompatibility on the dimensions of social integration and social regulation, she now began to focus on challenging the widespread assumption that fundamental social conflicts took root between empirical and particular identities such as religion and secularism, 'East' and 'West', Islamic and Judaeo-Christian traditions, or such adventitious and fleeting things as 'ethnicities', often and glibly described as 'cultures' (Richards, 2009). Logically, it also followed that to talk of 'multiculturalism' between, for example, African-American, native American, Hispanic American, Italian-American and WASP American identities was to seize upon the wrong level of analysis, if the argument is to be useful in understanding conflicts in the modern United States. It followed from her theoretical standpoint that all four elementary forms of social organization and their distinctive forms of cognition would be found within each of these supposedly distinct ethnic identities.

One of Douglas' key insights was that within-group institutional tensions might be as troublesome as those between groups, as a result of organizational differences among people who otherwise might share nationality, language, religion or ethnicity. This meant that she was well positioned to take account of the growing interest among social scientists in the 1990s in understanding civil wars. Civil wars pose a puzzle to conventional arguments about a 'clash of cultures', since the degree of bitterness can be directly proportional to the degree of cultural similarity. Hutus and Tutsis in Rwanda, for instance, speak but one language. Religious wars tear apart communities whose differences of belief may boil down to no more than a turn of phrase in a statement of faith. But according to Douglas, it is the competing organization, not the belief, that drives the hatred. In short, her theory gave her conceptual tools to tease apart within-group institutional tensions.

By the beginning of the 1990s, Douglas had recast her whole theory – first developed in *Purity and Danger* and *Natural Symbols* as one of distinctive, stable, but separate social and ritual practices – as one of conflict. Culture itself, she wrote, should be understood as 'a never resolved argument about rightness of choice' (1992a, 260). Indeed, 'argument is too soft a word for the struggle'. It followed that the normative imperative to which her own programme was a response was as much to contain, limit and offset culture quite generally, and not only those forms that produced collective effervescence, which had been her stance when she had first worried about witchcraft cleansing cults in central Africa in the 1960s or the most radical forms of environmentalism in the United States in the early 1980s. She now returned decisively to the original aspiration of her theory to treat all the elementary forms of institutional life symmetrically.

So, despite what seemed to have been suggested in *Risk and Culture*, each of the forms was likely to contribute as much as any other to the eternal clash of cultural claims. Conflict amplification could now be explained by action and counter-reaction among the four forms, and by self-radicalization, and self-reinforcement, within each. Although Douglas herself did not make the move explicit, it could be argued that instead of thinking – as she had done in *Purity and Danger* – only of the enclave as the case par excellence of mechanical solidarity, the logic of the theory required that each of the elementary forms was to be treated as a distinctive form of mechanical solidarity. Mechanical solidarity rests on classifying people within the ordering as similar to each other and dissimilar from others. Individualistic institutions, for example, cultivate classification of people as relevantly similar to each other as all being weakly integrated and separately responsible, just as much as enclaved institutions more obviously insist on the classification of people by identity or shared belief as being the most important thing we need to know about someone in order to know how to deal with them. Douglas had consistently argued (1966, 1986, 1992b) that similarity is not a thing given in nature, but an artefact of institutions selecting the particular respects under which things are classified as similar to each other. This kind of operation is performed in hierarchy, under individualism and in isolate ordering just as much as it is performed in enclaved contexts. So the question that Douglas now had to ask herself was, in effect, whether her arguments also yielded a theory of organic solidarity – an explanation of complementarity based on organizational difference. In effect, she now had to ask how the attenuation of conflict might be possible.

By Douglas' own definition of bias in culture as clashing claims of right, there is no normative position – even one for dampening conflict – on which to stand outside culture, for normative claims define the cultural. She concluded that 'a reflexive culture that takes all sides at once is a contradiction, but I don't think that the idea of a reflexive sociology is absurd'. The most that could be achieved normatively, then, would be to identify what it might take for each of the elementary forms to be sustained in sufficient articulation that it neither overwhelms the others nor is overwhelmed, but also where, instead of gridlock and permanent standoff, some sort of four-sided relationship is achieved in which some mutuality and provisional settlement might be possible, at least for a time. Douglas did later cautiously adopt the cybernetic theory used by Thompson and others. She seemed not to be entirely comfortable with the idea of 'requisite variety'. Perhaps she thought it had a worryingly 'just so' aspect. Yet Ashby's (1956) term is certainly relevant here. It denotes the principle that each and every element in a system must be controlled, and the controlling system must be at least as diverse as the elements to be controlled. But the match is not exact, and herein may have lain the difficulty for Douglas, because Ashby's concept envisaged a controlling system independent of the things controlled, whereas her argument is that there are only the four elementary forms to exercise some control over each other. There are no independent referees or controllers in the game of social life.

By the mid 1990s, in the papers in the final part of *Risk and Blame*, Douglas had formulated the problem clearly. But she had not yet formulated a way to address it. By this time, Thompson and Wildavsky had both begun to develop accounts of four-sided settlement. Wildavsky was writing shortly before his death, in papers that appeared posthumously, of the notion of 'coalitions of cultures' and of a renovating 'pluralism' in political science as a cultural affair rather than one of organized interests (Wildavsky, 1998, 187–213). Yet, typically, Wildavsky still wanted to take sides. By the end of his life, Wildavsky's animus against what he called 'egalitarianism' had only dimmed to the point that he was prepared to see its value in mopping up what he saw as the damaging rot caused by isolate ordering (or what he called 'fatalism'). His four-sided coalitions were still really based on the same hegemony of the 'centre' that *Risk and Culture* had presented, but now in altogether politer language (see e.g. Wildavsky, 1998, 209–12). By contrast, Thompson (1996, 1997a, 1997b) was already working his way toward the idea of what, after the turn of the century, he would call 'clumsy' institutions (Verweij and Thompson, 2006). These were institutions that articulated enough but not too much of each of the four elementary forms, even at the price of inefficient redundancy, and that focused on activities that, at least, were not unacceptable to any (Thompson, 1997a). 6 (2003) offered a typology of ways in which the four forms might be related to each other, of which Thompson's 'clumsy' institutions were but one case.

Douglas' own sole-authored writings contain little discussion of Thompson's 'clumsiness' approach, but in her last years, she did put her name to one coauthored paper setting out the argument for clumsy four-way settlements (Verweij et al., 2006). It was not her way to comment much in print on any doubts she might have had about the applications and extensions of her theory by those who drew upon her work, however sharp she might be in private conversation. Nevertheless, in her last sole-authored works, which we discuss in Chapter 4, she pursued an entirely different path toward thinking about the attenuation, channelling and dampening of conflict. Whereas Thompson concentrated on relations among the four elementary forms of social organization, Douglas asked herself in her final years the opposite question: what resources are there that might contribute to containing conflict, within each of the forms, and how can each form cultivate those resources from within its own capabilities? This direction, she announced, but could not yet follow through in the papers in *Risk and Blame* (1992a, esp. 255–70). In the limited time left to her, she decided to concentrate on the peculiar case of hierarchy, for which she proclaimed a lasting affection, based on youthful experience.

Before examining that turn, though, we look at the obverse of the work that Douglas carried out in her middle period from the mid 1970s to the mid 1990s. This chapter has been concerned above all with the development of the typological theory of social organization and of the ideas that are cultivated in each of the elementary forms. The causal engine beneath the typology was specified fairly schematically in 'Cultural Bias'. *Risk and Culture* had, if anything, obscured rather than clarified it. If Douglas were to achieve the aspiration she had set out of working out how resources might be found, cultivated, mobilized and configured within each form of organization (or even within hierarchy alone) that might contribute to the attenuation of conflict among the four, then it would be necessary to develop a much clearer and better specified set of microfoundations of causation for the theory. It was to that task that Douglas turned with especial energy in the second half of the 1980s, although a key book from the end of the 1970s began that development. The next chapter examines the microfoundations that she carefully constructed in these years.

3

BUILDING FUNDAMENTAL EXPLANATIONS
Rituals Do the Institutionalizing, and Institutions Make Change

This chapter examines the major work of Douglas' middle period, and provides an account of the microfoundations for her typological theory. These works set out the roles of ritual, institutions, functional explanation and dynamics in a tightly interlocking structure shaping and stylizing thought. First, we examine her negative critique of the microfoundations of economics, presented in a piece of deck-clearing work in the 1970s, before returning to examine in finer detail than hitherto the role of ritual in her causal theory. Then the chapter turns to her major work encapsulating this microfoundational theory, *How Institutions Think*. We show that several of her later works on microfoundations are extensions of the arguments she presented there. We look at her definition of an institution, at the causal theory she offered to explain the work of institutions in shaping thought, and at her 'dependent variable' of thought style and its relationship with the problem of agency in institutional theory. Two important but late contributions to the understanding of microfoundations are examined, including her final and – to some who misunderstood her as a theorist of 'culture', surprising – rejection in 2004 of the notion that the idea of culture can be put to any explanatory work. We examine her modelling work on positive feedback and ratchet effects in de-institutionalization and social disorganization, using sectarian terrorism as an illustrative case study for a more widespread process. Before concluding the chapter, we briefly consider some of the criticisms made of her microfoundational arguments and her replies.

Douglas only produced her major statements on these foundations after she had already developed the key concepts of social cognition, organization and anomaly, and her typology of elementary forms. Many of the microfoundational arguments are implicit in her early work, but only in the 1980s did she work them out systematically. She wrote that she might have been better understood if she had developed the microfoundations first, yet few theorists ever do arrange their work in such a systematically deductive fashion. Durkheim himself, for example, only provided the microfoundations for his own body of work in his major treatise *The Elementary Forms of Religious Life* (1995 [1912]), which was published only after many years of reflection. Douglas' career trajectory showed the same late move to microfoundations in order to integrate her arguments.

'Microfoundations' is a term borrowed from economics and now used more widely in social theory across the social sciences (Little, 1998). It is certainly not one that Douglas would have used. She disliked such terms, which she considered jargon, but our view is that it is in fact a helpful category. In economics it refers to basic theories of human interaction, motivation, and capacity to recognize and respond to information. Together, these form an aggregate on which all the field's substantive theories rest. For example, optimization under constraint in neoclassical economics and heuristic-driven 'satisficing' in behavioural economics (behaviour in which outcomes are adequate to the agents' own standards or reference points, if not the best attainable) are each particular aspects of quite distinct schemes of microfoundations.

In much economic theory, microfoundations have been developed within the framework of methodological individualism. First formulated (but not yet so named) in the eighteenth century by Adam Smith and by Condorcet, and recast by Weber, and then Popper and Hayek in the twentieth century, methodological individualism is the philosophical position underpinning social science traditions such as rational choice, neoclassical economics, prospect theory and even – perhaps surprisingly – Freud's psychoanalysis. It makes the foundational assumption that accurate and causally satisfying explanations of all human actions and their outcomes rest, and can only rest, on statements about desires, beliefs and intentions of individuals, and the ways in which these actions aggregate to produce patterns of outcomes. Even the social constraints that individuals face are themselves to be explained, according to methodological individualism, as the aggregation of previous individual desires, beliefs and intentions. (It is called methodological individualism to differentiate it from normative individualism – the claim that people ought to stand on their own two feet and know their own minds – and from substantive individualism, which is Douglas' term for that elementary form of social organization which is defined by weakly socially integrated and weakly socially regulated institutions.)

Durkheimian approaches differ sharply. Durkheim argued that social life was more than the sum of individual motivations. Rather, it rests on a presumed species-wide capacity to initiate and apprehend collective practices. Although not methodologically individualistic, Durkheimian arguments still require microfoundations. But in this tradition, the 'micro' elements cannot be individual agents who might be understood to be autonomous and discrete from each other. Nor, in a theory that is not methodologically individualistic, can people's preferences be taken as given in explanations. Instead, they are likely to be developed and eroded endogenously within patterns of interaction. The 'micro' elements in the foundations for such theories are practices, ritual forms and causal loops supporting explanations focused upon the endogenous group-based cultivation of preferences and emotions.

In Douglas' larger argument, the most important microfoundations are those that give specification to the mechanisms in the causal engine that turns the typology into something capable to produce explanations. By no means all the necessary microfoundations for her theory were supplied in her own writings.

The claim that there is a species-wide capacity to initiate and apprehend collective practices is an assumption Douglas inherited from Durkheim, and it is still something being worked out empirically by biological anthropologists, evolutionary musicologists and others interested in sociality and social coordination as an aspect of comparative primate behaviour. One key aspect that is highly relevant to ritual performance is the ability to follow a beat. This capacity, which is basic to dance and coordinated labour, has been reported in newborn infants, so is presumably innate in the human species (Winkler et al., 2009). Rhythm and repeated note and phrase structure are fundamental to whale song composition, and ritual bodily coordination is well developed among whales and dolphins, but as yet there is limited evidence of a direct equivalent of dance in the full sense among cetaceans. Whether it is found in primates other than humans is unclear. Can chimpanzees dance? More remains to be discovered. Douglas' sense that something foundational was as yet lacking in this area helps explain the close attention she paid in her last phase to developments in this branch of anthropology. On the view developed from Durkheim's late (1995 [1912]) work, dance provides a basic template for repeated rhythmic bodily coordination in communication with other people either in matched, or in responsive and exchanged, or in sequenced or ranked sets of moves, thus providing the foundations of human ritual action, on the basis of which capabilities for social life generally can be sustained, even in informal conversational settings when rhythms are attenuated or broken. Thus, we 'dance' our social organization into institutionalization, and the structures of our 'dances' – for instance, our handshakes, our meeting and averting of eyes, whether we rise or remained seated to greet (Goffman, 1967a), how we hold ourselves to give and receive gifts (Mauss, 1990 [1950]), and how we arrange our land, buildings, rooms and spaces as social dancefloors – in turn reflect the social organization they reinforce. Thereby collective practices emerge, which are ordered by a limited variety of elementary forms of ritual coordination. In turn, these basic forms of 'danced' organization stand towards each other in the paradoxical processes of conflictual mutual dependence that are at the core of Douglas' work. They sustain themselves and provoke each other by cultivating styles of thought that cognitively reflect features of their social relations. People must, as it were, know how to follow a beat, to dance and to sing before they can know themselves socially (Cross, 2003; Richards, 2007). Whether or not the evolution was a linear chronological development from simple dance to complex ritual social interaction, the capacities for ordered practices that make up the full variety of social relations depend at any one time on ritualized, rhythmic bodily coordination.

Other foundations were developed by collaborators. In particular, as discussed above, the theory of the dynamics of institutional change was developed by Thompson (1982a, 1982b, 1992; Thompson et al., 1990). But it was especially through critical engagement with economics and its methodologically individualistic microfoundations that she began to develop her own very distinctive foundational framework. Her own undergraduate training had been in economics, politics and philosophy. Perhaps being married to an economist – especially one engaged directly in politics and policy – also helped to ensure that this discipline was the primary point of reference for her critical reflection on microfoundations.

Circumventing the Microfoundations of Economics

From as early as her examination of Lele households, Douglas had been interested in why many people do and why some people very definitely do *not* want goods. She was fascinated by questions such as why most of us want to consume many things only at particular times and places and with particular other people. She wanted to know why there are prohibitions against the pursuit of some goods in some settings but not in others. In the same vein, she puzzled over how and why we distinguish between necessities and luxuries. An abiding interest for her was the effort to understand how in some contexts, the possession of many goods marks status or power, whereas in others, it is the eschewing of goods, or at least of particular goods, that marks status or, if status is rejected, at least attracts respect. These issues had preoccupied her earliest ethnography, when she had examined use by the Lele of raffia cloth in its role as an equivalent for money, as a vehicle for gift-giving and as a means of implementing men's control over women. When the 1970s presented her with opportunities to devote time to these questions comparatively, she saw a chance to develop her arguments as microfoundations for her own theory. Consumption was not chosen as a side-issue where anthropology could quietly supplement standard economic analysis by decorating a spare account with a little 'folk' colour without disturbing the hegemony of the economists over the supposedly more central issues of production, work, demand, wealth and price. Rather, it was chosen precisely as a means of challenging economic microfoundations quite generally.

Of course, anthropologists, like sociologists, had long engaged in critiques of conventional economic microfoundational assumptions. Collaborative studies resulting in edited volumes on uses of food in the early 1970s (Douglas, 1973c) and later on alcohol (Douglas, 1987) extended Douglas' earlier ethnographic work on food prohibitions among the Lele and in Leviticus (Douglas, 1966). In 'Deciphering a Meal' (reprinted in Douglas, 1999a [1975], 231–51), she was already exploring arguments about the limitations of conventional economic conceptions of consumption. Eating and drinking were not only utilitarian activities but also important ways of marking off time in cycles of festivities, of sustaining bonds with others, of marking boundaries and of ritually enacting social organization.

Yet Douglas did more than merely offer a standard anthropological critique of economic utilitarianism. Her aim was to use the study of consumption as a vehicle for developing a set of theoretical arguments about practices that would afford goals and constraints, which in turn would supply reasons and justifications, and patterns of relationships that would call for specific ritual acts. This work would supply a basis for her general typological theory of available variety in the elementary forms of social organization. The results appeared in a series of papers mainly on money and on food republished in excerpted form in the edited collection *In the Active Voice* (Douglas, 1982c, 16–134) and in the 1979 book *The World of Goods*, written with the economist Baron Isherwood. Isherwood was a trained econometrician who became a research fellow in the anthropology department at UCL in the early 1970s, before going on to work in the British government on poverty and inequality issues under the Labour administrations led by Harold Wilson and James Callaghan in the second half of the decade. The argument of this collaborative book was then reiterated and illustrated with further examples in a set of papers collected in *Thought Styles* (1996), several of which drew upon a major study of a large sample of households undertaken for the multinational company Unilever by Gerald and Valerie Mars.

Douglas' central argument was that routinely consuming, as well as periodically and excessively consuming in feasts and potlatches, while also at times limiting consumption or prohibiting others from consuming, are all acts of ritual communication. The ritual practice of consumption was a basic category of institution, and it would be modulated in different ways in each of the elementary forms. Ritual was now firmly understood as encompassing the etiquette of everyday ritual interaction, often in private and without formal staging, just as Goffman (1967; Collins, 2004) had understood it, and not only as grand public ceremonial. Human motivation was thereby endogenously cultivated in each ritually ordered practice, but the ordering was different according to the differing strengths of social integration and social regulation. More precisely, motivation for consumption was, she argued, as forensic in its own way as was worrying about risks and taking precautions. As consumers, people used goods or, for that matter, made a point of not using goods in order to 'construct an intelligible universe'. On this occasion, Douglas used the word 'construct' as a verb meaning to 'build' or 'assemble' rather than as a variant of 'construe'. Both experimentation and refusal to experiment with food, clothes, interior decor, consumer durable equipment, eating certain foods at festivals or possession of sacred and even academic books were ritual activities signalling group membership and nonmembership on one dimension, while signifying discretion or authority on the other, all the while marking participation and nonparticipation in particular kinds of relationships and institutions. Through ritual performance of consumption and fasting and other ways of deliberately limiting consumption, people engaged in learning about their social world while also acquiring the blinkers and partisanships that come with such learning. Categories of relationships, positions and opportunities are fixed through this kind of performance. Only when the social sciences can put the institutional ordering into the column marked 'independent variables' and examine the ritual mechanisms through which institutional ordering works will it be possible to model the endogenous cultivation of preferences, or, for that matter, the ranking of risks, as outputs in explanations of consumer behaviour.

Douglas credited the founding figure in Durkheimian anthropology, Marcel Mauss, with having fully grasped this issue. In writing an introduction for an English translation of Mauss' famous essay 'The Gift' (1990 [1950]), she advocated following gifts through society as a basic procedure for ethnographic analysis (Douglas, 1990, viii–ix). This requires not only formal network analysis of exchanges, but also careful attention to the *diversity* of ritual practices and the contexts of each transfer. Mauss had made something of a rod for his own back by assuming that every gift required a return. This is true only under certain forms of institutional ordering, well represented in the ethnographic reports around which Mauss had shaped his account. In other cases, gifts, honour and respect accumulate upwards or dissipate downwards. The actual pattern, Douglas notes, cannot be 'read off' from the ideas and rationalizations of informants, but is apparent only when the interactional tally of ritual exchanges is totalled and when we see to whom honour is due and, conversely, who is debased in what she calls the 'public drama ... directly cued to public esteem' of gift-giving (Douglas, 1990b, xiv). Neither Mauss nor Douglas mentions anonymous charitable donations, but these cases serve to remind us that under different institutions, the interaction order of ritual will be very different, but still highly ritualized. It is only when we appreciate the ritual performance of giving, Douglas remarks, rubbing in the point about the performative basis of institutions, that the songs and dirges typical of the institutional ordering in question can be understood. Ritual action tells us more than words, and runs ahead of and shapes, words and concepts. As Durkheim taught, we believe because we pray; we do not pray because we believe.

Because everyday household consumption behaviour requires more satisfying explanation than assumptions based on optimization by discrete autonomous individuals facing budget constraints, the microfoundations of neoclassical economics must be questioned. And yet this was the very terrain economics claimed as 'mainstream'.

Mainstream neoclassical economics could manage to ignore such things as the periodicities of Christmas or Ramadan, or jubilees and durbars, as though these were special cases with little impact for

the mass of consumption activity. The real world of retail economics, of course, makes no such mistake. It is common knowledge in
West Africa, for example, that prices of basic food items rise during
Ramadan, in anticipation of the end of the fast. But here we are dealing with the ivory tower. Academic economists could dismiss Veblen's
conspicuous consumption merely as a form of investment in pursuit
of social climbing. They might regard Roman and Renaissance sumptuary laws as quaint quirks or irrational responses now surpassed by
modern individualist maximizers of utility. They could leave aside
religious or political ascetics as similar anachronisms. This left a wide
space clear for Douglas to elaborate her theory of goods. It was not
difficult for an anthropologist to show how each of these behaviours
would be cultivated and, indeed, be entirely rational under the differing institutions associated with each of her four elementary forms
– ascetic restraint in the enclave, conspicuous consumption in individualistic ordering, opportunist scavenging or piecemeal accumulation in isolate ordering, and the many kinds of periodic days of feast
and fast associated with hierarchy.

Douglas clearly demonstrated that if the full range of social and
contextual constraints and imperatives she later termed 'institutions'
was modelled in the explanation of the formation of preferences, then
periodicity, excess and asceticism, restriction and selection, signalling and socially learnt preferences in consumption would emerge
as entirely rational and reasonable. Many rational choice theorists of
the 1970s assumed that when people engaged in behaviour that did
not maximize their utility, they were being irrational, and that this
irrationality lay beyond the explanatory reach of economics. Others
had already pointed out that this was tantamount to arguing that 'if
the theory does not explain it, that shows it is not interesting or important'. But whereas many anthropologists and sociologists simply
turned away from rationality, constraint and returns altogether, and
retreated into ideational interpretive and descriptive work, Douglas
used her machinery to show that if the full range of institutional constraints and distinct styles of rationality was to be admitted, then
gifts, sumptuary laws, abstention during Lent or Ramadan, hair
shirts, binge drinking and potlatches could also be shown to be institutionally rational – which, she would later argue in *How Institutions
Think*, is the only kind of rationality available. Moreover, if that were
done, then even the humdrum consumption of the weekly shopping
expedition, or the mundane and tedious ticking off of the seasonal
holiday gift list, acquired a richer and more comprehensive mode of
explanation.

Yet only a modest portion of *The World of Goods* is devoted to this part of the argument about microfoundations. A good deal of the second half of the book is about class or, at any rate, about consumption classes, and it offers a good deal of empirical and even some statistical evidence. Some readers may have thought that this was simply the part reflecting Isherwood's interests, while others perhaps assumed that Douglas was doing little more than anticipating by a few years the availability in English of Bourdieu's study *Distinction*, by showing how consumption marks social distinctions of class, turning some goods into positional ones (Hirsch, 1976).

It is true that Douglas did cite Bourdieu's writings in *The World of Goods*, and in the original French. Yet, in fact, without overtly targeting him, Douglas was also subtly undermining and complicating Bourdieu's claims that consumption is an indicator of class and social origin, and that consumption preferences are made stable by class. Two years after *The World of Goods*, she reviewed Bourdieu's work and made the argument much more bluntly (Douglas, 1982c, 125–34). She argued that far from being stable, consumption preferences are often periodic, episodic and even cyclical, in ways that have to be explained by reference to the ritual function of consumption as a category of human behaviour. Moreover, for her, class distinctions are not so much reflected by consumption as produced, recast and changed by them. By contrast, in Bourdieu's theory, class formation either happens well away from consumption in a zone of production supposedly insulated from it or else is not explained at all. Where Bourdieu conceived class as a matter of status, Douglas used her typology of elementary forms to show just how specific and restricted the emphasis on social status is, while the role of consumption in social organization runs much more widely. Nor could Bourdieu's theory cope as well with prohibitions and eschewing of goods as it could with excess, positionality and exclusivity. Therefore, *The World of Goods* explores restrictions and prohibitions on consumption as often as the phenomena of conspicuous consumption or the snobbery and inverse snobbery that preoccupied Bourdieu. Moreover, where Bourdieu would flirt with the idea that discourse, or talk and ideas about consumption, might be enrolled to do the explanatory work, Douglas rigorously treated talk and ideas as things to be explained, not as fundamental causal forces in their own right.

Class certainly matters, for Douglas, in *The World of Goods*. Indeed, Isherwood provided the book with its statistical resources and much of the detailed secondary analysis of empirical data on class. The inequalities of class and the peculiar humiliations it produces were the burden of the argument of the second half of the book, but Douglas' and Isherwood's argument is that the real humiliations and disadvantage for poor consumers have to do with relations and institutions from which they are excluded, not with foregone material satisfactions. In this regard, Douglas was a theorist of 'social exclusion' twenty years in advance of the popularity of that notion among other social scientists.

Whereas the microfoundations of Bourdieu's theory lie in class-based differences in access to many different kinds of capital, so that *habitus* is really a locale for their reproduction, Douglas' microfoundational argument is almost the inverse. It is in quotidian ritual interaction that the very resources that come to form and to be classified as different kinds of capital are sustained. Crucially, Douglas' argument is that class categories are not to be taken for granted as if they formed a fixed system. Rather, consumption classes, and perhaps other concurrent class orderings, are recursively recast over time by consumption, and therefore they need not map onto class structures in the workplace. In later decades, she would go on to borrow Thompson's cybernetic account of feedback loops resulting in change. But in 1979, she was concerned to emphasize ritual as a causal mechanism by which social organization selects consumption patterns and by which consumption changes social organization. Thereby a variety of different class systems is produced, which need not, and typically do not, map neatly onto each other as Bourdieu presumed they must. Just as Basil Bernstein once said that her argument in *Natural Symbols* took his own in *Class, Codes and Control* (Bernstein, 1971) and stood it on its head, not least with respect to the supposed simplicities of working-class speech, so in *The World of Goods*, Douglas could be said to have stood Bourdieu on his head too.

Douglas could not adopt Bourdieu's microfoundations of *habitus*, *praxis* and discourse. In the collection *Risk and Blame* (Douglas, 1992a), she would offer occasional olive branches to advocates of Bourdieu's concept of *habitus* and write that she admired his analysis of the ritual organization of symbolic order in Berber rural households. But she never endorsed his underlying theory, because he took the classifications embodied in class interests as being fundamental and because his theory of practice lacked a typological account of variation.

The microfoundational project was left incomplete at the end of *The World of Goods*. Douglas had yet to fully work out her account of how ritual served to cultivate categories and how in turn this process might supply goals to be maximized, which could then replace the undernourished account of motivation offered in conventional neoclassical economics. What remained to be done was to give content to the idea that there were distinct styles of rationality. What, after all, were the constraints that anthropologists and sociologists typically discussed under the headings of social structure, social context and social organization, if not styles of reasoning? And what did a style consist in, and what precisely was its relationship with ritual as a causal mechanism? Even if there were only four elementary forms, how and why were specific and distinctive styles cultivated, sustained or changed? Answering such questions took up much of Douglas' time during the 1980s and the first half of the 1990s, when she produced her most important microfoundational statements.

Institutions as the Unit of Foundational Analysis

Douglas' most systematic argument in answer to these questions was published in 1986, having been first given as a series of endowed lectures at Syracuse University in the spring of the previous year. *How Institutions Think* provides the theoretical statement of the microfoundations of her entire body of work, finally laying out the structure of the causal mechanism and recasting it as an institutional theory, and arguing that classification itself is the basic element for all the ideational panoply of symbol, culture and perception.

Unfortunately, the book attracted few admirers, and it is more often cited than fully engaged with. At first sight, *How Institutions Think* seems short, even slight, oblique in its argument and lacking the expected grand finale. The book puzzled the devotees of her fourfold typology because the matrix is only fleetingly invoked in one sentence in the sixth chapter (Douglas, 1986, 80). It baffled those among the risk scholars who thought of her as making a major contribution to their field, because the book avoids all mention of their topic. Anthropologists found it devoid of ethnographic input or illumination. Those in North America who thought of their subject as the study of culture could not see why Douglas appeared to go out of her way to avoid the term. Institutionalists in economics and sociology did not at first see how it connected with their concerns, though perhaps Douglass North (1990) was hinting at Douglas' argument as a distant influence when he flagged the importance of what he termed 'informal' institutional restraints. To the faithful Durkheimians who had regarded Douglas as a loyalist, albeit an eccentric one, her opening chapter, questioning the idea that institutions could have minds of their own, seemed to ditch the idea of the 'conscience collective', and her description of Durkheim as a 'broken reed' would have struck some as gratuitously insulting.

Yet *How Institutions Think* is the essential statement of Douglas' thought, and one that anyone seriously engaging with her argument ought to study most carefully. Those willing to embark on the journey face a number of obstacles, about which it is best to be frank. Though direct in style, *How Institutions Think* demands ferocious concentration. Each short chapter requires several readings in order for the true significance of the sometimes understated arguments to be seen. It also assumes a strong grasp of major theoretical debates in the social sciences. The reader needs to come prepared with at least a working knowledge of theoretical positions adopted by Hume, Durkheim, Merton, Evans-Pritchard, Mancur Olson and Jon Elster – perhaps a tall order for even the best prepared graduate student.

Douglas wrote that it was the book she should have written before almost all the others. It was the work of the year of her retirement and a pivotal moment in the trajectory of the development of her thought. It is essentially an unpacking of Durkheim's and Mauss' claim in the monograph *Primitive Classification* (1963 [1902–3]) – a work she took very seriously indeed – that 'the classification of things *reproduces* [replicates in microcosm] the classification of [people]'. Perhaps it was because of the difficulties Douglas and Wildavsky's *Risk and Culture* had got into that in *How Institutions Think*, Douglas largely avoided the word 'culture'; it does not even have an entry in the index. The decision makes the argument much clearer, for now there could be no danger of muddling up just what culture is, or whether it does the explaining, or gets explained.

The first stage in Douglas' programme of providing microfoundations is to offer her alternative to methodological individualism. Methodological individualists often took Durkheim's work as an example of the kind of argument they opposed, assuming that it advocates some kind of mystical 'group mind' autonomous from the minds of individuals. This is not the place to debate whether or how far that charge might have been (partially) true, apart from noting that it is not clear whether Durkheim's arguments concerning the 'conscience collective' or mechanical solidarity do imply anything like a 'group mind'. On the other hand, because Durkheim offered a series of only partly worked-out statements of just how we should understand the relationship between the individual and the social, later theorists such as Douglas, who saw value in Durkheim's work, chose to select carefully from his legacy. Despite Cherkaoui's (2008) ingenious reworking of Durkheim's arguments in methodologically

individualistic versions, Durkheim's own arguments were not methodologically individualistic ones. Durkheim's explanations treated
many aspects of social life as irreducible to individual beliefs, desires
and intentions. He argued at length that aggregation of individual
action is something that needed to be explained in collective terms;
aggregation through markets or through voting systems rests on collective institutions often developed over generations.

Moreover, it is false to assume that any theory not methodologically individualistic must make 'group minds' fundamental. After all,
both Durkheim himself in his discussion of native Australian peoples
during some hunting seasons, and Mauss and Beuchat (1979 [1904–5])
in their analysis of the ways in which the Inuit longhouse community
disperses in family groups over the tundra during the summer months
were very much interested in understanding the basis of isolate life,
precisely when collective life is most attenuated. Durkheim's and
Mauss' point about the hunting seasons in the Arctic and the outback
is precisely that people are scattered too far apart for any 'group mind'
to be sustained, but that even isolate organization during the hunt
is the work of their institutions. Institutions do not only arise when
people feast together in long houses or in great outdoor dances. Just
as Durkheim argued that the moral or substantive individualism for
which he argued in his normative writing would be a social achievement, so the isolate life of the Inuit summer was a social achievement.
The opposite special cases of very strongly bonded groups such as
religious orders or communes were the result of social processes that
required much expense and effort devoted to overcoming the difficulty of sustaining them. If the monastery or commune ever thought
'as one', then it was only after a very great deal of struggle, diligence
and vigilance. If there is anything at all in human life approximating
the group mind, then it would have to be the special case of effervescence in enclaves, where a kind of collective panic takes hold. But
this is not a fundamental or instinctive manifestation. Rather, it takes
deep institutional work to create and sustain the conditions in which
it propagates. No riot 'just happens', as the authorities are often keen
to affirm when they hunt for the organizers. Douglas had argued from
the 1960s onwards, through many years of studying potentially violent and destructive witchcraft cleansing cults and millennial sects,
that a *conscience collective* was the product of organizational effort. It
was no more to be regarded as causally fundamental in social explanation than it was to be admired politically.

The problem that Douglas had to address in providing microfoundations was to provide an account of just what would be causally

fundamental in explanation. Such explanation needed to be general rather than an analysis couched in terms of special cases. Also, it had to be genuinely social, by covering more than individual desires and beliefs and intentions. Equally, it needed to be free from reliance on invoking mystical and inexplicable entities.

For her answer in 1986, Douglas reached for the concept of an institution, borrowing from developments in social theory outside her own discipline. One reason for choosing this approach was precisely to answer to any charge of the kind made against Durkheim that her theory might have smuggled back in the notion of the mystical 'group mind'. For an institution, even if it is tacit and informal, is more or less an entrenched practice to which people become committed, and that, if it ever were made explicit as a social contract, would prescribe, proscribe or permit particular actions or relations. A group mind, if such a thing were to be sustained, would have to deliberate, form intentions and itself take action. By contrast, institutions simply cultivate a prescription. They generate not 'group minds', but 'club rules'. Then individuals either go through causal processes to arrive at an understanding and acceptance of the prescription implied, or do not do so, in which case (her theory of institutional variation posits) they will have to revert to other causal processes, associated with some other institution, in order to revolt against the first (Douglas, 1986, 9–19, 92). In short, rebellion cannot be freedom, as the student revolutionaries Douglas encountered in London and Paris in the 1960s had asserted. Revolt opts for a different set of institutional prescriptions, with all the baggage they bring with them. Robin Horton, a philosopher and anthropologist whose work Douglas admired, graphically described it as a choice to leap from the crown of one palm tree to another (Horton, 1967). No one floats free. A prickly, awkward landing is guaranteed.

In the 1980s, institutional theory was undergoing a revival in economics, organizational sociology, political science, public administration and some parts of development studies, even as it was being submerged in the flood tide of postmodernism in anthropology. The 'new' institutionalism of those years drew on various sources. In economics, Oliver Williamson (1985) was a leading figure in one of the schools defining institutions as equilibria in incentives (cf. Calvert, 1995). For him, even enforcement practices for contracts achieved stability, endurance, robustness and, in due course, legal authority only because of the balance of transaction costs. Another cluster followed North (1990) in allowing some institutions to be generated in politics, in part arising from other forces as well as transaction costs. For both these traditions, institutions were defined as rules providing constraints and specifying incentives. (North, 1990, 3). In organizational sociology, W. Richard Scott (1995) offered a richer definition of an institution as a 'social structure', although he also considered ways of defining institutions as cognitive frameworks or as rules, but his settled view appeared to be, like Douglas' earlier work, that the cognitive styles were to be explained by, rather than being constitutive of, institutions.

Unfortunately, in *How Institutions Think*, Douglas moved uneasily between several definitions of an institution. Moreover, none of these definitions really met the requirements of her overall argument in the book. Her officially stated definition (Douglas, 1986, 46) was that an institution is a 'legitimised social grouping' and excludes any 'purely instrumental or provisional practical arrangement'. This, alas, brought back the idea of the group when the purpose of her whole argument was to explain what makes both groups and ungrouped clusters possible. Worse still, legitimation, she argued, was achieved by 'authority' for the arrangement. This too was a circular argument; it was true by definition, but is not an explanation. Douglas' answer to the puzzle about where that authority comes from was also disappointingly circular, for she simply claimed that it is justified, ex post facto, by ideas – for example, about nature, about the supernatural, about social life, about morality or about the limits on the feasible set. Yet the whole point of the book was to show that institutions explain styles of justification, not the other way around.

In other passages in the book, she resorted to North's and Williamson's characterizations of institutions as rules. This did not help much, because rules too are 'if ... then' statements providing guidance on what is to be done or not done, or may or may not be done, in given circumstances; in short, they are also ideas and beliefs. So it is not clear that an argument that institutions explain ideas, classification and thought styles can avoid circularity if rules are to be invoked in their definition. Or, to put it another way, if circularity is avoided, then it is at the price of seeming to claim that certain special kinds of ideas explain other kinds of ideas.

If institutions are rules, and rules are 'if ... then' statements, then sincere operation under institutions has to be a case of implicit belief or acceptance of the statements. The result is that we end up attributing vastly more beliefs to people than they plausibly possess in any strong sense of the word. Indeed, Douglas herself (1973a) appeared to accept Garfinkel's (1967) critique of the intellectualist supposition that people deal with the social world with their heads already full of implausibly vast number of beliefs in propositional rule statements.

Although never formulated clearly, some sections of the book suggested a better answer to the question: 'What is an institution?' Douglas did not, in fact, abandon the idea that institutions are pieces of social structure, although in *How Institutions Think*, she did not use that term. In several passages, she wrote of 'institutional structures' (e.g. Douglas, 1986, 81). By this, she clearly means established patterns of positions and relations. Determined to distinguish institutions from mystical notions of group minds and to ensure that they can explain cognition, such as aspects of intention and classification, without being themselves intentions and categories, she argued in one passage that 'institutions cannot have purposes ... only individuals can intend' (Douglas, 1986, 92). Equally determined to resist the methodologically individualistic argument that they can only result from the aggregation of individual intentions or interests under constraints that are themselves the result of previous aggregations to the point of equilibrium (Douglas, 1986, 111), Douglas went on to argue that the stability, order and authority that institutions achieve is the result of processes of energy absorption and dissipation, which required adding the machinery of dynamic complexity theory to the model (Douglas, 1986, 112).

The origins of such energy managing systems are, Douglas hints (1986, 58), in social interaction. This move brings her significantly closer to Garfinkel again, for this makes social structure into something performed and enacted among people. However, whereas Garfinkel (1967) doubted that performance ever achieved either any great stability, or that it exhibited a limited variety of elementary forms, or that collective performance stylized thought, Douglas argued for all three propositions. Nonetheless, she shared with Garfinkel the view that established patterns of relations and positions are the work that processes of ritually performed interaction among individuals achieve. Before social interaction becomes ordered by conscious, deliberate intentional action – even, for example, to propose a simple convention – there have to be tacit *practices* of patterned relationships among people. Moreover, these patterned practices must be established to some extent and must have been attempted before being the subject of explicit representations, through which collective energies can be gathered or dissipated in a more controlled manner.

In short, institutions are practices (6, 2016a). By practices, for this purpose we do not mean skills or activities specific to an empirical domain (e.g., Shove et al., 2012), such as sailing a canoe or a trawler, or the document handling of lawyers. Instead, we are concerned with a particular subset of 'generic' or 'dispersed' practices (Schatzki, 1996,

91). These are activities such as blaming, praising, deferring, bargaining, instructing and teaching. We might helpfully call these sorts of practices 'operations', for these are entirely universal behaviours that people deploy to achieve a social result. They are used to bring pressure to bear on other people in ways that, when we perform them, we enact particular imperatives ('positive rites' for Durkheim (1995 [1912])) or prohibitions ('negative rites' for Durkheim (1995 [1912])). An explicit statement of an 'if … then …' type follows the prior informal establishment of a practice in this sense. This 'if … then …' formulation is usually offered in explanation, justification or exculpation (all themselves operations) to produce a 'rule', which is a type of idea or belief. An everyday or quotidian ritual interaction order (Goffman, 1967a; Collins, 2004) is then established as a pattern of performing operations exhibiting a common style. And this common style is the elementary form of the institution. One can think of a style of dancing as the elementary form, as opposed to the many kinds of actual dances that can be produced in that style. In other words, elementary forms are shared capacities to execute certain kinds of patterned operational practices. As Rawls (2004) has demonstrated, the most consistent reading of Durkheim's conception in *Elementary Forms* is that he used practices to explain features of cognition such as classification and categories.

Douglas' reference to 'conventions' (1986, 46) as the simplest kind of institutions, especially when they have yet to be formulated as rules, came closest to the concept of more or less established informal practices of patterned relations. In her (1980) book about Evans-Pritchard's work, she had used the word 'accountabilities'. Although that term suggested to political scientists and others the idea of a duty to provide explicit and retrospective accounts of actions to identifiable living others, if it had not had those connotations, it would have served well to capture the notion of combinations of bodily rituals in practice – the stance, comportment and interactive turn-taking involved in enacting patterns of social relations, and the imperatives and demands that these interactional practices impose or permit. Do you stand, look and move like a Nuer, etc? Then I can be accountable to you, or you to me, in terms of the social bonds you embody. Indeed, quite literally I expect you to act out and reinforce those bonds, as you behave toward me as Nuer do.

One thing is missing from this account of the causal engine beneath the fourfold typology, which readers of *Purity and Danger* and *Natural Symbols* might have expected Douglas to emphasize as part of a Durkheimian argument, even if one now freed from some of

Durkheim's own mistakes. What is absent is any account of the role of ritual in supporting either the mechanisms or the trajectory of institutional process, whether considered in terms of the enactment of social organization to reinforce practices or its capacity to inculcate categories through performative repetition. Ritual practice probably remains implicit in, for example, boundary-maintenance activity and in processes of sustaining social motivation. As *The World of Goods* had argued, physical objects, technologies or resources are used as notation systems for people to make sense of and interpret for themselves their placement within a field or trajectory of institutionalization. By the mid 1980s, Douglas appeared no longer to think it necessary to emphasize this aspect. This may have been a mistake. Perhaps she had overestimated the ability of her readers to follow the implications of her emerging train of thought? Perhaps she allowed too little scope in her presentation for new readers to join her halfway?

Yet the whole causal argument requires a particular understanding of ritual interaction if it is to go through at all. What we do in our ritual interaction in conversation, in meetings and even in written communication is to enact our social organization in microcosm. Of all the practices captured in an elementary form such as hierarchy or enclave or individualistic ordering, the face-to-face, speaker-to-listener and writer-to-reader ritual practices are the ones by which we cultivate, reinforce, implicitly convey and 'teach' that form's thought style to each other. The only consistent answer to the question '*how do institutions cultivate thought style?*' is 'ritually'. And this is why Douglas really needs a definition of an institution in terms of 'practice' rather than a set of 'rules'. Ritual interaction order crystallizes forms of practices in the little microcosm of everyday communication because it is itself a particular kind of practice. It does not and could not do so because somehow people approach each with huge sets of propositional beliefs about correct behaviour that they follow by direct transcription from intellectually accepted rules to particular local action. There is no grammar book for learning 'body language'. Rather, the framework of the elementary form of hierarchy, individualism and so forth is adapted to empirical circumstance through ritual interaction, such as everyday gestures of greeting, or knowing where to sit or stand, in order to socialize those present to the thought styles appropriate to the prevailing institutions.

In her later writings, Douglas increasingly emphasized performative aspects of institutional life, often using the word 'institution' to describe shared commitment to practices sustained by ritual interaction. A simple example – as summarized in her book on her teacher's work – would be Evans-Pritchard's account of Nuer bridewealth transactions. The marriage institution among the Nuer is summed up and made apparent on the ground by the redistribution of cows among all entitled members of the bride-giving family. This is captured in the simple aphorism learned by generations of anthropology students – 'the women are where the cattle are not'. Nuer marriage is made manifest not by grand ceremony or a portentous set of symbols, but by meaningful movement on the ground – of the women to her husband's camp and the evident movement of cattle in the other direction. It is summed up in the steps taken by the woman and by the animals; indeed, it is a kind of dance.

Yet nowhere in *How Institutions Think* was there a sustained discussion of practices in their full, performative, choreographic sense. Perhaps Douglas was worried that any such discussion would be too reminiscent of Bourdieu's somewhat circular conception of a practice as *habitus*, by which Bourdieu meant internalized habits and dispositions. Yet, without a clear definition of an institution, it became impossible for Douglas' argument to do the work being asked of it. It was there, but only by implication. For her typological theory of social organization had been, since *Natural Symbols*, grounded in Durkheim and Mauss' (1963 [1902–3], 11) claim that the classifications of things replicated the classifications of people, where the classifications of people really consisted in the more or less established patterns of their relations, as described in the mix of the four elementary forms of those patterns. *How Institutions Think* itself was principally devoted to showing precisely *not* that Durkheim's and Mauss' slogan can be cashed out as people modelling one set of ideas about the world upon another set of ideas about themselves; rather, its aim was to demonstrate that basic of aspects of thought quite generally, whether about the world or about other people, are cultivated by something more basic and practical than ideas or justifications. Perhaps rather than 'accountability', she might have used 'countability', as in counting the steps of a dance to know where to come in, or counting the cattle to know that a Nuer marriage is complete. As we will go on to show, the notion of timing or 'clocking' social performance becomes increasingly important in understanding her later work. It is already apparent in *How Institutions Think* that only a performance-based definition of an institution, as a template for what Goffman (1967a) had called interaction ritual, will do the required job. Douglas' distinctive contribution in her typological work in 'Cultural Bias' was to show that we dance our interactions into institutionalized commitments in a very small number of basic ways – not in one way alone, but not in very many ways either. Underneath the blooming, buzzing variety of social life, there are just four basic types of ritual interaction order. It is here that Douglas' implicit definition of an institution lurks.

An established practice of conducting a pattern of social relations is certainly a collective activity, and in Douglas' Durkheimian account, institutions in this sense are produced and recast, not simply by individual adjustment, but institutionally. In other words, the development of institutions as practices arises by what she would later learn to call feedback dynamics of reinforcement and undermining, or at least checking. These dynamics guide the capabilities of individuals into particular paths, even when they resist particular institutions. For, as Douglas' typological theory argues, there is no way to resist one kind of institutional pattern and practice that does not involve reaching for and falling under the influence of one or the other elementary institutional forms. But such practices of patterned relations require no mystical communion to achieve or sustain. Indeed, patterns and practices of weak social integration such as substantively individualistic and isolate ordering, by definition, lack any hint of a group mind. Rather, these patterns develop through the performative reinforcement of practices and relations. People learn from the experience of their position and their relations to think in ways that reflect that situation, until its frustrations become so great that they begin to look for other kinds of relations, in which case they cannot avoid learning to think in styles appropriate to whatever fresh relations they can find. Cultivation of thought style is the work not just of constraint but also of imperative and experience. Even to maintain isolate ordering, people must work in some kind of coordinated way, implicitly even if not consciously. A solo dancer requires spaces to be cleared and distances to be maintained. This institutional work is driven by the 'countabilities' of spacing and timing arrangements characteristic of (i.e. specific to) the elementary form in question. For this purpose, therefore, it did not help Douglas' presentation of her argument that she used the term 'latent group' to describe embryonic performative social arrangements. Before the institution becomes articulated in a rule or an explicit statement and before it has been subject to any great self-reinforcing dynamic, it may well be described as 'latent'. Yet it certainly need not be – on Douglas' own theory – a group, which has to be a strongly integrated arrangement. The group is the product, as it were, of performing a particular kind of dance many times over. Behind it all lies a species-wide capacity for coordination of gesture.

Functional Explanations as Mechanisms by Which Organization Cultivates Cognition

A key microfoundational question, then, is just *how* – that is, by what causal mechanism – do institutions do their work of cultivating cognition? The full performative 'turn' in Douglas' work lay in the future and was to be approached through the somewhat esoteric route of a concern for poetic compositional strategy in the Hebrew Bible.

In *How Institutions Think*, Douglas was still working through the cybernetic insights of Michael Thompson and others in her group of close associates. Her strategy was to lay out the sequential structure of mechanisms that work by a functional process. Institutions, precisely because they may well be informal, tacit practices not (yet) formulated explicitly as rules may lead people to enact outcomes not consciously intended by the actors. In fact, Douglas' theoretical statement posited overtly that people operating under institutions will *not* intend the outcomes, though in fact this requirement is stronger than her argument strictly required. The causal mechanism can be specified and its logic can be sustained provided only that it is not necessary that the process be wholly palpable to all those affected (cf. Stinchcombe's (1986) argument that Elster's (1983) requirement that institutional effects be wholly *unintended* is too strong).

Douglas showed that institutional outcomes can be arrived at by more than one route. A frequently encountered pathway, generalizing the logic of Rayner's (1982) paper in *Essays in the Sociology of Perception* (Douglas, 1982b), is that institutions – for example, in enclaved settings – present people with problems of maintaining the prevailing form of organization against threats to its cohesion. Individual deal-making, incentives, reliance upon authority and mere coping under blunt imposition cannot be used to sustain the enclaved organizational form, for these are precisely the ways of organizing that enclaves either knowingly reject or are otherwise cultivated to avoid. Given the institutional character of that form of organization, the only practicable way to solve those problems is to develop other practices and, indeed, perhaps even become consciously and cognitively committed to these other practices, which serve to reinforce the content of the original enclaved institution. In enclaved settings, that cognitive commitment will take the form of defining a principle with which to justify the practices. When authority and incentive and deal-making fail, only a shared commitment to beliefs in principles can hold the enclave together. Douglas' example of this situation is the way in which many enclaves must try preserve a rule of equality among their members, but *only* among the members. In order to do so, people must strongly to mark and reinforce the external boundary between members and nonmembers. Another pathway into an institutional form works by way of motivation to defend existing institutional commitments. Again, using the example of enclaved organization, Douglas shows that people working under a particular institutional form will have reasons to defend each aspect of the arrangements it specifies. If, for example, boundary-maintenance is required, in order to rationalize effort, members will develop an account of the world in which the boundary appears under great threat.

Threat, perhaps even exaggerated danger, plays several roles in the theory. First, the form of cognition motivates agents by giving reasons for urgency of action that would, if the institution were an explicit one, be institutionally prescribed. Second, the cognition is a rationalization. Third, that rationalization proceeds by the generation of an anomaly – a perception of a threat, when people in other settings might recognize the conditions as representing a less severe or less probable threat. Anomaly is no longer just a methodological priority for diagnosis, as it was in *Purity and Danger* and in *Natural Symbols*. It has now become part of the causal mechanism underpinning the theory. Fourth, problem-setting and constrained solution-finding, extending motivations among aspects of organization and rationalizing existing commitments are all processes that avoid any suggestion of society having 'needs', in the manner that made functionalism so suspect. Fifth, because only one institutional form is at work in any given mechanism, there is no question of any concept as ill-bounded as 'society' being required to make the theory work. Certainly, now that no one would map nations or states or even nation-states on to societies, Durkheim's too-easy use of this macroscale notion can no longer be sustained. The formative trajectory envisioned by her theory, she argues in the second chapter, will be found to be true at any scale, from the smallest to the largest. There is no 'macro-micro problem', as some sociological theorists have suggested (Alexander et al., 1987). By concentrating on institutions, she showed the value of functional explanations running through feedback loops by which institutions reinforce styles of thought that lead people to act in ways that reinforce the institution (Douglas, 1986) even to the point of actually disorganizing it (Douglas, 1992a). But functional*ism*'s static consensual view of social organization is entirely avoided.

Douglas' final step in the argument is a critical one. She assembles her series of examples of functional causal mechanisms within enclaved ordering in a set running from the weakest to the strongest cases of enclaved organization and cognition. Each example, she suggests, is a 'cycle', though which a given ideal-typical case might pass. The sequence of mechanisms now constitutes a trajectory. That trajectory of self-generated deepening and exaggeration and reinforcement of organization and cognition by prior initial organization is equivalent to what is meant by positive feedback dynamics in cybernetic accounts. Taken together, then, the series of mechanisms forms a discrete dynamic by which a case moves from nearer the centre of her two-by-two typological matrix towards one or other of the outer corners. In this regard, Douglas had not only finally adopted Thompson's formulation of a dynamic theory for her originally static account of socially available variation in elementary forms. Now she had grounded that cybernetic dynamic by reducing it, in the strict analytical sense, to a sequence of mechanisms of the functional kind with which she had long worked. Moreover, in showing that the trajectory linked each organizational form to the outer corner solution, she was able to show precisely why, correctly understood, functional explanations undermine functionalism; they explain the tendency toward self-radicalization in thought and organization that sustains endemic conflict with rival organizations drawing upon other elementary forms.

The step *not* taken in *How Institutions Think*, but postponed for later work, was to show how Durkheim (1984 [1893]; 1951 [1897]) might have been right in his remarks on sacred contagion, namely that this positive feedback can explain *dis*organization, if taken far enough. Douglas deepened and extended her account, bringing out more explicitly the cybernetic character of the trajectory as one of positive feedback, in an important article on terrorism with Gerald Mars (Douglas and Mars, 2003). This used a degree of formalization to which she resorted only sparingly. Now flow diagrams carefully distinguished stages, 'forks' and alternate pathways. The diagrams enabled her and Mars to present the sequence of steps through which an enclaved political group might resort to increasingly extreme manifestations of its own cognitive style and engage in increasingly drastic action, including acts of terror, to solve its *own* organizational problems. The argument proceeded by showing that membership, information, material resources and opportunities are each successively controlled by rejection, in order to buttress social boundaries between the enclaved group and non-members. Pointedly avoiding the too obvious case of Islamist terrorism – the great preoccupation of the time after the attacks on New York and Washington DC, but that might have diverted attention from the generalizability of her argument – Douglas used examples from Northern Ireland, from ancient Israel, and from colonial and postcolonial Africa, thus emphasizing the continuity over human history of the same dynamics in the elementary forms, as well as allowing her to draw upon cases she understood empirically as an ethnographer. The dynamic was shown to explain not only conflict with other groups, whether enclaved or otherwise, but also the Durkheimian process by which schism could bring about its own disorganization. In effect, she had developed a theory covering the outpourings of the effervescent and otherwise incomprehensible violence often associated with the endings of civil wars and sectarian implosions (Richards, 1996, 1999, 2012).

What remained to be done, when she began her work on ancient Israel, was to develop a full understanding of the thought style of the disorganization that arises from this functional dynamic. That would indeed require returning to Durkheim's concept of sacred contagion, which captures the thought style in which accusations of similarity by outsiders and claims of similarity by insiders lose all anchoring in institutional controls (Douglas, 1996a). Accused of being similar to those whom the enclave mistrusts, outsiders may face the violence of revolt; increasingly suspicious insiders may insist on similarity being enforced by sanctioning the least divergence from the shared principle of identity (Rayner, 1982, 1988). As the self-reinforcement dynamic proceeds to radicalize, ever more similarity is demanded from members, until exhaustion or schism follow. Uncontrolled similarity in thought style mirrors the density and bounded of the social relations in the enclave. Social contagion is its thought style, collective effervescence is its style of feeling and disorganization is its eventual outcome.

Of course, in sacred contagion of this kind, words literally meaning 'similarity' may not be the ones used by the people being studied. The anthropologist must diagnose the dynamic from the institutional context and then identify the ways in which categories are used to do the job that 'similarity' does in the theory. For example, consider the ways in which, when people are subject to blame of a kind that is used to justify physical attacks, boycotts or intimidation, those who blame them will often accuse their victims of 'complicity' in some crime or imagined or supposed crime, which may have been committed even before their victims were born or thousands of miles away in another country. In using that literally far-fetched concept of complicity, the accuser claims to be able to diagnose some connection that would seem tenuous in the extreme to people who do not operate under the accusing enclave's institutions. It might consist in some claim that the accused have in some indirect way benefited from the supposed crime, even if the accused do not think of themselves as having done so. Connections of trade and economic development over history are of course so common that every individual is linked to every other by such transactions, which would, if simple logic were all that mattered, make everyone complicit in every crime or supposed crime in human history. Only under the institutions of the accusing enclave can the selection of some of these tenuous connections for blame seem intelligible. 'Complicity' in these cases does the work of selective making of similarity, for it makes tenuous classificatory connections between the accused seem as dense as the real and dense social ties among those within the accusing enclave: as with other elementary forms, people apply the assumptions of their own social organization to other groups with whom they interact and even to the world as a whole. Outsiders are represented as being similar to each other in relation to the symbols used in blame, in order that the similarity of the insiders to each other can seem as dissimilar from that of the outsiders as possible. Thus, accusatory emotion is stirred. The term 'contagion' is simply a metaphor for this reckless spreading of blame and accusatory excitement along connections that would seem tenuous to those outside the accusing enclave. This process of 'moral panic' (Cohen, 2002 [1972]) is exactly what Douglas means by the institutional cultivation of thought style. When the Lele were accused by others of being witches unknowingly, the institutional dynamic was not different from that shown in 1930s National Socialist Germany when justifying boycotts of Jewish businesses.

This reworking of Durkheim's concept of sacred contagion appeared only after Douglas had returned to the Congo and to the Hebrew Bible, but *How Institutions Think* provided the microfoundational theory for the trajectory of change. Moreover, that trajectory was one that showed de-institutionalization and disorganization to be the result of even further extending the positive feedback dynamic that produced institutionalization. Most theories of institutionalization simply treat it as some combination of the growing explicitness of rules and the increasing internalization of prescription (e.g. Levitsky, 1998). Douglas' microfoundations, by contrast, showed more clearly than most so-called 'new' institutionalist theories just what the causal relationship was between rules and prescription, and what provokes and sustains this relationship. Her argument described rigorously how Durkheim's insight might be developed about institutionalization and de-institutionalization, for she showed that the functional loop generates a cybernetic process that, when understood dynamically, reveals organization and disorganization as different phases of the same process rather than as the opposites they appear to be when static definitions of their states at any one point in time are adopted.

It is important to recognize here just how big a departure Douglas makes in this argument from the conception of institutions offered in the writings of the institutional economists to whose debates one part of her argument was offered as a contribution. We noted above that for Williamson, whose major statement (1985) was published just before Douglas' *How Institutions Think*, an institution is an equilibrium that is only self-reinforcing to the extent that incentives make it so. For Williamson, any account of those incentives must take full account of the costs of transacting, as well as the direct costs of goods and services. Dynamics, in Williamson's account, are simply driven by transaction costs that are more or less given for the type of transaction to be undertaken (or not to be). Douglas had already argued that people are sometimes willing, in some kinds of social organization, to bear very high transaction costs for some kinds of relationship or simply not to perceive them as salient, or are willing to accept deep sacrificial losses in transaction costs for relations they are institutionally cultivated to regard as vital. Moreover, the self-reinforcing dynamic that her functional account of causation affords undermines any attempt to confine dynamics to cases of equilibrium-seeking behaviour. On the contrary, institutions disequilibrate as much as they cultivate equilibria. Any institution is self-reinforcing, to the extent that it ever is, only by feedback dynamics of social organization. True, transaction costs are objective matters, but variation in the importance given to them cannot be explained by the objective scale of the costs themselves. Those who institutionalize their enclaved ordering in collective effervescence to the point of self-destruction do not do so because of the relative balance of transaction costs, but rather because of the way that their sectarian ordering shaped their tolerance for transaction costs. This affords a much deeper and more genuinely dynamic conception of institutions than the economic institutionalists developed.

The third chapter of *How Institutions Think*, in which this formulation is presented, is often remembered mainly for a negative strand of argument – namely, its reply to Jon Elster's then recent (1983) critique of functional explanations. Indeed, Douglas shows that the circularity of the loop is causally sequential, not logically vicious, that although functional explanations are demanding in regard to evidence, they are not inherently flawed, and that social science literature exhibits as many good examples as bad ones. Yet the really important contribution of the chapter is to the microfoundations for her larger theoretical project, not merely its technical answer to Elster. The student of Douglas' thought is counselled to reread what she wrote in this chapter, paying less attention to the foreground drama and more to the positive argument developed underneath.

What is it about Thought That Institutions Explain?

But what, precisely, is the dependent variable? The claim in *Risk and Culture* that institutions explain 'culture' understood as political ideology led to all sorts of problems. Douglas realized that it was a cul-de-sac. That step left it impossible to explain why people who agreed on ideology might agree much less about what, practically, to do. Conversely, it also made it impossible to explain why people might think in such similar ways, even in politics, when they could not disagree more in fundamental ways about ideology. Moreover, ideology is not a central factor in explaining the depth or shallowness of many conflicts. For example, even people who share an environmentalist ideology might worry about boundaries in different ways, exaggerate the severity or probability of risks differently, disagree about the importance of precedent or a very long planning horizons, use important categories rigidly or flexibly, or weigh justice and pragmatic considerations of prudence differently. Equally, libertarians might be as sectarian as their socialist opponents, or social democrats might be individualistically organized, leading them to be as pragmatic in thinking through their decisions as any market trader (6, 2016a). Even people who agree on what substantive risks to worry about can bring very different emotions, ways of classifying and senses of time both to fearing things and to justifying the decisions they make about those fears to their peers and to others.

Douglas therefore needed a measure of the ways in which people think that described just how worried they were about whatever topic concerned them, just how rigidly they handled their categories and just how gingerly they handled anomalies or – picking up on Rayner's (1982) development of her own argument – whether they looked at their problems with a long-term or a short-term collective memory or future planning horizon. Her own argument about the nature of the functional causal mechanisms required her to show that political ideology could be an ex post facto rationalization for commitments driven by social organization. In that role, it was unlikely also to be the primary dependent variable. Something else about cognition had to be more directly explained by the work of institutions.

Douglas found the concept to provide her dependent variable for the work of institutions in the work of the scientist, historian and philosopher of science Ludwik Fleck, whose best-known philosophical and historical writings on science were published in the 1930s (Fleck, 1979 [1935]), but were translated into English more recently. From him she borrowed the concept of a 'thought style'.

Unfortunately, nowhere in *How Institutions Think* did Douglas define a thought style (nor, frustratingly, did she do so in the 1996 collection entitled *Thought Styles*). It was variously characterized loosely as equivalent to Durkheim's 'collective representations' (Douglas, 1986, 12), a set of standards for what counts as a candidate for being an answer to a question (1986, 13), a style of reasoning (1986, 14), a thought world (1986, 16), a mode of thought (1986, 17) and a 'communicative genre for a community speaking to itself about itself' (Douglas, 1996b, xii), but she avoided precision. Nor did she cite any of the psychological literature on the concept of 'cognitive style' (although this cannot be mere disciplinary chauvinism, because her chapter on memory shows her interest in both classical and recent psychological work in that area). She may also have taken the notion partly from the social phenomenologist Alfred Schütz, whose writings on the 'cognitive style' she had anthologised thirteen years previously (Douglas, 1973a, 227–31). At any rate, it is clear from her examination of analogizing, classifying, and remembering and forgetting that she intended to capture a measure of the *manner* in which people cognize, as opposed to the *topics* they think about, or the substantive empirical or political *claims* they make.

This is a significant shift in Douglas' account of her own theory. *Purity and Danger* had rather vaguely indicated that social context, at that stage still lacking definition or typology, explained the recognition of anomalous things as being salient, troublesome and requiring treatment, ranging from suppression of the thought of the anomaly to prohibition of the anomalous thing itself. In *Natural Symbols*, it was the symbols that were explained by social organization. By 1982, *Risk and Culture* had offered to explain the 'perception', meaning heightened recognition and fear, of particular risks, leaving implicit for readers to work out for themselves the fact that risks were, for Douglas, anomalies in precisely the sense identified in *Purity and Danger*.

Recasting the theory as one of thought style makes two quite distinct and very important claims. The first is that what the elementary forms of social organization really explain is the *manner* in which people think, but without predicting the *topics* about which they think (these are explained by the empirical institutions that make up their livelihoods, family life and so forth) or even the substantive normative, ideological *beliefs* or claims they make about, for example, justice, liberty, property, equality, punishment, economic protection or the protection of the natural environment or ecology. A central plank of the programme of *Risk and Culture* therefore falls away. Now it becomes possible to understand how the theory can explain something centrally important about the thought of small enclaved groups of, for example, radical libertarians, monetarists or free marketeers in an exactly symmetrical fashion to the way in which it might explain the enclaved thought of religious sectarians or British Maoist diehards (cf. Rayner, 1982, 1988). Despite their opposed beliefs, these groups share a common style of thought. That common enclaved style can be seen in a number of manifestations, such as stances regarding anomalies, the long past and foreshortened future, disdain of fallback or second-best positions, the degree of emotional fervour applied to beliefs and the rigidity with which classifications are deployed. The same approach can be used to understand common thought styles despite contrasted substantive bodies of belief among hierarchically ordered functionaries in government or companies, in big international voluntary organizations and among individualistically ordered groups as apparently diverse as bonus-hunting Wall Street traders, ancient Roman patrons and 'big people' engaged in competitive feasting in highland New Guinea.

This recognition is missing in approaches such as that of Kahan (Kahan et al., 2011, discussed in Chapter 2) that measure assent to statements of belief, but do not follow practice to see how, if at all, people actually use their beliefs in conflict or mutual accommodation.

The second important claim made by the shift toward thought style is that the 'cultural' phenomenon explained by the theory is a systematic one. In other words, a single underlying stylistic syndrome underpins the ways in which people think, under the institutions of a particular elementary form, whether we are considering stance towards anomaly, toward time or space, toward fallback options or toward links made among concepts. Of course, in many empirical cases, people will exhibit stylistic inconsistency precisely because the prevailing institutions involve mixes, hybrids or conflicting formal structures. But that is a quite different level of analysis from the level within each elementary form at which Douglas can now identify the integrity of that form's style.

How Institutions Think did not put the point in this fashion, perhaps because, as we have seen, Douglas wanted to distance herself from Durkheim in order to appeal to the 'new' institutionalists of the 1980s. But this later shift to thought style actually brought her argument back to the deepest level of Durkheim's sociology of knowledge.

For now, with the concept of a thought style, her argument can be restated in direct relation to the two Durkheimian dimensions of social regulation and social integration underpinning her typology of forms, but that *How Institutions Think* carefully avoided mentioning. The core of her theory, as restated, is now that people's style of thought is regulated and integrated *cognitively* as people's organization is regulated and integrated *socially*. This relationship between social organization and thought style is one of ritual cultivation in everyday secular interaction. The ritual interaction order sustains a feedback loop. Institutions of a given form lead people to enact the form of that organization in ritual microcosm in their dealings with each other, and this in turn cultivates a style of thinking, which then leads them to act in ways that reinforce those institutions (positive feedback) and that thereby come into conflict with other institutions formed differently (negative feedback). The interaction of these two institutional dynamics – of positive feedback within each elementary form and negative feedback among the distinct elementary forms – provides the forces for Douglas' theory of change. She now understood (borrowing from Thompson, 1982a) the dynamics of feedback in cybernetic terms. But whereas cybernetic social theorists conceived of feedback as moving information, her theory focused on feedback as applying institutional pressure. Forms of thought style and practices of classification were what the theory explained, not its driving force. The trajectories of feedback are derived directly from her functional explanation of how latent groups reinforce their social organization.

The core of Douglas' causal theory can therefore be presented as a two-phase feedback loop consisting of a primary relation in which institutions ritually cultivate thought style and a secondary impact by which people's thought style leads them to reinforce institutions of the prevailing elementary form and, correlatively, react against and undermine institutions of other forms (Figure 3.1).

Now it should be clear why Douglas wished she had written *How Institutions Think* before her other books. Had this machinery been in place in the 1960s and 1970s, the role that fears about nuclear power or celebration of pangolins play in building the theory would have been stated much more precisely. Without this machinery, the choice of topics appeared at best opportunistic and at worst whimsical and capricious, as if the anthropologist was ever the trickster, trying to disrupt serious, sustained analytical thought with ethnological curiosities or attention-grabbing issues of the day.

Moreover, set out in this fashion, the subordinate place of the typology in her theory also becomes clear. Figure 3.2 (cf. 6, 2003, 401; 6

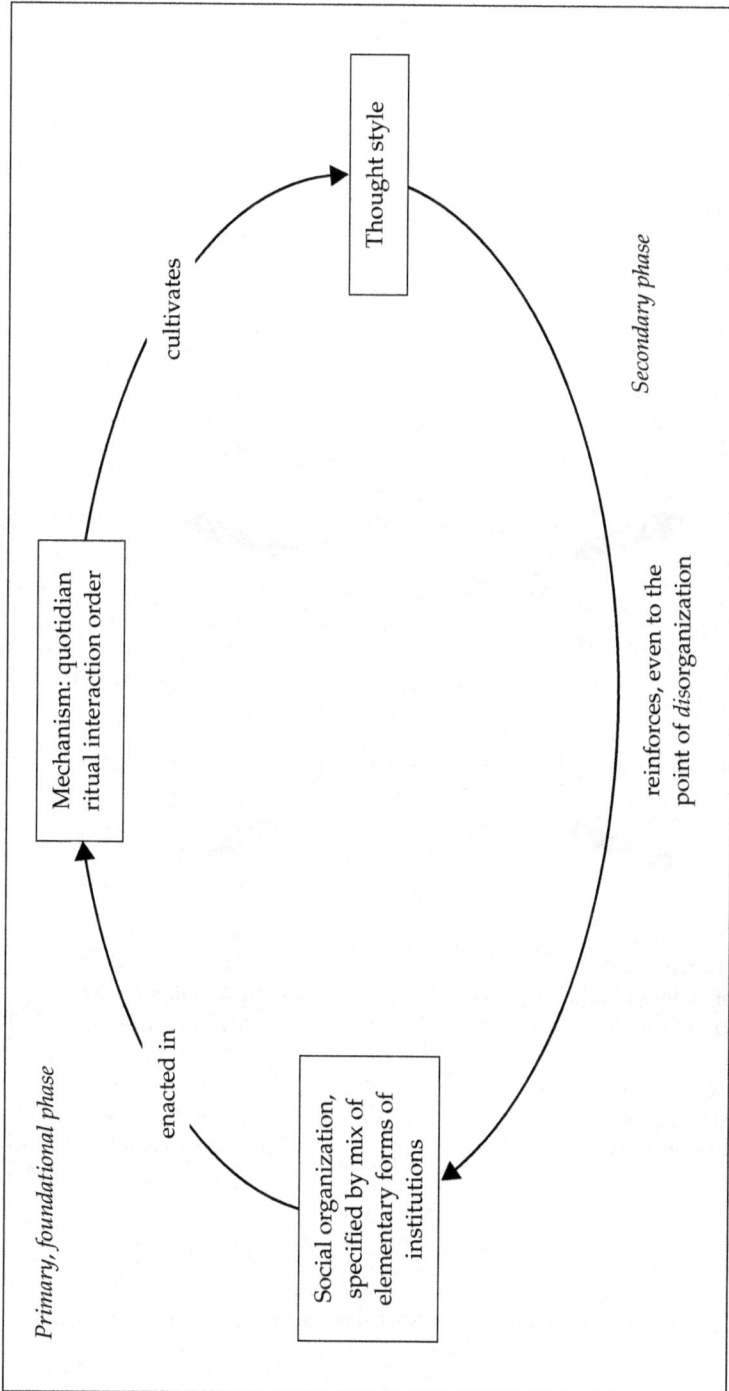

Figure 3.1 The causal mechanism in Douglas' theory: a two-phase feedback loop. Source: 6, 2014, 'Explaining Decision-making in Government: The Neo-Durkheimian Institutional Framework', *Public Administration* 92(1), 87–103, at p. 93, reprinted by kind permission of John Wiley & Sons.

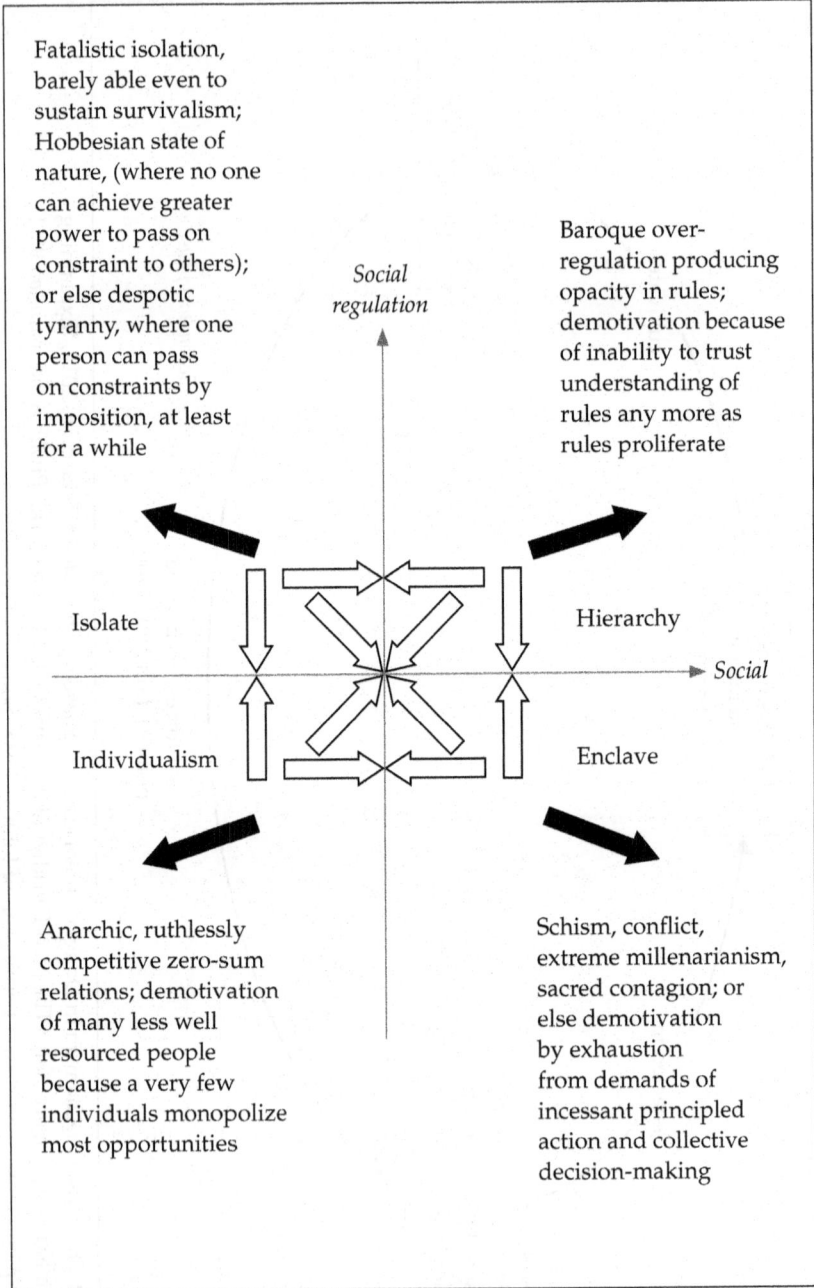

Fatalistic isolation, barely able even to sustain survivalism; Hobbesian state of nature, (where no one can achieve greater power to pass on constraint to others); or else despotic tyranny, where one person can pass on constraints by imposition, at least for a while

Social regulation

Baroque over-regulation producing opacity in rules; demotivation because of inability to trust understanding of rules any more as rules proliferate

Isolate

Hierarchy

Social

Individualism

Enclave

Anarchic, ruthlessly competitive zero-sum relations; demotivation of many less well resourced people because a very few individuals monopolize most opportunities

Schism, conflict, extreme millenarianism, sacred contagion; or else demotivation by exhaustion from demands of incessant principled action and collective decision-making

Figure 3.2 Positive and negative feedback dynamics of the four elementary forms

et al., 2006, 70; Hendriks, 2010, 139) presents the structure of Douglas' dynamic theory, using the typology that was discussed in Chapter 2. First, the four elementary forms are deduced from the coincidence of strong and weak forms of the two basic dimensions of institutional ordering – namely, Durkheim's (1951 [1897]) concepts of 'social regulation' (shown as the vertical dimension) and 'social integration' (shown as the horizontal dimension). Self-reinforcing dynamics of positive feedback are represented with the filled arrows moving social organization to the corners of the chart, which represent its extremes. At those extremes, we find distinct kinds of disorganization. By contrast, as people react against any form of ordering (for example, precisely because it is already tending toward disorganization) and must therefore reach for another form or indeed for a hybrid of two or even three other forms, the result will be conflict among elementary forms. The institutional reaction of each against its neighbour is represented in the figure by the outlined arrows pressing inward within the chart.

From a careful reading of *How Institutions Think*, it becomes clear that far from being merely a typologist, Douglas was a causal theorist who found that her mechanism needed a typology. Her general claim that social organization influences the way in which people think is widely accepted today. Perhaps only the most dedicated of genetic determinists would deny it outright. Some other traditions neither affirm nor deny that social context shapes thought, but simply argue that we can explain all the really important behavioural outcomes without needing to refer to the way in which people think at all. For example, that remains the position of many rational choice theorists working in political science and international relations. If, however, we accept that institutions of social organization, including informal ones, shape the manner in which people think, then it follows from the variety of those institutions across history and geography that there is a plurality of ways for people to think and still to be counted as sane, competent, intelligent and rational within the particular contexts in which they operate. Thus, against both postmodernism and the methodological timidity of merely piling up local descriptions, Douglas could now use institutional arguments to show – as she had only asserted in *Purity and Danger* – that humanity is one species subject to many of the same basic constraints. Therefore, she concluded, variation in thought styles must be limited. And if that variation can be captured on a small number of dimensions, then an exhaustive typology is not only necessary for the theory to provide explanations, but also achievable.

With these functional explanatory foundations in place, *How Institutions Think* can now proceed to present its series of illustrative instances of the ways in which institutions specify the manner in which classification and categories are treated, confer identities, and cultivate remembering and forgetting. No grand conclusion is needed because the argument is fully presented at the beginning and then illustrated through comparative case analysis.

For example, classification – quite straightforwardly understood as the business of determining that distinct things fall under the same category on the basis of their recognized similarity in some respect – is explained as itself being a creature of institutions, not something given. Similarity and identity, Douglas argues, structure human thought only under particular institutions that require people to treat some things as relevantly similar to, or dissimilar from, or identical or nonidentical with, each other for the purposes pursued by those institutions. Replication is shown to be institutional similarity in formal, structural features of thought rather than a feature with overt propositional content.

How Institutions Think requires its readers to do a lot of work for themselves. They are left to work out how Douglas uses institutionalist ideas while subverting their conventional applications. Few readers familiar with institutionalism in economics or organizational theory would have expected to find the institutional engine coupled to a transformative gearbox of thought styles. Readers must also work out for themselves that the causal engine is one that works in structurally identical ways in each of her four elementary forms. This is something she perhaps over-optimistically expects the reader to supply from a detailed knowledge of her other writings. It is not that the diligent student has not read these items, but that the lessons are at times hard to retain in sufficient detail for those who do not have the grand vision at their fingertips. Alas, she does not even deign to help them work out the central place of ritual in the causal mechanism driving classification and selective attention to ideas, although an account is there for those who read sufficiently closely. It is her most profound book, and one that anyone interested in her work should tackle. But just as it was not in fact written first, it probably should not be read in isolation from her other writings either.

Thought Styles Provide Styles of Agency

How Institutions Think showed how a refurbished Durkheimian project could avoid 'group minds', 'society' or 'society's needs', and also how a set of causal mechanisms and trajectories driving interactions among elementary forms could be specified with clarity and rigour. However, there remained some old charges for which the new work had not presented exonerating argument. One of those charges in particular had long preoccupied Douglas. Many institutionalist theories have faced a charge levelled at Durkheim and the structural-functionalists – namely, in Garfinkel's (1967, 68) much-cited phrase, that such approaches turn people into 'cultural dopes'. By this he meant that they become passive creatures, lacking 'agency'. The same debate about institutions and the 'institutionalized' in which Durkheim himself engaged continues today in organization studies (Lawrence et al., 2009), in general sociology (Archer, 2000; Martin and Dennis, 2010) and in political science (Hay, 2002, 2009; Béland and Cox, 2011). In 1979, Douglas had argued strongly against what she had called 'passive voice theories' in the sociology of religion (Douglas, 1982d). But what was the 'active voice'? Only toward the end of the 1990s did she publish a major statement concerning her conception of the microfoundations of agency linked to her theory of styles of ritual performance cultivated by institutional structure.

The statement in question is *Missing Persons*, a book written with Steven Ney (Douglas and Ney, 1998). It compresses a series of closely interlocking arguments into a small space. First, Douglas argued against neoclassical economic assumptions that institutions could be understood simply as equilibria, with preferences understood to be primarily utilitarian in content. For anthropologists, sociologists and even many political scientists, this was not news. Once again, the book targets economists and lays out a critique of economic models of rationality and of methodological individualism. Impact on the field was negligible, when set alongside not-dissimilar critiques, such as Daniel Kahneman's experimental demonstrations of the gap between economic rationality and everyday thinking, for which the psychologist eventually won a Nobel Prize in economics (Kahneman, 2011).

Douglas' argument about agency in *Missing Persons* was that it is only by recognizing the differences that institutions make that we can we give content to agency. The problem with agency from a perspective of methodological individualism is that it is left as an unexplained residual after constraints have been accounted for. 'Bringing agency back in' to institutional theory by simply relaxing constraints to allow people to become 'institutional entrepreneurs' – a fashionable fudge (see e.g. Lawrence et al., 2009) – does little or nothing to explain who might exhibit entrepreneurial agency and who might not, or to predict in just which kinds of institutional setting relaxation of control and extension of discretion will be exhibited, and where it will not.

Instead of the conventional accounts of agency as some entirely general space for choice, Douglas offers a substantive theory of the available variation in the styles available for agency. Agency, for her, cannot simply be the discretionary space marked out by constraints. This is because that would mean, within her theory, that only in the weakly socially regulated contexts of individualistic and enclaved ordering would people exhibit agency, while people in hierarchical and isolate settings would become the 'institutional dopes'. This was contradicted empirically, because her early work on hierarchical strands in Lele life had shown, and her later studies on hierarchy in the priestly order in ancient Israel would further document, individuals operating within hierarchical institutions exhibit all the key indicators of agency. Likewise, a classic anthropological study by Banfield and Banfield (1958) on Calabria had shown that people in isolate ordering actively make decisions and pursue goals, but in ways that are stylized by their isolate institutions. The voice of agency stylised by isolate institutions is still distinct in the musicological record of chattel slavery, as documented by Radano (2003).

By agency, we generally understand the exercise of choices and individual decision-making, the exhibiting of creativity within the guidance of the peculiar local constraints, and the capacity for people's choices to form a pattern that is coherent when analysed by an anthropologist or, in Radano's case, the musicologist.

In the special case of isolate life, that pattern may not be clear to the people being studied, in part because the strong social regulation and weak social integration leave them experiencing their coping as a response to events that may seem to them to be random, even if an analyst can discern patterns predicted by the theory of their institutions. In the other forms, people themselves are expected to exhibit some recognition of the pattern of their choices, either as an individual project or as a group or community commitment.

Douglas argued that each of the four elementary forms cultivates distinct forms of agency in just this sense. A thought style, for Douglas, is already a style of agency, without any further cycles of causation being required. Aspects of thought style, such as time horizons referenced to a long or a short past as the reference point, or the degree to which action is rule-based or discretionary, or the way in which anomalies are recognized and responded to, specify quite distinct styles of decision-making, choosing and acting. In a hierarchical setting, agency will be rule-based and authorized, or else grounded in authorized sanction for others taking unauthorized action. In isolate ordering, agency will be coping and short term in orientation, and will also exhibit guile (see Radano (2003), who even entitled his first chapter on this subject 'Telling Stories, Telling Lies'). In enclaved settings, agency will be principled, urgent and require extensive moral justification. In individualistic contexts, it will be oriented toward the medium-term future against a foreshortened past and toward the control of resources.

With this argument, a key defensive bulwark against an old enemy had been extended into a part of the microfoundations of the theory. Moreover, Douglas had now offered a much richer and more substantive answer than any other institutional theorist to the ancient question about just how the concept of agency can play a full and central role in a theory that emphasizes institutional cultivation of preferences.

Next, Douglas turned to attack the ruse for which fashionable social theory was beginning once again to reach at the end of the twentieth century – of appealing to emotions (cf. Douglas, 1993b), or ideas, or indeed culture in an ad hoc fashion, to explain deviations from rationality, while leaving the supposed core of rationality itself unexplained. Emotion, as Herbert Simon (e.g. 1983, 29–30) had argued, entrains attention and sustained rational reflection. Treating feelings simply as ad hoc explanations for particular supposed deviations from too narrow a conception of rationality makes no sense. For rational people, as Hume (1969 [1739–40, 462]) argued, can only exercise their rationality in pursuit of goals that sustain their emotional commitments; 'reason is and ought only to be the slave of the passions', and reasons for action must motivate. The idea that emotion is merely irrational, Douglas argued, risked dragging social theory back in time to the elitist frameworks of such thinkers as Lévy-Bruhl or Le Bon, in which the underclasses (whether colonized peoples or riotous urban masses) were regarded as deficient because they were possessed of emotions, ideologies or culture, unlike the superior and rational agents of a ruling imperial or bourgeois elite. Instead, she argued, we should focus less on how emotions are felt and more on how they are deployed, either forensically when people accuse others of feeling some objectionable emotion, or else in exculpation when they insist on claiming for themselves some more admirable feeling as their motivation.

Nevertheless, there are very strong reasons to doubt whether this apparently reductionist view of emotions was Douglas' final word on the subject. Indeed, her late works on ancient Israel show that she regarded both the fears, jealousies and millenarian aspirations cultivated in enclaved settings, and the calmer solidarities of forgiveness

and reconciliation that she thought the priestly hierarchy of post-exilic times sustained, as being genuinely felt, for all that they were the
work of institutions and for all that they might sometimes be feigned,
or that some emotions such as malevolence or jealously might be used
strategically in blame and accusation. Even in *Risk and Culture*, for
all its weaknesses, there is a clear recognition that the fears being explained are sincerely felt. The late writings show even more clearly
that she took emotion seriously, as important stylized products of
institutionalization, although she remained consistent in refusing to
treat feelings as fundamental and independent causes. Even when we
claim to feel an emotion or accuse someone else of being driven by a
supposedly less creditable emotion, we are engaging in practices that
rest in part on *another* emotion of our own – usually, one to which we
do not admit, but that is involved in our desire to exculpate ourselves
or blame someone else. In 'Terrorism: A Positive Feedback Game', for
example, Douglas and Mars (2003) clearly recognize that the self-radicalization process in enclaving does not only sustain self-attribu-
tions and accusations; rather, it also cultivates actually felt emotions,
including those aroused in collective effervescence. In the chapter
'Traditional Culture: Let's Hear No More about it', Douglas (2004a)
devotes a section to discussing the emotions *other than* apathy that
are cultivated in isolate ordering, precisely to emphasize the alternate
pathways possible, contingent on particular conditions, in the generation of genuinely felt emotion. Her piece with Michel Lianos entitled
'Dangerization' is likewise concerned with fears sincerely experienced
and their explanation. Presumably, she intended both attribution and
cultivation to be understood as outcomes of the same quotidian ritual
interaction processes of cultivation. In the event, however, her mature
view of the emotions was subtler. In *How Institutions Think*, she had
shown that our feelings associated with our beliefs are part of our
thought style. For example, if we feel fury and resentment at the least
suggestion that our ideology – whatever that ideology is – might not
provide the most perfect solution to our immediate practical problems, then our emotions are an index of our style of thought and show
it to be very different from a style of thought in which challenges to
our views provoke our curiosity that someone wishes to debate with
us and so might be open to persuasion. Here presumably is an important difference between some 'jihadists' and the patient style of
doorstep persuasion adopted by other conversion-minded sectarians.
Douglas' argument is not that emotion is insignificant; nor is it that
the whole vocabulary of emotions is a kind of sham, or that emotions are not really felt but are only the subject of accusations against

others and of our own excuses. Rather, emotions and the manner in which they are felt and their contribution to commitment to decisions are important enough to require explanation. That explanation has to based, she argues, in the ritual cultivation of feeling in institutionalised styles.

In the 1990s, Douglas took this argument about emotions further to show that each thought style cultivated by its elementary form also cultivates a particular style of agency which in turn requires a style of feeling (6, 2002b). A style of agency must include a style of will or desire to perform an action, but also distinct ways of feeling the motivating emotions for agency of (for example) stoicism in a hand-to-mouth coping style of agency in isolate ordering, or emotions of resentment against external social regulation and passion in commitment to shared principle, in the style of agency cultivated in enclaved settings. True, in such styles of agency, we often do use feelings as weapons. More precisely, we may claim to feel certain things (altruistic, philanthropic feelings, perhaps, or admirable determination), and accuse other people of being motivated by particular emotions that are disreputable in our own elementary form of organization ('the politics of envy' or 'the politics of greed', perhaps). But when considered as a whole, Douglas' later writings show that she appreciated just how sincerely emotions are felt and that she could use her theory to explain how that sincerity of feeling is cultivated, just as she could, symmetrically, explain insincerity in emotional claims and blame.

Douglas' presentation of the concept of culture now focused on showing that there is no default position, no single reference point from which deviations are to be plotted and no explanatory content that such deviation-plotting can capture. Thus, she was able to cut the ground from under the feet of those who shared Leach's suspicion of her 1970 work *Natural Symbols* that her work was an extended apologia for Catholic ritualism (see Lemos, 2009; Schmitt, 2008). None of the four elementary forms is unambiguously rational or irrational. Each channels and rejects information to provide enlightenment and cultivate ignorance in commensurable, causally explicable ways (Thompson and Wildavsky, 1986). Douglas argues that the institutions that serve to define the elementary forms each specify what she calls moral purposes, thus reconnecting her argument with Durkheim's uncompleted project for a science of social morality. Moralities necessarily conflict, and come to temporary accommodations, in what she now called 'the adversarial mode'. This was an altogether more robust conception than the 'forensic' usage of danger and blame, which had been the tone of her argument only a few years before. By implication, the 'global absolutism' inherent in modern definitions of universal human rights was under challenge. Those anthropologists who had worried about the hegemonic character of the UN Declaration of Human Rights in 1948 had perhaps found in Douglas a fierce advocate.

In *Missing Persons*, moral conflict was illustrated most powerfully in rival claims on poverty and justice. Although poverty was an important concern in *The World of Goods*, the issue of poverty, understood as a question of injustice, had not been central to Douglas' theoretical interests in the 1960s or 1980s, save perhaps for those sections of *The World of Goods* that examined inequality and social exclusion from access to those goods that furnish dignity. Yet by the mid 1990s, these issues returned to the fore. Her final intervention in the debate about what culture does, causally speaking, was both centrally about poverty and itself highly adversarial in style. The book chapter 'Traditional Culture: Let's Hear No More about it' (Douglas, 2004a) presents several of the arguments in *Missing Persons*, but with a controlled vitriol that she showed only rarely.

The chapter begins with a blunt moral condemnation of the long-standing idea that the poor remain in poverty because of their culture, an idea implicitly suggesting that the better off do not suffer from such self-inflicted afflictions as tradition. Then Douglas moved on to undermine the claim both theoretically and empirically. Her argument was pitched firmly against those development experts in the World Bank and elsewhere who held the view that culture was an obstacle to development. She attacked the 'subcultures of poverty' argument sometimes used in international social policy debates. Not only was this patronizing and offensive, it was also a misunderstanding of the causal status of culture. Culture, she had argued in *How Institutions Think*, is not a fundamental driver in its own right; it has to be explained by basic forms of social organization. Nor would she allow that her own theory could be used to smuggle the objectionable idea back in. Again, the issue comes down to a correct understanding of the substantive character of styles of agency. Not even isolates, she insisted, are necessarily apathetic. On the contrary, isolate life is an ordering sometimes requiring the hardest and most determined work to ensure its survival; it is despite coping, not because of it, that institutions perpetuate poverty.

Equally, though, Douglas insisted that poverty itself must be understood and measured by institutions, not by universally applicable standards of living. Extending her argument from *The World of Goods* (1979), she insisted that the precise meaning of poverty differs, but commensurably so, under different institutions, even if the core concept of poverty remains constant as exclusion from the main systems of exchange. In the late 1970s, British politicians such as Keith (later Lord) Joseph, a leading ideologue of the Thatcher era, had sought to explain poverty in terms of a culture of fecklessness. Douglas had only given an oblique answer to Joseph in *The World of Goods* by emphasizing the ritual periodicity of poor people's consumption and the ways in which positional goods (Hirsch, 1976) meant that the services they consumed continued to mark them as excluded. In the 1990s and early 2000s, a structurally analogous argument was still being offered in some areas of development assistance, according to which the poor in developing countries were held back by their 'traditional' culture. In this confrontational piece, Douglas argued not only that the claim is empirically false, but that it is based on the theoretical misunderstanding that culture is a cause (see also Douglas, 1999d). However, the way forward is not to evict the concept of culture altogether from the argument about poverty; rather, researchers should show that culture is part of what has to be explained. What they should not do is to allow it to be used as if it were an explanation, for that only turned the concept back into another instrument for blaming the poor for their poverty (Richards, 2009).

There is one work by Douglas cited neither in *Missing Persons* nor in 'Traditional Culture'. Ironically (given that *Missing Persons* was published in a series of lectures given in honour of Aaron Wildavsky), this is the 1982 book she had written with Wildavsky, *Risk and Culture*. The silence is telling, for if any book of Douglas' had left some readers with the impression that poverty was the voluntary choice of an ascetic enclaved 'culture' or that a particular form of culture was in some cases a blameworthy thing, then that surely was *Risk and Culture*. What 'Traditional Culture' added to the series of corrections Douglas quietly made to restore her theory was its demonstration that her account of institutions and culture was also morally decent.

Criticisms of Douglas' Theory and Douglasian Answers

It is striking that most of Douglas' critics who addressed her microfoundational arguments did so by writing in response to her work on risk or else her arguments in 'Cultural Bias' rather than directly about *How Institutions Think* or about the microfoundational part of her argument in *The World of Goods*.

It is worth noting, with some surprise, how little attention is paid to Douglas' microfoundational work in other traditions stemming from

Durkheim, such as that running from Goffman to Randall Collins (2004) and his students, or ethnomethodology following on from Garfinkel, or indeed mainstream Durkheim scholarship as a whole. Perhaps this is because of one rather prominent, early expression of disagreement with Durkheim (Douglas, 1970a). Douglas later came back to the notion of sacred contagion, but, as we have already made clear, her later work on the Bible, in which this recantation occurs (see in particular Douglas, 1996a), is insufficiently well known among social scientists. Thus, for the most part, Durkheim scholars continue to make polite reference to her arguments without really engaging in debate or critique or development with them. One notable exception, however, was Robert Bellah, who described Douglas in his important essay on 'Durkheim and Ritual' (Bellah, 2005) as 'the most interesting living Durkheimian'. This was generous, since for many, Bellah might at the time have qualified for exactly that kind of endorsement himself. Regrettably, Bellah did not engage with Douglas' late work where ritual dynamics are of key significance to the development of her theory, but his essay nevertheless devotes a substantial section to 'Ritual in the work of Mary Douglas'. It was based on assessing *Natural Symbols*. Bellah was one of the few commentators to have truly grasped the significance of the research agenda she announced in that complicated and much-criticized work. So clearly did Bellah understand where she was headed that he hardly needed to reference the later work where she finally felt she had accomplished what she had set out to do.

Others, though, were less generous, especially those with few Durkheimian sympathies. Mainly with 'Cultural Bias' in mind, but also responding to a specially commissioned paper by Douglas, the philosopher John Skorupski (1979a, 1979b) charged her with cultural relativism, meaning the thesis in philosophical epistemology that there are no determinate facts and that statements can only be 'true' or 'false' within the frameworks of particular ways of thinking, such as those cultivated – on Douglas' account – within particular forms of social organization.

Douglas' own (1979) reply to Skorupski is discussed in Fardon (1999, 252–61) and develops the following answer. The theory does not in fact imply relativism; indeed, it no more entails any particular philosophical position than does any other scientific theory. Douglas offers a causal theory of bias and expects her own theory to be true or false depending on whether it conforms to determinate facts of the matter about causation, cognition and organization. People's beliefs, classifications and thought styles may well be right or wrong, but the theory is designed to explain why they come to use sound or unsound classifications, beliefs, etc., not to identify particular errors. Moreover, her theory of variation in elementary forms is designed precisely to provide comparability among thought styles, whereas many forms of relativism claim that stylistic features are strictly incommensurable.

Some of Douglas' allies, such as David Bloor (1991 [1976]), were actually content with the conclusion that her account led to relativism, but Douglas herself was not. Nor did her thesis that institutions explain thought style require her, in logic, to accept Bloor's conclusion. First, the theory of dynamics and surprises developed by Thompson showed that it is false to claim that any given form of social organization is a 'prison'. The fact that people make shifts in their organization in response to disorganization, itself a response to anomaly and adversity, does not make the process unreasoned, 'decisionistic' or arbitrary. Second, there is a deeper reply to Skorupski's charge. The work of institutions does not just explain human error. If that were the case, then an institution-free world would free its inhabitants from error, an experiment few seem willing to try. Rather, the capacity for reaching objective truths rests on thought styles too. The dwellers in the institution-free world would be unable to direct their attention and unable to cultivate relations through which to learn valid procedures of inference. For the explanation is symmetrical between error and accuracy. Not least, this is because each elementary thought style cultivates capacities for noticing different things, for undertaking inquiries in particular ways and for making valid inferences, just as much as they enable the making of mistakes. The third reply to Skorupski derives from Verweij and Thompson (2006) rather than Douglas – namely, that people reduce their chances of error, *overall*, and increase their prospects of intelligent noticing and valid inference by developing institutions exhibiting requisite variety, and thus some degree of balance and creative interrelations among the forms. More work is needed to ascertain whether this third answer will be borne out. But at least it has the merit of making the philosophical debate about relativism into something amenable to enlightenment from the results of empirical inquiry – a hope of great importance to Douglas and something that should motivate any of those who aspire to be social scientists.

A related charge, made by Renn (1992) and Nelkin (1982), is that the theory is deterministic, meaning that it must entail the proposition that once organized under a particular institution, people *cannot but* think in the ways cultivated under that institution; in other words, given the organizational conditions, the cognitive formation emerges with a probability of one. This is a variant of the 'cultural dopes' critique of Durkheim. Douglas' treatment of the concept of agency in *Missing Persons* is perhaps her most developed answer to this charge.

In any case, Douglas' general framework makes no more claims about conditional probabilities in particular cases than do other general frameworks of explanation, such as rational choice theory, the Weberian tradition or historical institutionalism. Moreover, the theory of dynamics developed by Thompson (Thompson et al., 1990; and Thompson, 2008 discussed above; see also 6, 2003) shows why conditional probabilities of one in particular cases are highly unlikely on the theory's own assumptions. For example, institutions will disorganize themselves when they go into positive feedback (as Durkheim himself argued about forms of division of labour and pathways into suicide) and they will generate surprises. This is because the biases cultivated in each thought style will sooner or later find it increasingly costly and cumbersome to explain away anomalies, and people will begin to look for other ways of organizing and therefore other mixes of biases. Thus, organizational and cognitive change will follow changes in experience. Because the combinations and velocities of positive and negative feedback cannot be specified in advance, conditional probabilities approaching certainty are highly unlikely in all but the very shortest run.

A widely cited critic is Åsa Boholm, whose 1996 article is a compendium of many of the arguments above, including those by Nelkin and Renn, with two additions. First, she claims that Douglas' account is not an institutionalist theory, but one that seems to suggest that people can choose what to fear. This is simply a misreading. Selective attention to anomalies is not predicted to be a free or still less an arbitrary choice, but explicably patterned.

Second, Boholm suggests that this is not a fully institutional theory, because it smuggles into its characterization of individuals a theory of personality types. This is simply untrue; Douglas offers no theory of personality at all. Third, Boholm claims that Douglas' theory is really circular because it explains ideas by reference to other ideas – the elementary forms of institutions are really just worldviews. Again, this is a misreading, apparently made without taking account of the argument of Douglas (1986) at all.

There remain differences, though, among those who draw upon Douglas' legacy about how far to follow her microfoundational theory. Some, such as 6 (2011), remain committed to Douglas' strategy in 'Cultural Bias' and in *How Institutions Think*, of seeking to measure social organization and thought style independently, so that the former can explain the latter. 6 (e.g., 2011; Peck et al., 2004) and Richards (1996) cleave to Douglas' own Durkheimian view about the centrality of ritual, not just to the 'dependent variable' of what the theory explains, but also to its causal mechanism. For example, 6's (2011) argument is that political judgement, understood as the mix of thought styles, is cultivated ritually. However, this strategy is perhaps a minority view even among those who draw upon Douglas' work.

By contrast, Thompson (2008) and Verweij (2011) doubt that this separation can be sustained. Thompson and Verweij therefore work with 'cultures' as manifolds of relations and ideas, and treat the evidence of consistent systematic correlations among them as evidence for the explanations offered that general cultures explain particular cultural strands.

Although 6 (2011, 2014a, 2014b) places great emphasis on the distinction between ideology and thought style, others using the theory reject the distinction, arguing instead that the concept of discourse, covering both substantive and stylistic aspects of political cognition, provides a workable 'dependent variable' (e.g. Thompson and Rayner, 1998; Thompson et al., 1998).

More detailed consideration and rebuttals of criticisms are given by Fardon (1999), and in the editorial introduction to 6 and Mars (2008 – see above) and 6 (2011, 2014a).

Conclusion

This chapter has sought to demonstrate that Douglas' microfoundational work is of considerable importance for the social sciences as a whole. At least implicitly, Douglas argued that social science is essentially one enterprise. The basic forms of organization, of styles of thought, of causal relation and dynamics are common, not just to the well-established pairing of anthropology and sociology or to their fragile and desultory partnerships with political science, but even – as she argued in *The World of Goods* – to the largest field in social science, economics itself.

Douglas' microfoundational argument should be considered to be one of the major approaches to explanation in social science alongside rational choice, historical institutionalism, social interactionism, ethnomethodology, theories of ritual action, and the frameworks supplied by Bourdieu and Foucault. Its replies to the criticisms made of it are at least as powerful as the answers that any of those traditions can offer to their critics. Like them, it has developed both a body of empirical studies offering supporting evidence for the theory and a set of theoretical arguments that continue to prove fertile, as well as a cluster – but never quite a group in Douglas' own sense of the word – of scholars and researchers seeking to take aspects of her agenda forward.

Douglas' great contribution to the microfoundations of explanation in the social sciences consists in her very particular view of the virtue of causality. The elementary forms are distal forces in explanation, not proximate ones. Douglas argued throughout her life that distal explanations are both more accurate than those that use proximate factors, because they avoid banality, and that they are more powerful, because they also best support the virtue of generality, over the course of a research programme. The four elementary forms are all present in any context, albeit in differing degrees and with different relations among them. Therefore, they are constants. Explanation by reference to constants is something about which many social scientists have reservations, but Douglas showed that the fear that it misses critically different contingencies with significant explanatory force is quite misplaced and that methods can be found for achieving the required capture of critical contingency on variations in constants.

Pursuing distal explanations, such as invoking elementary forms of social organization, makes it especially likely, although not logically necessary, that the researcher will have to look for and try to test functional explanations. For if our aim is, as it should be in all science, to capture the most fundamental causal processes, and if the hypothesis is that the most fundamental causal processes are not well explained by taking preferences, particular constraints and payoffs as given, but rather by trying to explain those things too, then it is very likely that we shall need to show how preferences, constraints and payoffs emerge, and are then either sustained or undermined in the course of processes structured as causal feedback loops. Douglas' strategy was to defend functional explanations as valid, holding them to be not guilty of the charge of vicious circularity and capable of being evidenced. Moreover, her aim was to use methodologically good functional explanations to show why functionalism, as a substantive theory, was false. Encouragingly, for the hope of convergence, some methodological individualists in the rational choice tradition now recognize that functional explanations can be specified in valid ways (Pettit, 2000), and leading philosophers of social science methodology have also followed Douglas' strategy of argument (Kincaid, 1990, 1996, 101–42). The growth of interest in the application to social science of complexity theories taken from biology, meteorology and oceanography has reinforced the argument for devoting attention to functional explanations of the kind that Douglas proposed – namely, those that provide the basis for self-reinforcing and self-undermining feedback loops, as well as those that specify conflict and checking among different looping structures (see Byrne (1998) for an early synthesis; Jervis (1997) for analysis of social feedback processes; and Room (2011) for a recent integrative application).

Nonetheless, Douglas' Durkheimian argument provides a vital corrective to the commonest use of positive feedback loops in social science in recent years. Typically, positive feedback is invoked to explain why things become stable. In economics, the self-reinforcing network benefits of technologies – path dependency – are often invoked to explain near-universal adoption of technologies (from the QWERTY keyboard to popular operating systems or electrical plug-and-socket standards). Pierson's influential (2004) study on successful institutional development uses positive feedback explanations in the field of politics to the same end. By contrast, Durkheim's argument in *Division* and in *Suicide*, developed by Douglas in her work on enclaves in *How Institutions Think, In the Wilderness* and the 2003 article with Mars on terrorism, was that beyond a certain phase, positive feedback produces disorganization. The central importance of this trajectory is still too little appreciated, even among those who might be expected to be sympathetic to Durkheimian, functional or complexity-oriented arguments.

Durkheim (1995 [1912]) had argued that ritual should be conceived as a part of a causal mechanism for explaining the fixing of categories, not just – as already well understood – the sustaining of bonds. His focus was generally on formal, public ceremonial, and his analysis of data on Australian peoples in the outback tended to concentrate on the phases of their lives when they operated under enclaved institutions. Yet his mechanism could, with appropriate modifications, be generalized and given adequate typological variation. Douglas also took very seriously Goffman's (1967b) precise transposition of Durkheim's argument to everyday interaction ritual, as occurs in the consumption of goods or eating a meal, or in practices of politeness or the telling of jokes. Only in her late work did she find a way to reintegrate the argument into her larger account of explanatory mechanisms. The challenges of evidencing explanations using quotidian ritual mechanisms for category fixing remain immense, but these are challenges that remain of great importance for understanding the most basic processes of social interaction.

144 • *Mary Douglas*

A key contribution Douglas made to understanding causation in social life was that she treated the emergence of anomaly, and the manner in which anomalies can be managed or not managed, as central to the mechanisms by which thought styles are cultivated, sustained, reinforced or undermined. In her early work, attending to anomalies was simply a methodological maxim for finding places in fieldwork where pressure gauges could usefully be deployed. By the middle and late periods, the concept had become much more important. The feedback loops by which systems of classification both face anomalies and also throw up new anomalies for each other, which then become surprises, thus giving rise to negative feedback dynamics, were moved to the core of her account of the relationship between mechanism and trajectory in causation. Classification and its anomalies are not, she showed, only worth examining as cross-sectional curiosities about how people think; rather, anomaly is the spark-plug that fires up the causal engine.

It is unfortunate that *How Institutions Think* has not been widely read and that many of those who did read found it difficult to understand fully. Douglas did not use 'microfoundations', nor did she want to distract herself from her own argument by engaging in close debate with the 'new' institutionalist theoretical literature. The decision to excise from the book nearly all discussion of the fourfold typology, and of culture as a topic, was strategically adroit in many ways. It enabled readers who were prepared to work hard enough to appreciate the basic principles of her argument to see its relevance, even if they had, for whatever reason, found the typology hard to use or were sceptical of the analytical value of so loose and rhetorical a term as 'culture'. Yet these decisions also made it difficult to appreciate the extent of her achievement in providing a richer and more precise set of microfoundations for institutional theory, and the tight intellectual integration of arguments running through her work as a whole.

Douglas' microfoundational arguments provide the basis for her contribution to the understanding of the dynamics of conflict. The final chapter of *How Institutions Think* emphasized that conflict among the elementary forms, and within them, is endemic, and that their positive feedback turned what was epidemic into something pandemic. The institutional basis of the explanation shows why conflict is so hard to break. Positive feedback dynamics push conflict to the fore. When reacting against any of the forms, people have to reach for one of the others; there is no neutral position in which to reflect upon options. Mere intellectual persuasion alone will not change thought styles entrenched by causative positive feedback loops, or by negative feedback among the four elementary forms producing endless struggle or gridlock; 'only changing institutions can help' (Douglas, 1986, 126). Yet neither *How Institutions Think* nor the other microfoundational writings from this period have much to say about *how* institutions can be changed in ways that might attenuate or channel conflict, or about how positive feedback dynamics might be arrested before they result in disorganization and violence. It is this issue that came to dominate the final phase of her work.

If Douglas was perhaps not fully convinced that Verweij's and Thompson's (2006) strategy would be sufficient of trying to work out the kinds of relations among all four elementary forms that avoided flight to the outer corners, or conversely mutual gridlock then she would need to develop an extended account of her own to address attenuation, channelling, diffusing and defusing conflict that began by looking within the capabilities of each elementary form. In her final years, she devoted a great deal of work to this problem. Yet she tackled it in a way that surprised even some of the researchers who worked with her and used her theory. In the 1990s and the 2000s, she turned to the books of the Hebrew Bible as a source of new ethnographic data about the people of ancient Israel. This 'fieldwork' answered at length Melford Spiro's (1968) charge that her data in *Purity and Danger* were insufficient. Douglas insisted she remained an anthropologist and that ethnography would be the acid test of her theory. She also brought to this new series of empirical cases many reflections from her ethnographically based arguments of thirty years earlier, even going so far as to compare the Jews of the exilic and post-exilic period with the Lele she had known in the 1950s and had visited once again in the 1980s.

4

The Analytic Method is Also Ritual Peace Making
Thinking in Circles Helps to Defuse Conflict

In this chapter, we examine the significance of Douglas' late work on ancient Israel using books from the Hebrew Bible as her sources of data. We examine its significance for her theory and especially for understanding conflict and its containment. We begin by describing her project. Then we set out the very distinctive development of her own theory of the dynamics of conflict amplification and containment that she undertook in this phase of her work. In particular, we trace her arguments about conflict amplification through what Durkheim had called 'sacred contagion' in enclaves. We show that Douglas discerned a certain kind of hierarchical ordering, performatively and ritually enacted, that was capable of containing and attenuating conflict, even between people organized in opposed hierarchical and enclaved institutions. We show how this late corpus of work constitutes an ethnographic capstone for her whole project. Last, we consider how her arguments were received by experts in biblical studies and by historians of ancient Israel.

Douglas' late books develop an approach taken from semiotic structural analysis about cosmographic forms in literature and the social settings in which such forms might be cultivated. Shaped by debates conducted among biblical scholars, Douglas' arguments from her late period might be thought to show her turning away from her earlier interests in social theory of organization, classification, ritual, institutionalization and de-institutionalization. Her biblical studies were doubtless seen by some as the quintessential retirement project – an absorbing but gentle pastime equivalent to gardening or chess. This misperception perhaps explains why few social science readers have yet paid close attention to these later writings. Certainly, her vocabulary in these later books largely avoided privileging such terms as risk and consumption. Nor did she frequently cite her 1950s and 1960s fieldwork in central Africa. But any sense of disjuncture is superficial. The Books of Numbers and Leviticus in the Hebrew Bible provided her with empirical case studies for a novel and compelling synthesis of her previous typological and microfoundational studies. Although the Lele were rarely mentioned explicitly, Douglas' biblical studies also provided a means through which she could return to the ethnographic concerns of her early African work. Her last book is called *Thinking in Circles* (2007): it showed that her own work had come full circle, but with its theoretical scope now fully apparent.

Three books published over a decade from the early 1990s – *In the Wilderness* (1993a), *Leviticus as Literature* (1999b) and *Jacob's Tears* (2004b) – appeared to be taken up mainly with close textual analysis and literary structure. This second topic is also the apparent main burden of *Thinking in Circles*.

Yet this attention to literary form represented no reversion to ideational explanation. On the contrary, Douglas was pursuing the same questions as those that ran through all her previous work. Now, however, she was applying her recently won theoretical resources to understand the dynamics of conflict and its containment or attenuation. Her interest in literary forms lay in the purposes to which they might, ritually, be put in situations of deep conflict. We shall show that she returned to the Durkheimian corpus of explanations for effervescence and social contagion. Indeed, she now gave a fresh centrality to Durkheimian arguments about the role of ritual processes in the causation of social change. The cybernetic dynamics of positive and negative feedback are often implicit rather than explicit in Douglas' later works, yet nevertheless play a key role in her arguments. Now, though, she understood those arguments in a new way, enabling her to use documents from ancient Israel as a source of valuable ethnographic data for framing hypotheses about ritual dynamics of accusation and accountability, but also of conflict containment. Indeed, in *Leviticus as Literature* (Douglas, 1999b, 21), she studied again a work that she argued should be regarded as a masterpiece of analogical writing, which she demonstrated to be a model instance of writerly intervention in reconciliation. In the last book of the trilogy, *Jacob's Tears*, she applied these hypotheses, as tested in the Hebrew Bible, to contemporary conflicts in Africa and across the globe.

In this chapter, we show that Douglas was as intensely preoccupied in these later works with the same theoretical problems that had
driven her career up to this point. Indeed, it was precisely *because* she
shifted her empirical focus and began to work with new and different
kinds of data sources that she was able to use the later studies to make
very major intellectual progress on questions that had centrally preoccupied her early and middle periods. Anthropology, for Douglas'
generation, had been developed on the assumption that it was possible to undertake temporary but deep immersion in the perspectives
of the people being examined without being intellectually captured
by the people studied, and also without myopia or loss of attention
to questions about universal human social ordering. Douglas and her
contemporaries examined people and situations of empirical unfa-
miliarity in order to achieve the distance to be able to see through
the careful reconstruction of empirical detail to quite general trends,
dynamics and processes. The strategy is sometimes known as the 'ethnographic detour' (Richman, 2002, referring to Durkheim's late jour-
neyings through the Australian ethnological literature) because the
apparently circuitous route to insight involves simultaneous distanc-
ing from and immersion in local empirical arrangements. Whether
the aim is ever satisfactorily achieved can be argued. What is in less
doubt is that Douglas remained fully subscribed to a tradition of ethnographic research in which close attention to detail was combined
with relentless commitment to comparative generality. The whole discipline was, in the mid twentieth-century modernist form to which
Douglas remained loyal, a systematic practice of parable writing, and
her later works are parables, but now using cases from the kind of
source material from which the concept of a parable was itself drawn.

The challenge for the reader is to master the necessary the ethnographic detail well enough to grasp the theoretical implications of the
argument Douglas erects. Of these late works, *Leviticus as Literature*
presents a particular challenge because it simply stops. 'Are we spin-
ning round in circles in the wilderness?', the frustrated reader looking for a summary and conclusion is likely to ask. But the antidote is
to turn to *Jacob's Tears* as quickly as possible. At that point, we shall
show, the grand vision begins to come into view.

An Old Problem Recurs: Accounting for Witches

In the year following the publication of *How Institutions Think*, Douglas
made her long-delayed return journey to what was then Zaire (now

the Democratic Republic of Congo) to visit the new generation of Lele, whose parents and grandparents she had known thirty years before. The experience seems to have shaken her to the core. The visit yielded two articles, of which the second (Douglas, 1999c) is a key to understanding her last books and requires extended comment.

In *The Lele of the Kasai* (1977 [1963], Chapter 13, 'On Control of Sorcery'), Douglas had explained that the poison ordeal was once decisive in allocating guilt for sorcery. When it was banned in 1925, endless wrangling took its place, periodically to be replaced by witch-finding episodes. Douglas had then closed her ethnography with the remark that 'all this must have changed ... when the Congo became independent' (1977 [1963], 269). The 1999c paper picks up where she left off. The 1987 visit showed that matters had not changed as much as she had supposed. In the late 1980s, Lele society was still riven by sorcery fears and was still shaken by witch-finding movements. What was especially distressing to Douglas was to discover that the latest witch purges had been led by two young Catholic priests. The Church had earlier encouraged Lele converts to abandon belief in sorcery. Now it was out and about hunting demons. Suspect sorcerers had been tortured and had died in the resulting vengeful effervescence. Douglas doubted whether she should publish what she had found, and sat on the paper for some years. Later, she changed her mind. She is not very explicit about why. Perhaps events in Rwanda in 1994 played some part, when ethnic massacres again attracted some involvement by priests.

Douglas' paper (1999c) summarily despatches anthropological relativism. All esoteric forces are imaginary; any accusation of sorcery is false accusation. She then considered two explanations for the recurrent upsurge of anti-witchcraft cults. One is social change and disintegration. But this – she claimed – goes on all the time, so cannot explain why witch-finding movements erupt at intervals. Ignoring economic cycles, she looks instead to 'rivalry between a dominant religion and one that it has suppressed' (Douglas, 1999c, 189). Essentially, a witch-finding movement led by priests represented a failure on the part of the Catholic mission to attend to its duty of pastoral care, and this in turn was linked to theological failure. When Cardinal Ratzinger (the future Pope Benedict XVI) visited the Faculty of Catholic Theology in the University of Kinshasa, he tasked its theologians with problems posed by the challenge of the Protestant churches in Zaire. The faculty might have been better advised, Douglas suggests, to have invested its efforts in understanding and defusing the local beliefs and social tensions that gave rise to witch-finding effervescence. In effect, Catholic theologians in Zaire needed a better theory of how to proceed when rival systems of social accountability clash and come into deadly confrontation.

Douglas' encounter with the ferocity and violence of the anti-sorcery cults among the Lele in the 1980s led her to return to Durkheim's concept of sacred contagion. Now she to cast aside the shallow understanding of it she had entertained when writing *Purity and Danger*. Instead, she understood it afresh as the thought style in which the similarity that mechanical solidarity rests upon and enforces is then amplified in uncontrolled ways when enclaved social organization goes into drastic positive feedback, as she had modelled in the third chapter of *How Institutions Think*. In order empirically to understand the mechanism by which this process worked and how it might be contained, she decided to examine cases from ancient Israel for which the Hebrew Bible provided information over a fuller historical cycle than she had the chance to examine in her work on the Lele.

Conflict Attenuation and Sustaining Viable Social Organization: One and the Same Problem

Douglas' middle period writings had left one central puzzle with no adequate answer. Explaining the fact that conflict is a defining feature and institutionally critical fact about human life had become increasingly central to her project. Yet if conflicts were the main likely outcome of institutionalization and de-institutionalization processes, then how was it possible that humanity had avoided utter collapse and breakdown? Durkheim's answer in *The Division of Labour in Society* was that the self-reinforcement of mechanical solidarity or organization based on the institutionally classified similarity to each other of the people involved had steadily been offset by growing organic solidarity in which mutual exchange, dependence and involvement of people classified by their local institutions as different from each other was cultivated by different kinds of institutional regulation and integration, such as contractual agreement. Thus, he thought, the fissiparous tendencies of the mechanical solidarities, of which Douglas had identified four elementary forms by resynthesizing Durkheim's own materials, had been offset, and (as Durkheim saw it) human capabilities for large-scale organization had even grown over the course of history. Durkheim certainly recognized (1984 [1893], 135) that mechanical solidarities and their conflicts persisted even in the presence of organic links, exchanges and dependencies among them. Indeed, he devoted the last book of *The Division of Labour in Society* to show-ing that positive feedback in each one of the four forms continued to produce social disorganization by excessive self-reinforcement. Having seen the disorganization process at work in the Congo in 1987, Douglas appreciated afresh the power of Durkheim's insight, at least for people working in enclaved institutions. But Douglas' ur-gent question was this: how was Durkheim's general trend towards 'increasing preponderance' of organic solidarity and capacity for con-flict attenuation made possible? In *The Division of Labour in Society* Durkheim's answer had been sketchy and unconvincing. Part of his strategy was a rather weakly evidenced functional explanation about the imperative for access to goods and services only available on a sustainable basis from others by way of a system of specialized divi-sion of labour, assuming the other people involved were not simply coerced (1984 [1893], 136). In the second edition, he gave more em-phasis to the speculation, in some way still to be worked out, that religion might be key to the process. Yet by the time he wrote *The Elementary Forms of Religious Life,* he had only succeeded in deepening his account of the role of religion in sustaining one particular kind of mechanical solidarity – namely, that of enclaved ordering where ritual life cultivated collective effervescence. In deepening and resynthesiz-ing Durkheim's own work through her middle period and producing much more carefully specified microfoundations for it, Douglas had merely succeeded in arriving at the same problem that Durkheim had failed to solve, only more starkly illuminated in the political formu-lation that Douglas used rather than the economic formulation with which Durkheim had worked.

Michael Thompson had offered Douglas an answer to the prob-lem, which he went on to develop with Marco Verweij (Verweij and Thompson, 2006). The notion was that each of the mechanical solidar-ities might be articulated sufficiently to offset and check the others. By negative feedback and countervailing institutional pressure, each should be able induce action and representation of events that would administer small surprises to the others (in other words, information that is anomalous within the classification system used by people in the other mechanical solidarities). These small surprises would serve as 'wake up!' calls to those so wrapped up in their own form of solidarity that they failed to sense trouble was looming from those working in rival forms. Multiplex settlements would thus be encour-aged. Four-sided settlement would sustain the ability of the different solidarities to see round their institutional blinkers and receive and act on anomalous information. Being able to receive small surprises and to adjust to the information received should, Thompson argued, increase the robustness of settlements among the four elementary forms to withstand major surprises and shocks. Thus, these 'clumsy institutions' would exhibit greater resilience and greater viability. Thompson's 'clumsy institutions' argument about viability could also be understood as a proposal for a mechanism for conflict attenuation.

Although Douglas did not criticize Thompson, the fact that she never herself published a sole-authored version of his argument, but only put her name to one multi-authored article on the idea of clumsy institutions in which all authors but the first were ordered alphabetically (Verweij et al., 2006), and that her later works pursued a different strategy suggests that she must have thought it an incomplete explanation, or perhaps that 'clumsiness' was at best a necessary but not a sufficient condition for conflict attenuation.

Douglas' own strategy, announced in one of the papers of her middle period (1992a, 266), was instead to consider whether within each of the four mechanical solidarities, there might be capacities for cultivating self-restraint as well as self-reinforcement and perhaps even capacities for making reconciliatory moves toward the other elementary forms. In this regard, she was particularly interested in hierarchy. She did not claim that hierarchical institutions uniquely cultivated capacities for conflict attenuation. That would have been entirely contrary to her theory that the four elementary forms should be understood as each having their strengths and weaknesses. The point of her theory was precisely to enable the analyst to identify each set of biases with equal facility (e.g., Douglas, 1999e). However, time was limited; in the time that remained to her, she was concentrating first on what she knew best, and that meant focusing on the institutions of her own acknowledged religious commitments (Douglas, 2005).

In the previous chapter, we noted that there was a puzzling lacuna in Douglas' account of causation in *How Institutions Think*. Ritual seemed oddly absent. Or, rather, its presence was either implicit or else considered only in the form of 'ritualism', or a very strong articulation of explicit, formal, grand public ceremonial forms, as one 'dependent variable' on the side of thought style, and thus as something to be explained. In the traditions of theory developed to understand institutionalization inspired by Durkheim's work, there are two distinct functional explanations in which ritual is invoked. These explanations are directed toward ritual both in the sense of grand public ceremonial and in the sense of the quotidian interactions that fascinated Goffman and Garfinkel. The first explanation emphasizes, following Durkheim's argument in *The Elementary Forms of Religious Life* that people come to fix categories by repeatedly enacting social organization in microcosm. For example, Goffman (1967a) showed that as people enact idioms of politeness, respect and backstage manoeuvring, these ritual practices cultivate the category of individuality. This is the everyday form in which Durkheim's idea of the 'cult of the individual' is displayed, enacted, reinforced and learned. In the same way, Douglas' own earlier work showed that the ritual management of the distribution of appropriate consumption goods in festivities or in display conveys messages about one's aspirations and commitments to others. The second approach to showing how ritual makes institutions emphasizes the ways by which performance reinforces bonds. In *Purity and Danger*, Douglas had examined the ways in which ritual practices reinforce the strongly integrated bonds of enclaved groups by recognition and circumscription of anomalies. *Natural Symbols* had looked more briefly at the ritual reinforcement of hierarchical bonds. Nevertheless, in both her earlier and middle periods, Douglas had shown much more sustained interest in the category-fixing than in the bond-reinforcing functions of ritual.

A question that Douglas asked in her later works is whether the links between the two functional processes running from ritual could be used to build social organization, as it were, outwards, from one elementary form toward the others, to provide microfoundations for the kinds of four-sided settlement Thompson was trying to model from the outside in. In this way, ritual processes would once again become central, not just to the 'dependent variable' of a particular thought style, but also to the functional causal mechanism itself. Put another way, if Thompson's argument is that hybridity – or, rather, hybridity of the right kind – is essential for attenuating conflicts, then we still need to know more about the internal institutional capabilities of each of the elementary forms to accommodate hybridity, and about the ritual processes through which emergent hybridity can be sustained, in order to arrive at a provisional working prototype of a durable organic solidarity. In her lecture on 'Other Beings, Post-colonially Correct' (in Fardon, 2013b: given to an audience of Catholic mission theologians in Chicago in 2001), Douglas presented the message she presumably wished Cardinal Ratzinger might have earlier conveyed to his Kinshasa audience. There, she discussed a number of examples of how certain notions of spirit forces, shaped as beliefs by the social solidarities and systems of social accountability of African rural enclave communities, might be incorporated within larger cosmological systems espoused by the Christian missions, and attuned to the social and economic complexities of modern Africa. Demonizing old gods of Africa without attempting to create new, more complex pathways of for establishing social accountabilities ran the risk of outbreaks of sacred contagion associated with mechanical solidarity, especially in the register it assumes under enclaved institutions. Incorporation, not confrontation was required, and this would require the imaginative use of the kind of poetic, compositional tools she had glimpsed through her studies of the priestly manuals of the Hebrew Bible.

Hierarchy Transforming Purification into Reconciliation

Having worked so extensively in *How Institutions Think* and, indeed, as far back as *Purity and Danger* on enclaving, it made sense for Douglas to begin the new phase of her work on the bilateral relationship between hierarchy and enclave. So the particular question to be addressed in the first of her studies drawing on materials from the Hebrew Bible would be whether those strands in ancient Israel that supported hierarchical organization exhibited capabilities for both self-restraint in avoiding the stasis of too much regulation and integration, while also developing ritual practices and interventions that could reach out to enclaved institutions and attenuate their self-radicalizing tendencies. The right examples might help her to locate key causal mechanisms. This would be the ethnographic detour through which a powerful account of conflict attenuation could be attained, just as her exposure to a terrifying witchcraft-cleansing cult on her return to Africa had allowed her, first, to understand how Lele self-radicalization and collective effervescence had led to conflict amplification and then to see how the some of the wilder spirits recognized in some African peoples' thought might be domesticated within a newer more complex postcolonial pantheon (a task, by implication, for Lele theological and ritual creativity). In the spirit of reusing some of her own earlier ethnographic work, she went back to the concept of purity in enclaves that had preoccupied her in *Purity and Danger* in order to examine the bilateral relation between hierarchy and enclave over the transformation of purification rituals.

Douglas had first been drawn to compare the Lele and the ancient Israelite religion in *Purity and Danger*. But some of her critics had implied that she was ill-equipped for the task. Now she set about dealing with that charge by mastering a new ethnographic challenge with enormous energy and determination. She learned biblical Hebrew and for the first time read the complete Hebrew Bible. Progressively she absorbed, with the help of an impressive group of distinguished scholarly mentors meticulously thanked in her various prefaces, an extensive and demanding scholarly literature on its first five books.

Douglas' approach was to develop anthropological hypotheses she thought were illuminated by biblical case material, buttressed by reading in the scholarly literature and by supporting linguistic or textual evidence provided by her expert mentors. The major first fruit was her monograph on the Book of Numbers, *In the Wilderness* (Douglas, 1993a).

Much of the book is concerned with what might be termed Douglas' ethnographic apparatus. This is the close attention she pays to the complex literary organization of Numbers, adding substantially to work by anthropologists such as Goody (2010) and Finnegan (2012 [1970]) on oral and early written forms of literature. Numbers, she argued was an example of an early (but largely forgotten) poetic genre known as 'ring composition'. In several places she notes or implies that ring poetry was intended for ritual performance. The modern 'linear' reader tends to get easily lost as the ring is rounded and parallels are drawn across the circle, but early performers, perhaps brought up to understand that ring dancing was an important way of celebrating community solidarity, would readily follow the performative logic of the poetry of Numbers. Thus, the ritually entrained reader might understand that the structure of the text, performed by being read aloud or perhaps sung, reproduces its inclusive argument that God's promises were extended to all Israel and not some narrow sectarian group.

Douglas argues that both Numbers and Leviticus should be dated, at least in their final form, to the postexilic period of the Second Temple, and that both books were the work of a group of priests, not of prophets or a sect. This is in fact quite a sizeable empirical bet because there is no full agreement among scholars about when Numbers and Leviticus were written or about their intended audiences. She claimed that the books were completed in the period of the governorships of Ezra and Nehemiah. In effect, she argued, the two works were priestly protests against a 'land grab' by Assyrian-sponsored returning exiles at the expense of a more diverse population that had continued to occupy the land in the meantime, but shared community and cult with the exiles. 'Holier than thou' enclavism was the means by which the returned exiles sought to impose their own hegemony. Numbers and Leviticus countered these claims. Douglas argues that these works were written for deeply political as well as for religious purposes – although, of course, in this period the distinction would have been difficult one to draw empirically within the emic categories of the people of ancient Israel.

All this detail has to be followed attentively and kept in mind in order to then make sense of the few but absolutely crucial moments at which Douglas advances her broader theoretical concerns. The central argument in this respect is that, among the institutional capabilities, hierarchical ordering brings to the arena of conflict attenuation its peculiar capacity to find internally distinguished rule-bound statuses and roles for a variety of activities. Even some enclaved groupings such as the regimes of Ezra and Nehemiah can thus be accommodated in particular niches if they are prepared, as a result of ritual processes yet to be examined, to compromise. To show how niches might be sustained, Douglas was inspired by the work of her Oxford contemporary, Louis Dumont (1980 [1966]). From Dumont, she borrowed a crucial emphasis upon 'contrapuntal' and complementary institutionalization in hierarchical ordering. By this, she meant that hierarchy integrates by accommodating, in constrained rule-based tension and complementarity, such rival principles as those of priesthood and kingship or caste and profession (in classical Hindu thought as Dumont (1980 [1966], 65–108) diagnosed it) church and state (in the mediaeval empires), sacred and profane, lay and clerical (in the church), profession and organization (in the National Health Service or, indeed, the civil service), staff and line (in the armed forces), carrying out the instructions of the government of the day and speaking truth to power (in the upper echelons of the civil service), double unilineal descent systems in the Cross River of eastern Nigeria (ones in which there is inheritance in both the male and female lines, an example she had learnt from her UCL colleague Daryll Forde), solemnity in grand ceremonial and self-mockery in carnival, and so on (Douglas, 1993a, 67–74). In hierarchy, each of these forms has its peculiar status. There is a multiplicity of levels, quite contrary to the common misconception of hierarchy as comprising only high-status commanders and the commanded who lack status. By these means, anomalies are adjusted for and alternative imperatives are each given their appropriate place and role, without reduction to a single metric.

But how could any of this bureaucratic tidiness appeal in part to people working in enclaved institutions? Part of Douglas' answer was that hierarchy provides transformations of ritual behaviours already engaged in within enclaves. Gradually, hierarchy introduces transformations by making ritual practices themselves specialist affairs rather than the all-consuming effervescent ones of sacred contagion displayed in the most self-radicalized forms such as the corroboree-like events described by Durkheim in' *The Elementary Forms of Religious Life*. In the case of ancient Israel, Douglas showed that enclave rituals of debarring anomalies as 'defilement' of members of the sect were the subject of work by the priestly strand of ancient Jewish life which turned ritual practices to correct defilement into something that instead accommodated and reintegrated the formerly polluted into a community in which hierarchical ordering contained the excesses of the sect.

The priestly group, Douglas argued, took responsibility for editing the body of texts possessed by the community both from the enclaved sectarian traditions and from the more individualistic, patrimonial kingly sources. This group used its editorial opportunities, she went on to claim, to rewrite the meaning of the purification rituals to correct defilement. In the enclaved settings, those rituals had been used to enforce boundaries against foreigners and others; thus, they had amplified conflict. For example, one of her ethnographic concerns was to show how Numbers queries a narrow interpretation of the returned exiles over marrying 'foreign' wives. Ezra in fact instructed that these wives were to be abandoned by all men who wished to worship at the restored Second Temple. Douglas made good use of her anthropological training at this point to suggest that what was at stake was land inheritance. Ezra's decree ordered that the abandoned women should be accompanied by their children. She recognized that, in effect, the decree disinherited the male children. This, it can reasonably be surmised, would have freed land for the returnees. A more recent equivalent of the kind of enclave about which she was writing would be the white settler regime in colonial Rhodesia and the way in which it framed land law to its own advantage. This led to a bitter, long-running and apparently irreconcilable conflict that has not yet fully ended.

The priestly editing of Numbers and Leviticus, Douglas argued, sought to take the vocabulary developed in the enclaves about purity and purification, but to transform the rituals into ones that were about re-integration rather than exclusion and into much less chauvinistic processes. Instead, the rituals would recognize forgivably inadvertent error and would provide purification opportunities for people less on the basis of ascribed characteristics than on the basis of achieved work, even for strangers. Now purification would help to make boundaries porous (Douglas, 1993a, 157–59, 164–67). In the theoretical argument that underpins her account, purification ritual works to defuse sacred contagion in a very particular way. In hierarchical ordering, we all stand in need of purification, not just a particular group of us. Moreover, under hierarchical institutions, we are all responsible for purification becoming a collective and shared commitment. Therefore, the purification ritual addresses the tenuousness of the connection between the accused and the supposed sin or crime directly. In hierarchical purification, the ritual reminds us that we are all connected just as tenuously to sins and crimes, and we are all, in a common community, responsible for ensuring that we do not make these tenuous connections bear greater responsibility for evil than our own. Whereas the rival enclave might challenge the accusing enclave by dismissing their own tenuous connections as trivial or irrelevant, purification ritual takes even tenuous brushes with pollution and allegations of guilt seriously. Yet, at the same time, the ritual points out that accusers have as many connections with sins and crimes as those they accuse and blame. Complicity is not simply denied, but instead it is defused by being diffused throughout the community. Instead of becoming a category used for divisiveness, the similarity of complicity is reinterpreted as one for wider social integration to be achieved through the social regulation of the purification ritual. The ring structure of the poetic composition is itself a way of symbolizing this. The ring structure of Numbers itself spoke to the inclusive nature of God's promises and provided much textual challenge to the overdraconian and racist interpretations of endogamy supplied by Ezra.

In enclaved ordering, schism is a highly likely form of disorganization arising from conflict over claims to represent, more so than others, the true and pure principles or identities around which the strongly integrated and weakly regulated group is organized. In enclaved communities committed to the retention of key assets by true members, such schisms can be bitter and violent. This occurs even among those who consider themselves to be members, let alone those classified as outsiders altogether. One reason for Douglas' interest in the Book of Numbers was that it describes a series of such schisms within Israel of its period in which claims to land are centrally at stake. The priests who edited the Book of Numbers reworked older records, she argues, to stress the forgiveness granted for such schismatic behaviour. In the first instance, that forgiveness was ordained divinely, of course, because thereby it became mandatory on the people of Israel. In particular, it was extended to those classified by the enclaves variously as cursed, as rebels or traitors or as sinners. These rituals of atonement and forgiveness played a central role in the hierarchical work of bringing accommodation to mutually mistrustful shards of the enclave, just as rituals of purification did for the integration of strangers. The priests even developed a major periodicity of ritual reintegration, namely the idea of the forty-nine-year cycle culminating in forgiveness of debt and of slavery at the fiftieth year, the Year of Jubilee (Douglas, 1993a, 235–47)

In the Wilderness also introduced an argument that became central to Douglas' later works – that the priestly work of reconciliation, as she called it, was achieved not only by classification but also by composition. By composition, she means more than just fine, poetic writing. Her central notion is that the priestly editors were constructing a ritual ordering that spoke to social cohesion through the skilful compilation, editing and balanced structuring of a range of often well-known sacred textual source materials originating with different factions. These texts would, she suggests, be intended in the first instance for performance, either by reading aloud or perhaps singing at least for certain passages, or presented in some other performative way (perhaps as a kind of community pageant). Only then were the texts used for individual and private reading in silence. Private reading might well typically have been undertaken as preparation for participation in performance, whether as priestly reader or perhaps by participants (Baumgarten, 1985). Formal balance and rhythmic energy impelled the participant to move to the tune of the text. The sacred composition thereby opens up a discrete and hitherto hidden mental space for interaction in which participants are enabled to envisage many otherwise hidden and underappreciated aspects of the community's complex and interdependent life. In consequence, the ring was carried around 'in the heads' of the community as well as the priests as a microcosmic model or cosmogram to guide private reflection.

In this way, the values thereby encapsulated would eventually be turned into social practices. The performed character of social order is a key insight of Durkheim and his group. Henri Hubert, a key member of the Durkheimian school and often coauthor with Marcel Mauss, wrote a short but highly innovative study on time (Hubert, 1999 [1905]), which argued that the ritual marking of calendrical time by means of high days and holy days is key to the maintenance of all social organization. Hubert described the way in which the ritual calendar 'clocks' and regulates the alternation of quotidian activity and periods of sacred excitement, via the chiming of the church bell, or call to prayer, and the regular procession of sacred days and holy festivals (cf. Corbin, 1998). Douglas (1993a) was very clearly building on this Durkheimian insight into social life as a sequence of recurrent, temporally ordered shared practices. Therefore, the editorial process of composition in the form of the ring, with material distributed around it in a precisely balanced way, with the key message at the mid point, where the ring turns back on itself, rather than at the end, as modern readers might suppose, enacts and exhibits the integration of rival elements within itself. The compositional structure of the writing is itself a ritual act intended regularly to produce and to reproduce a system not merely of classification, but of narratively managed tight coupling of shared interests, exemplifying the complex ties linking rival factions and thus serving to dampen violent factional emotional excess. Everything, and everyone, has a recurrent place; even secessionists and prodigals will one day make their way back home and rejoin the cycle of community life. In a ring, there are no 'final solutions'.

Checking Enclaved Effervescence without Confrontation or Coercion

In the Wilderness provides only part of the causal mechanism by which institutional capabilities latent within hierarchy can operate ritually to provide interventions that might attenuate conflict. Douglas' book makes this argument by showing how careful composition and editing can themselves make and remake a ritual form. She demonstrates that the priestly editors of the Hebrew biblical Book of Numbers took fragments of enclave memory and transformed them into an integrated performable composition. The integrated structure of the composition mirrors the structure of its argument about how social institutions maintain viable organization and attenuate conflict. The internal boundaries of the sections of the composition are used and given due weight, but are then related to each other in the ring structure of the composition. They mirror the argument that social boundaries can be used not for permanent exclusion but for managing integration or re-integration. The emphasis is now on admitting outsiders or re-admitting those who have been excluded by, or who have excluded themselves through, schisms.

In this manner, *In the Wilderness* presented an account of internal capacities within one elementary form for *appealing* to another in ways that people working in the second elementary form might recognize and perhaps accept. After her return to the Lele in 1987, if not long before, Douglas was deeply alive to the recognition that capacity to appeal may well not be enough by itself to attenuate conflict or to dampen its amplification. Mechanisms may be required for *checking* positive feedback and collective effervescence in enclaved sectarian groups, as well as for accommodating those willing to consider the more moderate positions available in niches afforded by hierarchical differentiation within an overarching scheme of integration. Checking cannot take the form of confrontation or coercion, for anthropology and sociology had documented over many decades the ways in which these strategies tend only to give rise to even deeper revolt, greater bitterness and further episodes of effervescence in those enclaves that are confronted or coerced. The most that these strategies could realistically expect would be a temporary crushing of aspirations and shifting people for a period into a dynamic of isolate ordering, from which they might eventually emerge only to resume more ferocious enclaving. What mechanism of checking might be available within hierarchy?

In *Leviticus as Literature*, Douglas (1999b) suggests that the priestly editor or author of Leviticus was writing at a time of deep disorganization, schism and perhaps even civil war among the people of ancient Israel in the wake of the end of the Babylonian exile. There were many difficulties between returnees and those who had remained behind. Readers familiar with Douglas' African ethnography will not take long to get their bearings. The Lele peer out from many a page. 'One family suffers a loss … The friends and kinsfolk … want to know … was it an accident or should someone be arraigned …? Some deflect blame … by holding the dead responsible, or by blaming capricious demons and ghosts. When the community is divided bitterly no closure to disputes is within sight … Divination can … either repair the social fabric, or intensify hostilities' (Douglas, 1999b, 119).

Douglas argued that in ancient Israel, the Book of Deuteronomy, not the Book of Leviticus, provides the legal, administrative and bureaucratic machinery for the project of reconciliation. Leviticus provides a different, more poetical and theological strategy for the same end and, in particular, for controlling the risks of effervescence (Douglas, 1999b, 107).

Leviticus is consistent with other books in the Pentateuch in its three principles of religion – the justice of God, the covenant between God and his people, and blood as its sign (Douglas, 1999b, 113). However, many other beliefs or practices to which ancient Semitic communities resorted in attempting to live together while reconciling themselves to life's dangers and misfortunes were explicitly excluded or rejected. Douglas therefore asks: why were these other beliefs and practices rejected and how does the cult of Leviticus manage without them?

Leviticus has no place for demons and witches. The community has no cult of the dead. Indeed, cults of the ancestors were among the sectarian practices that its priestly editor sought to check. There are no sodalities or secret conclaves. Divination is possible only in very special circumstances. There are no images or shrines other than the tabernacle in the wilderness, and this is an idea to be reproduced in the virtual space of writing itself rather than a single physical place, because the editors' or authors' audience had long since settled in towns and villages. Instead, religion now inheres in a completely fresh conception of what sacrifice is, and in a complex set of purification rituals for social reintegration. Moreover, these are for individuals, not for marking a permanently pure group off from the permanently impure.

The features Leviticus excludes Douglas had expected to find as a result of her experience as an Africanist anthropologist. Comparative reading on ancient Semitic and Middle Eastern cultures showed that they were also widely distributed features of other societies in the region. Thus, their absence in the Hebrew Bible was a shock to her expectations and triggered a search for explanation. In essence, her answer is that all these practices – whether included within or excluded from the cult – made sense in terms of real practical problems of community cohesion. They were all problems of what today might be termed 'postwar reconstruction' – how to integrate long-divided communities or refugees and those who never moved, but survived a period of anarchy or war through developing characteristic local survival strategies. The problem is well known from studies of intercommunal tensions after modern civil wars, where enforced division of communities causes a reversion to the four basic forms of mechanical solidarity (for a case study of postwar rural Sierra Leone, see Archibald and Richards (2002)).

The exclusions from the cult, as propounded by Leviticus, are all directed, Douglas argues, at damping the risks of disorganization potentially stirred up by postconflict regression toward separated and polarized elementary forms on a divided landscape. The nub of her argument is that 'fears of civil breakdown would give Deuteronomy and Leviticus and their supporters good reason to outlaw divination in the already divided communities of Israel and Judah'. The priestly code of Leviticus thus reworks ancient Hebrew cults in such a way that effervescence has no scope to take hold. How was this supposed to work? Here Douglas deploys her feeling for the compositional analysis of myth to good advantage.

Leviticus has a particular literary form that is obscure to modern readers. Much of *Leviticus as Literature*, just like *In the Wilderness*, is devoted to setting out in detail the structure basic to the composition of the biblical text. Unlike Numbers, Leviticus is not a ring, but it is a cosmogram. The text traces out a picture or map of the tabernacle and allows the reader to take a tour, as if actually visiting the site. The structure models the proportions of the tabernacle in the wilderness. Following the map provided eventually leads the reader on a virtual pilgrimage to the inner sanctuary. A certain excitement builds as the tour approaches the holy of holies. Is the secret about to be revealed? Will god appear behind the smoke? No, there are no secrets. The cult of Leviticus is aniconic. 'Even going as far as we can go into the interior of the tabernacle, expecting to unveil its secrets, what we find is ... still, only and always, the justice of God and his fidelity to the covenants' (Douglas, 1999b, 244). Douglas documents closely two parallel sets of 'rungs' of ladders – sequences of passages along which the reader of Leviticus moves to its grand conclusion about the holy of holies. The parallelism of these two 'ladders' makes it possible to present the ritual response to and correction for conditions identified by the other sequence, made up of laws, stories and reflections. The enthusiast, wildly excited to be visiting the shrine of shrines, is held fast by the strict structuring of the hierarchical text.

What, then, does the believer do? Douglas is very clear that religion relieves fear and anxiety by mandating action. The afflicted engage in ritual action. Durkheim (1995 [1912]) taught that collective ritual action comes before shared meaning. But trouble lies in this direction. Collective action generates group excitement. A positive feedback effect, which, in *The Elementary Forms of Religious Life*, Durkheim had labelled 'sacred contagion', can sweep all before it, as in the case of Lele witch-finding rampages. Leviticus introduces the renovated practice of purification as a bulwark against effervescence. The effervescent mourning ritual that Durkheim (1995 [1912]) called the piacular rite is banned. Any involvement in sacred rites is risky and subject to strong constraints. The Pharisees – a sect important during the Second Temple period, but after the priestly editors of Leviticus had done their work, and who significantly influenced the later rabbinic movement – considered that handling sacred scripture rendered the reader's hands ritually unclean (Baumgarten, 2016). How could this arise, Douglas asks, when the object itself is holy? The answer to such puzzles, for her, is to be found in the remedy prescribed in Leviticus itself. It is purification. Purification, in the priestly recasting of the concept, is not about being dirty. It is a ritual that 'brings home' to the believer the greatness, benevolence and complete otherness of God. It expresses acceptance of deity through care for the cult. Purification ritual is the answer to fear and dread, and the cure for effervescent outrage. No magic – just housework, and lots of it. Those citizens who went out on to the streets of riot-torn London in 2011 with brooms aloft, hoping thereby to restore respect to their communities through a clean-up ritual, were acting entirely consistently with Douglas' understanding of Leviticus.

However, this was a new approach to taboo and it brought home to Douglas that in *Purity and Danger*, she had been wrong about the abominations of Leviticus. The prohibited animals were not to be demonized. The cosmology of Leviticus has no room for demons. Animal taxonomy in Leviticus is a total system, manifesting divine benevolence. Most animals are prohibited for food and human use, and this prohibition is protective. It prevents human exploitation and abuse, and demonstrates the deity's care for all of creation. There is no room in the cosmology of Leviticus for phantasms, but there is room for all of creation. *Leviticus as Literature* ends with a striking allusion to the parlous predicament of the Lele: 'Demerit does not explain misfortune. Disease or barrenness is not the fault of the victim' (Douglas, 1999b, 251). Leviticus taught that the only protection needed against misfortune is a cult of ritual cleanliness.

The mechanism by which enclaved effervescence is checked, then, is the obverse of that documented in *In the Wilderness*. The earlier book showed that purification was changed to allow social structure to be shifted to accommodate groups in niches and to integrate outsiders. *Leviticus as Literature* presents the other mechanism by which the same ritual works to check effervescence. The recast purification ritual adopts the very vocabulary of the enclave about 'purity', but stands it on its head. Now, it turns the ritual process of achieving purification into one in which fervent fury is calmed and the reintegrated person attaches to a status in a law-bound community. If the renovated purification ritual in *In the Wilderness* is about making openings in *structural* boundaries, in *Leviticus as Literature*, it is about using atonement and forgiveness to harness the *emotional* energy that might otherwise erupt into effervescence. In both books, what hierarchy does is to allow the enclaved concern about boundaries to be accommodated within the differentiated structure of contrapuntal complementarity in niches and compartments of an overarching hierarchical order.

The hierarchical twisting of enclaved concerns extends directly to the issue of violence. Leviticus builds steadily through laws of restitution and reciprocity towards a grand injunction against eating anything containing blood, because that constitutes the essence of life, and alludes to the violence through which life can be ended – the shedding of blood (1999b, 231–34). After animal sacrifice, when violence is ritually rendered sacred in character, the blood on the altar is unclean. Indeed, she argues (1999b, 247–51) that in the collective atonement ritual, the 'scapegoat' is not in fact killed, but simply released into the wilderness. Contrary to Girard and Smith's (1987) much-cited neo-Freudian theory of the treatment of the scapegoat as a violent elemental act defining of subsequent social organization (a view that did not fully reflect the critique of psychoanalytical and phenomenological explanations of religious life that Smith presented in other writings: cf. Smith, 1987), the rite of sacrifice itself is turned in Leviticus into one of accommodation and reintegration, not one of violence at all (see Douglas, 2004b, 38–60).

The agenda of understanding hierarchy's contribution to reconciliation or, when that is too much to ask, to conflict attenuation was made explicit in the title of Douglas' third (2004b) book on the Pentateuch – *Jacob's Tears: The Priestly Work of Reconciliation*. No longer was the argument restricted to particular books (Numbers and Leviticus) or even to a third member of the Pentateuch (Deuteronomy) recurrently referred to for contrast in *Leviticus as Literature*. In *Jacob's Tears*, Douglas focuses directly on the conflicted parties. These included the returnees from exile claiming to be the true Israel, the descendants of those who remained in the promised land at the time of the Babylonian captivity. Douglas concluded that many of them had come to adopt a variety of ecstatic and effervescent cults. She is blunt about Ezra, the populist governor of Judah and leader of returnees, and his followers. She accuses him of misrepresenting the law and even of being a racist. Some of his ire was directed at the tribes of Ephraim, later grouped as Samaria, the rival polity to Jerusalem, whose residents he no longer saw as part of the Jewish community, but where priestly organization remained strong and where the editors of Leviticus might have sought allies (Douglas, 2004b, 23–23). In *Jacob's Tears* (2004b, 82), she recognized the influence of Ezra's vision and the fact that the priestly work of reconciliation argued for in her reading of Leviticus would not unite the Jewish people in the longer term. Moreover, that book spells out much more clearly than the previous studies that she was writing about the Pentateuch in order to study the dynamics of civil war and disruption quite generally, and now she drew the parallels with Africa very explicitly.

The period in which she wrote was one in which several extremely violent African civil wars and ethnic pogroms had made international headlines. The violence and emotional recklessness of these conflicts had shocked and puzzled a global media audience, and Douglas felt that she held the explanatory key. Although the third book recapitulates many of the arguments in the 1993 and 1999 studies, in part because it is a reworking of earlier preparatory essays – a circumstance that clearly establishes, if any doubted, that Douglas' late project was part of her long-term intellectual agenda – its anthropological focus is given over to the tension between ancestor cults and monotheism.

This tension is explained as the result of a conflict of institutions, between enclaved sectarians demanding the unity of absolute similarity (in other words, extreme mechanical solidarity of the enclaved kind) and a priestly hierarchy pursuing grand unity within rule-based schemes of accommodation. The argument provides a clearer macrocontext for the attention to micromechanisms in the earlier studies. Monotheism is a potentially effective hierarchical strategy for dealing with enclaves experiencing positive feedback because it at once insists on grand unity, appeals in its austerity to the purity and cleansing concerns shaped by enclaved schemes of classification, and also allows scope for atonement, reintegration and a more porous conception of the community open to individual or local group commitment and efforts to join (thus, Douglas recast Morton Smith's classical 1952 argument on why monotheism emerges as a solution to political difficulties into an explanation driven by conflict management). By contrast, an ancestor cult insists on ascribed characteristics and evidence of descent to mark difference, and tends toward both exclusivity and chauvinism in its pomp and violent fury under threat. The enclaved cult of the dead lacks the ability to atone or forgive. Feud is all too likely, because ascription is all that is counted, marked and sacrificed in violence or celebrated in effervescent exultation. Ethnic conflict, whether in Africa or the former Soviet sphere, turns out to look much like a certain kind of enclaved religious conflict. The problem is an excess of mechanical solidarity based on spurious marks of descent, inheritance or inclusion (skin colour-based identity, at its most extreme).

One example from *Jacob's Tears* may serve to make the point (Douglas, 2004b, 28–31). Early in that book, Douglas re-examined the biblical story of Jacob. As an Africanist skilled in dissecting the complex institutional problems and relations between pastoralist families trying to work out ways to live in larger, but rather fragmented political communities, she immediately recognized the dilemma facing the pastoralist Jacob. Jacob had been trying to mend fences with the kingdom of Shechem by reviving an old Abrahamic shrine and trying to sustain some agreed ritual practices, in the hope of securing concessions for his grouping. Then a prince of Shechem raped Jacob's daughter. Rather than seeking vengeance, Jacob negotiated a settlement in which his community would keep the peace if the people of Shechem agreed to male circumcision, thus indicating common membership in a ritual community. But then Jacob's sons, Simeon and Levi, led an attack on Shechem in a vendetta. Jacob, furious less about the fact of the killings per se than about the fact that the Shechemites – whose goodwill he needed and with whom he was trying to build a common ritual community – had now been turned into implacable enemies, disinherited his headstrong older sons. Douglas shows both the roots of the conflict in the political economy of pastoralist communities on the edges of larger polities and the process of enclaving and feuding that undermines efforts to sustain organic solidarity by ritual means across boundaries of identity. Simeon's and Levi's effervescent fury and refusal to forgive went through precisely the positive feedback dynamic of enclaving that Douglas had examined in her 2003 work with Mars on terrorist sects.

Douglas was too well trained an anthropologist, of course, not to know about fictive kinship and sodality membership as ways of transcending some of the most obvious limitations of ancestral cults. Indeed, it was a core part of her theory that enclaves, like other solidarities, always have some internal resources for dealing with excessive effervescence. Her central focus, however, was to draw attention to and explain the skills of priestcraft displayed by those who understood the dangers and could compose ritual disciplines with the capacity to capture and entrain the squabbling, fighting, feuding or massacring factions. Conflict mitigation required ritual composers of great skill and political adroitness. We should be grateful for that skill wherever it is to be found. As an Africanist, she knew that many of the most spectacular masquerades and public ceremonials for which the continent's rural communities are famous, and that are now regarded as an encapsulating the richness of local cultural heritage and welcomed as life-enhancing events, were born of bitter conflicts and were in effect dances of peace. This was to her also the key to understanding much of the Hebrew Bible, and essential guidance for those who seek to *make* peace.

Douglas' final work, *Thinking in Circles* (2007), was devoted almost entirely to the analysis of ring composition as a literary structure in the Hebrew Bible, *The Iliad*, *Tristram Shandy* and elsewhere. Only in the final chapter did she turn to the question of what kind of intervention it is for a text to be composed in that form, especially when it is intended to be read aloud in performance, whether at once or over a protracted cycle of performances. That performance is a ritual intervention, especially when what is read is a cycle of poems, laws and stories about who the listeners are and what they can hope for, such as that offered in Leviticus. The elements of her argument are already familiar from the studies on the Pentateuch. The ring is very highly rule-ordered. Elements on the two sides of the ring must be finely balanced, in order to lead in complementary, contrapuntal ways to the ending that provides the microcosm in which the second side of the ring develops reconciliation for the problems, risks and excesses set out in the first. The balancing of the elements on the two sides exhibits reciprocity. That reciprocity may be either punitive or restitutive; at its best, it may be redemptive. The ring structure presents a microcosm of reconciliation. Its use for literary content that examines this social process is therefore especially apt (for that reason it is perhaps more debatable than she admitted in *Thinking in Circles* whether *The Iliad* and *Shandy* are the most apt uses of the form). The very rhythms of elements set out in parallel on the two sides of the ring composition structure are presented in the rhythms of the performance, as an intervention in the conflicts of those who are asked to listen, or who are asked to attend to a performed reading.

The hierarchical institutional context from which the integrated, rule-bound, balanced, contrapuntal ring composition springs and that it exhibits in microcosm is important for Douglas' argument in two quite contrasting respects. On the one hand, her *In the Wilderness* and *Leviticus as Literature* studies show it to be critical in understanding what kind of ritual intervention it was, and still is, to write, read and perform a ring composition to a community of listeners who are going through civil war, dislocation, exile and return, and bitter conflict of ideas, and where there are organized cults of extreme purity liable at any time to boil over into violent hatred. In that setting, the performance of the ring-composed text embodies, in the interaction between readers and listeners in which parallelisms and the closure of the ring are marked, the ritual actions through which effervescence can be controlled.

On the other hand, in *Thinking in Circles*, Douglas asks why the literary form is now both rarely used and hard for contemporary readers to recognize in ancient texts. Her anxious answer (2007, 139–48) was that hierarchy, or at least its mode of offering overarching and background unification with openness to reintegration, may be in decline in contemporary Europe and North America. Perhaps its fate in other parts of the world, at least in the short term, will be different. But her concern is that with growing individualism come aspirations for open-endedness and for exploitation of anomaly rather than for closure and the integrative adjustment of anomaly. Douglas' late period work had addressed the bilateral relations between hierarchy and enclave, not those with individualism. The problem of whether positive reinforcement within individualism can be constrained to make it less invasive, triumphalist and ultimately intolerant she left to her successors.

Conflict Attenuation and Reconciliation

Did the strategy adopted by the priestly editors of Numbers and Leviticus actually work? Was the violence of the effervescent enclave tamed by a causal mechanism sustained by the hierarchical priesthood in ancient Israel? By some combination of forces, we are told, Ezra's movement was apparently defeated and its sentiments sidelined. But because we only have the accounts written, on Douglas' argument, by the priests themselves, we cannot be sure (see remarks by Lester Grabbe, in Heald, Grabbe, Handelman, Segal and Hendel, 2004).

Douglas' account of the causal mechanism may therefore be fairly criticized as speculative. On the other hand, given that we lack good rival accounts of mechanisms that are really much better evidenced about the means by which conflict attenuation might actually be achieved in bilateral relations among elementary forms, her approach of trying to use a kind of causal process tracing on a rich literary data set may not have been the worst one with which to begin.

However future biblical scholarship might eventually assess the particular claims that Douglas advanced in relation to the Pentateuch, the significance of the later work for her social theory should now be clear. Her later works were devoted to a central problem left unanswered in the microfoundational studies of her middle period and that was also left inadequately explained by Durkheim. This is the question of just how an institutional theory of the dynamics of conflict can also help to explain the fact that human societies have found ways – indeed, *institutional* ways, and not merely short-term expedients of interests, payoffs and utilities – to contain, attenuate and channel conflict generated by institutional imperatives.

Douglas' later works have helped to bring to the surface ritual's role in causation, a role that was submerged in *How Institutions Think*. In fact, although they do not announce the fact in the manner of their writing, which is very different from any conventional treatise of social theory, Douglas' later studies were still preoccupied by microfoundations. For the question she sought to answer through them was one about the institutional capacities and capabilities within just one elementary form, acknowledged by her to be as much a mechanical solidarity as the other three, how these capacities could be harnessed for a project of organic solidarity and, in particular, how these capabilities might be used to attenuate conflict in just one bilateral relation among the forms.

Douglas did not and had not expected to live long enough to go on to pursue the same strategy in examining all the twelve bilateral relations possible among the four elementary forms. But she had at least set out the programme by which microfoundations might be found for some of the patterns of four-sided settlement that Thompson had argued would be normatively valuable.

Turning her explanatory social theory into a normative one proved genuinely difficult. Although it is easy to allege that Douglas' theory somehow smuggles in unacknowledged normative baggage, in fact, dragging normative implications out of explanatory social theory is genuinely difficult. It requires painstaking work on mechanisms, on distinguishing different kinds of normative outcomes, and on tensions and tradeoffs. She had barely begun that programme of normative work before her death. Typically, she did it without simple moral commendation of any one elementary form, even of the one (hierarchy) that she tended personally to favour. Instead, her strategy was to pursue normative implications by concentrating on causal mechanisms for conflict attenuation, beginning with just one of twelve generic types of case her own theory suggested. The result was not a comprehensive theory of conflict attenuation, let alone of full reconciliation, but a tiny microcosm of what could and still might be done.

Douglas was always mindful that anthropology is the examination of case studies as microcosms. Her own Durkheimian argument was that people's thought styles are a further microcosm of their own social organizations. Whatever makes microcosm a viable and sustainable practice for the people being studied also matters among the social scientists who research them. She wrote that 'a microcosm allows a community to establish some conventions about meanings ... without a strong community a microcosm cannot flourish' (Douglas, 2004b, 155). The series of microcosms to which she devoted her efforts, from the Lele of the 1950s to ancient Israel, from environmental risk conflicts in the United States of the 1980s to the shoppers of 1970s Britain, were offered to what in the 1960s she had once hoped would be a strong community of anthropology. When that community diversified, turning in particular toward the humanities, she offered her insights to other social sciences, in the hope that they too might be interested in how institutions ritually cultivate thought styles and in turn how styles specify action. She did not create a strong community around her own neo-Durkheimian and institutional approach. But her hope that one might be developed on a much larger scale by accommodating and adjusting a variety of intellectual traditions in a larger programme remains a reasonable one, and perhaps a necessary condition of progress in the social sciences.

The Reception of Douglas' Work among Biblical Scholars

The focus of our book is on Douglas as a social theorist. But theory, she always insisted, cannot stand without empirical grounding. As an anthropologist, she thought that good ethnography was the proper way to test social theory. Her ideas would mean nothing, she once stated to one of us in conversation, unless competent ethnographers endorsed them as ways of helping to explain their data.

Whether Douglas herself possessed the requisite data to support her early theoretical inferences had been questioned in Spiro's review of *Purity and Danger*. The later work on the Hebrew Bible, we have suggested, was perhaps intended to address this concern. A biblical scholar, Alan Segal, appositely refers to this body of work as representing Douglas' 'fieldwork among the ancient Hebrews' (Segal, in Heald et al., 2004). Whether this new fieldwork supported her theory depended, by her own standards, on whether other 'fieldworkers' accepted evidence she had assembled as valid. Thus, her reception among biblical scholars is a matter of significance for those interested in her social theory. If her data were found to be weak, the theory would remain unsupported.

Of course, the biblical data are not the only test. We have shown that Douglas' theoretical understandings arose from and drew upon, in the first instance, her work as an Africanist ethnographer. Other Africanist ethnographers have continued to revert to her theoretical contributions ever since, including applying them to emergent fields such as the ethnography of African civil wars (Richards, 1996, 1999), and her theory could perhaps continue to thrive empirically on its Africanist credentials alone.

To date, rather little theoretical work has been done by social scientists to develop the insights of Douglas' late work. Richards (2009) extends her argument about the performance of ring composition and their implications for reconciliation by linking them with developments in ethnomusicology and in the anthropology of dance. He argues that her late arguments are consistent with the speculations of some evolutionists that a human capacity for music and dance may have emerged as a domain for the rehearsal of sociality (Cross, 2003). The technical properties of ring composition extend to musical resources. His article ends by pointing out the historical relevance of masquerade traditions and the ring dance in reducing the power of memory to revive African deadly conflicts. Like war, peace was also danced into being.

Nevertheless, there is a whiff of circularity hovering over theoretical ideas that emerge from a single setting. Douglas understandably hankered after comparative confirmation. This was why she felt it so important to move to a distant thematic area such as the analysis of risk in industrial society. However, *Risk and Culture* proved to be a dead end. Whatever defences may be advanced for that book, a close and diligent analysis of an extensive body of systematic empirical data was not its strongest suit. New data were needed. 'Fieldwork among the ancient Hebrews' must have appealed in part because *Purity and Danger* had already had a major impact on the field of biblical scholarship. Also, it was a field tilled by a large and vigilant community of scholars. There could be no slacking on language and text. The facts would be scrutinized with great care.

How well, then, has Douglas' work been received among biblical scholars? The broad answer is 'very well indeed'. It is true that a few, such as Larsen (2014), a scholar with an avowedly Christian apologetic agenda rather than a principal concern with Hebrew texts, simply do not accept her account of Ezra's position. Yet it is hard to make any other sense than Douglas did of Ezra's insistence on forced divorce of all 'foreign wives'. Reconstructing the ritual and social life of communities at the distance of several millennia can never be an exact science, so it is unsurprising to encounter disagreement about details. But the overall insights she brought to the field have been welcomed and readily acknowledged as being plausible, if not always fully substantiated. Here we refer mainly to three major critical overviews. One is a symposium in the *Journal of Ritual Studies* (Heald et al., 2004), consisting in papers by three biblical scholars and two anthropologists assessing *Leviticus as Literature,* and a response by Douglas (2004c). A second collection of short review essays appeared in a symposium in the *Journal of Hebrew Scriptures* (2008) that Douglas was too ill to attend. The third is the seminar resulting in Sawyer's (1996) edited collection on Leviticus where Douglas (1996a) presented her reworking of the concept of sacred contagion. Most of the papers in these collections not only endorse her findings but also actively enlarge upon them. One or two are more sceptical. We focus on the sceptics.

Lester Grabbe (in Heald et al., 2004) strikes a major blow when he wonders whether Leviticus documented a living religion or was a utopian work by a priestly 'cell'. Douglas admits that she had an open mind on this issue (Douglas, 2004c). In effect, neither Grabbe nor Douglas has the evidence to decide. However, the question matters because if the answer is 'utopian', then her theory is endorsed only by another (ancient) theory, not by data from a real, if ancient society.

In the second collection, an essay by Rüdiger Schmitt (2008) on magic and monotheism is especially critical of Douglas' later work, comparing it unfavourably with the position adopted in *Purity and Danger*. Schmitt sees no evidence for Douglas' argument in *Jacob's Tears* that the priests of Leviticus were seeking to abolish an older cult of the dead. He considers the idea espoused by Jacob Milgrom, perhaps the leading contemporary expert on Leviticus, as well as by Douglas that the priests rejected magic and divination as playing no part in true religion to be a relic of an old Durkheimian prejudice that magic was somehow bad because it was individualistic, in contrast with religion, which for Durkheim was a reflection of communitarian values. Aligning himself with postmodernism and perhaps unaware of Douglas' argument that postmodernism must be seen as just one more socially determined interpretive perspective, Schmitt claims that recent anthropology has overcome this prejudice. His own work admits magic and divination to the ancient Israelite religious pantheon. Accordingly, he repudiates or simply fails to see significance in Douglas' claim that magic and monotheism are distinct and socially determined styles of thought.

This leaves us with the problem that argument based on facts is also a reflection of assumptions based on theoretical positions, and in the end the test of empirical accuracy is often less decisive than hoped. The dangers of slipping into circularity are real. Whatever remedies might be sought, the problem cannot be resolved by piece-meal quibbling over detail. Douglas' empirical claims will have little appeal to those who reject or refuse to see the larger explanatory canvas. What would be interesting, however, would be to know more about Schmitt's own larger reasons for rejection. Perhaps the mask slips slightly when he accuses Douglas of apologia for the priests and hints at her Catholic bias. Douglas (2005), herself, admits to a bias for hierarchy, but does not accept that her Catholicism affected her social science. Rather, it is the case that she sees her theory as being devised as a safeguard against any such priors having undue influence in interpreting anthropological evidence.

Schmitt is not alone in considering Douglas' later work on the Bible to be revisionist backsliding from the heights attained in *Purity and Danger*. Klawans (2001) praises the beneficial impact of this earlier book in directing attention to ritual and sacrifice as symbolic systems, and accuses fellow biblical scholars of having lost sight of its insights when getting down to interpretive details. In his own work, he is interested in substantive issues of purity and sacrifice. Like Hayes (2002), Klawans (2003) makes some use of Douglas' arguments about the ritual content of purification, but takes them further to distinguish varieties of purity in ancient Jewish thought.

Here, Klawans appears to align with others who wonder why Douglas has got herself bogged down in the Bible when her approach appears tailor-made to contribute to key interpretive and comparative debates in religious studies more broadly. One such broader debate is the groundbreaking comparative work on ritual by Bell (1992), McClymond (2008), Smith (1987), Staal (1990), Zuesse (1979) and others, some of it explicitly neo-Durkheimian in orientation. Why is Douglas not among them? This is the question that Ivan Strenski's seems to ask in his somewhat ambivalent endorsement of Douglas' biblical 'holiday' in a wide-ranging essay 'Durkheim Sings' (Strenski, 2006), a title seemingly positively calculated to grab her attention.

Doubtless, Douglas was interested in these wider debates by scholars of comparative religion, and her work is regularly referenced within them. However, her reason for sticking to the Bible was not a newfound, textual narrowmindedness. Even less was it Catholic bias. Rather, it was that as a theorist, her methodological concerns overtook her substantive interests. The Bible allowed her to test her theory. It was like an expensive and elaborately designed experiment that could not be abandoned halfway through.

Lemos (2009) is perhaps the most stringent of Douglas' critics in the field of biblical scholarship. He is much more explicit than Klawans in expressing the view that her later work represents a step backwards. For him, *Purity and Danger* was a revolutionary breakthrough. Her later work is adjudged thinly disguised theologizing and priestly apologia. He regrets that Douglas, whom he claims as one of his intellectual heroes, died before she could answer him in person as he had hoped.

The annotations in *Leviticus as Literature* suggest that Douglas relied most heavily on the edition published as the *Jewish People's Torah*. There is a tendency in some conservative annotated texts to imply continuities between the Torah and Judaism, which many biblical scholars would now criticize. Lemos (2009, 213, 247–48) makes the same criticism of Douglas – that she wrote as if the Bible and Judaism were synonymous.

Probably, Douglas would have welcomed Lemos' call for more comparative work. She might well have accepted his charge that she had collapsed the topic of ancient Israelite religion into Judaism, and Judaism into priestcraft, and then replied that this criticism was a stimulus to broaden her canvas. Surely, she would also have welcomed the challenge to pay closer attention to Islamic purity laws.

Indeed, Gauvain (2005) sought to use Douglas' theory and method to understand that very topic. But in terms of the empirical test she hoped that her theory would pass, Lemos provides a strong if unintentional endorsement. He and James W. Watts, he claims, are among 'the very few biblical scholar [*sic*] ... to critique Douglas' latter day work'. If her critics are so thin on the ground in such a rigorous and combative field, then her fieldwork data must be deemed to have passed the test of initial professional scepticism. According to Lemos, Watts also complained that her later work drew 'on her anthropological background relatively little'. Surely this is further indication of how hard she worked to make her biblical fieldwork a truly independent test of her theoretical deductions. Spiro's (1968) reproach was finally assuaged.

§5

DOUGLAS' CONTRIBUTION TO UNDERSTANDING SOCIAL THOUGHT AND CONFLICT

In this final chapter, we offer an integrated statement of the central explanatory argument underpinning all Douglas' work and what this can offer for the social sciences. Douglas believed that thinking was a collective task, so it is also important for us to say something about how her argument drew from and was further developed by her collaborators.

The formulation of this argument took Douglas a lifetime of work. In each of the previous chapters, we have shown how each of her projects contributed to it. We have also described the ways in which each stage left gaps or opened up questions that she would only later be able to resolve. Key to this chapter's synthesis is the appreciation that to explain human thought is to explain human conflict: the two themes of this book turn out to be one. Douglas' achievement not only offers a fresh and profound account of how conflict is amplified. In her later writings, she drew out from her theory an account, using the same causal mechanism, of the manner in which conflicts are contained, channelled and abated, until they become tensions managed through civil and restrained practices.

After presenting our synthesis of Douglas' theoretical achievement, we examine the extent to which her theoretical arguments about conflict amplification and containment have been extended by the scholars who have drawn upon them. This enables us to conclude the book with an appreciation of her achievement and her approach's potential. We offer some reasons that researchers should pay attention to her arguments now. Her arguments continue to matter both for their substantive contribution to understanding of human thought and conflict, and for the route that she opened up beyond some of the methodological impasses encountered in social science today.

How Conflict Amplifies and is Attenuated: Douglas' Argument Summarized

Having presented the development of her theory over the course of her writings in the previous four chapters of this book, we can now summarize the fundamentally Durkheimian argument running through Douglas' whole oeuvre. This argument fully integrates her methodological and causal innovations both with her explanation of human thought and with her very distinctive account of human conflict.

People ritually perform their social organization (Douglas, 1966), in each of the available elementary forms (Douglas, 1982a [1978]), in ways that cultivate their styles of thought (Douglas, 1986). Social organization consists in informal institutions, described by the strength and weakness of social integration and social regulation (Douglas, 1970a, 1982a [1978]). Thought style describes *how* people think with whatever substantive propositions they may accept (Douglas, 1986). Quotidian, everyday ritual interaction order is the causal mechanism by which elementary forms of social organization cultivate styles of thought (e.g. Douglas, 1972). By performing our social organization in its weak and strong bonds and constraints, we channel our emotions and train our patterns of thought to follow the forms of our account-abilities to and from each other. By enacting their strong or weak social integration and social regulation, people cultivate in themselves and others a style of thought that is as weakly or strongly *cognitively* integrated and regulated as they are themselves weakly or strongly *socially* integrated and regulated (Douglas, 1982a [1978]). Having been ritually cultivated by forms of social organization, thought styles lead people to act in ways that reinforce their form of social organization, even to the point where ritual insistence disorganizes it and leads people to react assertively against other forms. The feedback loop begins with social organization and runs to thought style. Only secondarily and by a different causal mechanism does it run back to shape social organization (see Figure 3.1 above; and 6, 2014a).

This feedback loop constitutes a functional explanation for conflict and even for dysfunction rather than only for stability or consensus

(Douglas and Mars, 2003). Explaining thought explains conflict precisely because there are multiple elementary forms and by cultivating one, we react against others. Moreover, even within each elementary form, conflict arises from the form itself. Hierarchical ordering within one set of socially integrated boundaries will always be in tension with any adjacent hierarchy: for example, the history of medicine is structured by tensions between the hierarchies of the profession and of hospital management. Rival enclaves (for example, in Beirut, Belfast or Bosnia) may exhibit similar styles of thought, but each of their efforts to mark out their boundaries against the other will lead to conflict. In individualistic ordering, rival patrons will emerge and will soon come into conflict, whether among ancient Roman politicians or among the rival 'crown princes' in twentieth-century cabinet governments (cf. 6, 2016a). Explaining conflict is not an extra step in the argument after explaining the styles of human thought; rather, our thought styles are inherently conflictual.

But all is not lost. Humankind need not collapse in universal disorder, even though in some periods we seem to come close to it (Parker, 2013), for by the very same ritual mechanism, each may cultivate its own ritual practices of conflict attenuation and containment. This is often observed (for a classic study, see Gluckman, 1955) but harder to prove. Some support comes from simulation modelling work done using Thompson's dynamic reformulation of Douglas' theory of elementary forms reinforcing themselves and reacting against each other (Ingram et al., 2012). This suggests that there will be periods when the mutual countervailing of the forms against other, and also fissiparous rivalries among enclaved groups, rival patrons and clashing hierarchies, will lead to general disarray followed by periods of greater accommodation, thus cycling from generalized conflict amplification to containment and back again over time.

It is the style of thought that matters much more in explaining what, when and how we decide to act rather than the substantive ideas we claim to believe (Douglas, 1986). Rival styles encounter each other as generators of anomalies. Ritual enactments provide reinforcement for disputants, each to the point of disorganization. Each rite is a fight. Conflict and anomalies proliferate.

Tension, chaos and destruction then mount up until a tipping point is reached. The very dynamic in human social organization and thought that amplifies conflict also explains how it is attenuated (Douglas, 2004b). If rites build fights, they also quieten them. The original scapegoat was not sacrificially killed in blame and symbolic retribution at all, but was ritually released to wander freely (Douglas,

2004b). Anomaly is ritually accepted and thereby tamed. It is also by ritually enacting organization in response to the disorganizing experience of conflict that tensions and rivalries are attenuated, contained and channelled into more creative, more civilized practices, through which apparent incompatibilities in behaviour and rites can be seen as part of a larger frame. Formal and explicit negotiations and debates about substantive propositions may be effective or may fail. But in either case, their success or failure will depend on the informal, quotidian ritual interaction order sustained as we listen to and respond to the rhythms of other performances, and as we respond to the stylistic features of other modes of thought. The greater long-term and underlying importance of style over substance is absolutely not a triumph of the trivial over the tremendous, but its reverse; ritual performance is not an empty sham, but a token of deep sincerity (Douglas, 1970a, 1982c). We judge each other's commitment to the rites of peace by the style of thought that we, within the blinkers of our own thought style, can detect in others. In peace making, we make inferences about others' style of thought from observing them perform, whether those performances are the dance evenings through which the diplomats at Vienna in 1814 appear to have negotiated the treaty that gave Europe peace after a generation of slaughter (Vick, 2014; Zamoyski, 2007) or the planting of the *rumbim* bush in peace making by the Maring people of highland New Guinea (Rappaport, 1999), or the more ruggedly individualistic squaring off in private bilateral conversation that was the hallmark of the Paris Peace Conference of 1919 after the Great War (MacMillan, 2001).

Anything really important in human life will be ritually enacted with flags and totems, but even more crucially with gestures, demeanours, ways of eating and not eating (Douglas, 1975a), styles of speech and genres of writing. 'As a social animal, man is a ritual animal' (Douglas, 1966, 62). The notion that in 'modernity' we dispense with style and ritual and organize ourselves entirely around logical and explicit causal relations among substantive propositions is misguided. Yet in its continuing recurrence throughout human history, the notion of the rational transcending the ritual is itself revealing of a certain style of thought. Rationalities are limited in plurality. But each of them is institutional. It is not true that once we were ritually primitive in debarring anomalies and now we are propositionally modern in calculating what is to be done with them by force of logic (Douglas, 1966). On the contrary, throughout history we could not avoid doing both. As Douglas (2007, 146) wrote, '[w]e tend to assume that postmodernism is something that has only happened to ourselves', but this is quite unhistorical. For without a foundation of quotidian rites of conversation and exchange, we cannot know what other people, or even we ourselves, are effectively doing with whatever substantive propositions we deploy.

In the final years of her life, Douglas returned to reading Durkheim's last writings on the origins of the Great War, where in his little-known (1915) pamphlet *'Germany above All'*, he made much the same argument about the way in which the social organization behind Wilhelmine German militarism had reinforced itself not only ritually within the army but also in the thought style exhibited most overtly by some of the most influential thinkers in Germany before the war, such as Treitschke. On the one hand, German preparation exhibited all the appearance of rigorous military calculation and planning in Tirpitz's expansion of the navy and in the refinements of Alfred, Graf von Schlieffen's plan for the invasion of France. Yet this was done in ways that were blinkered by the very thought style on which it rested. Durkheim showed that the underlying embittered enclaving cultivated the rigid use of categories, the unchallenged assertion of the superiority of the members of the German enclave and the rejection of all external moral restraint, including those of rule-based law. Despite the contrast of empirical context (militarism versus religious sect), this self-assumed freedom from moral restraint of German state elites before the Great War is reminiscent of findings in a classic sociological work, much admired by Douglas, on religious enclaves in deep positive feedback, namely Karl Mannheim's account of the utopian mentality of Thomas Münzer and his grouping of radically communal Protestants at Mühlhausen, and also the embattled Anabaptist commune at Münster led by Jan Matthys and John of Leiden in the early sixteenth century. Douglas valued Mannheim's *Ideology and Utopia* (1936) precisely because it presented an integrated explanation of thought style as driven by forms of social organization, which also thereby explained conflict. What Douglas found important in Durkheim's account of the thought style in Treitschke's writings is that it provided a compelling example of the intimate relationship between calculating rationality in its toughest and most rigorous format in military planning, and the ritual cultivation of the most drastic feelings for the sacred and against the profane. This was the hallmark of enclaving. The German high command felt itself walled off from the wider world and freed from certain moral restraints.

Both in *Purity and Danger* and in her later work on ancient Israel, Douglas' argument is that this intimate connection between the supposedly rational and the supposedly irrational is no recent affair.

There is, in fact, no contrast between the modern and the primitive when it comes to understanding the basic social dynamic of human conflict and conflict attenuation. This recasts Durkheim's own argument leading to the same conclusion about sacred contagion and collective effervescence in *Elementary Forms*. If positive feedback ritually amplifies a thought style, which in turn makes calculative judgement into an instrument for its particular method of handling anomalies (6, 2011, 19, 297), this is exemplified among modern terrorist groups and in the ancient world alike. For example, Thucydides (1954) showed that Athenian thought style, ritually reinforced in great set-piece debates in the *agora*, had so blinkered the city's leaders' capacities to calculate that reliance on the short-term weighing of coercive resources proved catastrophically misleading in the conflicts in Sicily and with the former ally, Melos. In her 2003 work with Gerald Mars on terrorist enclaves, Douglas points to the same kind of ritual reinforcement contributing to strategic overreach. Here she draws on a cybernetic analysis to trace the causal pathways through which processes of reinforcement and destabilization occur. By implication, analysts of modern security threats also need conceptual tools to link ritual and material resources if they are correctly to infer the trajectory of rebellions as superficially different as those in Syria and eastern Ukraine.

Distinguishing the elementary forms of human social organization and thought style from each other and showing the feedback loops among them is therefore analytically essential in understanding the structure of conflict. But its importance does not consist at any very fundamental level – as is too often assumed – in identifying clashing worldviews, and then offering to explain people's particular and conflicting judgements as specific cases. In moving from Mannheim's (and perhaps also from Wildavsky's) concept of ideology to her own concept of thought style, Douglas made a vital innovation with great explanatory power. The importance of her theoretical achievement is that it provides a method by which to diagnose how far the process of ritual self-reinforcement of thought styles in each of the forms has gone in any situation and, conversely, what capacities and capabilities in performance and thought style are being cultivated, or have ritually been left to atrophy, in performing the attenuation of conflict.

In the next section, we examine why Douglas' account of how conflicts develop and abate is so important for the social sciences, and specifically for any social science-based contributions to the practice of efforts to channel and contain conflicts. Then we show how her argument has been extended and deepened by those who have drawn upon her work for inspiration. We examine how her understanding of particular causal mechanisms – first for conflict amplification and then for conflict attenuation – has been advanced. The chapter concludes with an assessment of Douglas' achievement, and legacy, and of the agenda for future work.

Why Douglas' Theory of Conflict Amplification and Containment Matters in Social Science and in Conflicts

In this section, we make the case that Douglas' arguments about how conflicts amplify and are contained are crucially important for social science because they offer a route beyond the weaknesses and limitations of all of the prevailing strategies that social scientists have inherited from the eighteenth- and nineteenth-century thinkers who first devised the basic ideas of social cohesion. And if Douglas' arguments are sound, then they also matter for the practice of conflict mitigation. To learn how to contain conflicts, we must devise ways of *performing* peace long before we work out schemes of mutual concessions on substantive demands. For peace treaties not based on a grasp of the organizational drivers of thought style and of style performed ritually will either fail to be accepted or will soon atrophy as the rites of conflict are reasserted.

In many of the disciplines of social science, conflict studies have been hived off to a special subdivision or field. If the organization of academic departments and journals are any indication of what we think we understand, then the novice social scientist might conclude that conflict is a separate problem, requiring quite different tools from those deployed for understanding peace, or perhaps even that peace is the normal condition from which we can measure conflict as an exception. The argument running through each of Douglas' writings is that both assumptions were among the mistakes that sank structural-functionalism; however, they persist, if in new forms across the social sciences.

One influential conventional explanation of why conflicts erupt and deepen falls into a modest number of schools. One body of work stresses the importance of interests by which people, organizations or nations are motivated and that are supposedly enduring and amenable to being regarded as fixed (e.g. rational choice theorists of conflict among nations, such as Bueno de Mesquita (2009), or of wars among absolutist monarchies, such as Rosenthal (1998), or bureaucratic politics theorists of conflicts within executive organizations such as Halperin et al. (2006) [1974]). 'Greed' theories of civil wars (e.g. Collier and Hoeffler, 2000) similarly rest on the same conception that interests can be taken as durable and fundamental.

At the opposite extreme are scholars who emphasize irrationality, either as the result of individual non rational factors in the biographies of particular leaders, or in the notion that people of all kinds are seized by the power of symbols (Edelman, 1985 [1967]), or simply that there is a large menu of particular but universal constant psychological biases (Kahneman et al., 1982; Kahneman, 2011), any one of which can be used to provide an explanation of a specific case (e.g. McDermott, 1998). A third group explains conflicts by reference to ideas as being the result of grand clashes of abstract theoretical beliefs or worldviews (Béland and Cox, 2011; Blyth, 1997; Huntington, 1996).

Douglas' account provides the most searching critique all these theories. She begins by building on Durkheim. Durkheim's (1984 [1893], 151–52) objection to the utilitarian or rational choice theories of his day was that interest is inconstant and, by itself, cannot bind even one side in a conflict. People have so many potentially internally conflicting interests that choosing which one to pursue, or even to pay attention to, is a problem that interest theory alone cannot solve. Even today, game theorists struggle to know which of a great many equilibria people will settle upon. Some of these theorists have resorted, in a fashion that Douglas would have called 'hand waving', to invoking a vaguely defined notion of 'culture' to explain such choices, but without a theory of what 'culture' is, or how it works, to help them explain which interests get picked (Eriksson, 2011, 101–39; and for Douglas' withering critique of such loose notions of culture, see her 2004 chapter discussed in Chapter 3 above, 'Traditional Culture: Let's Hear No More About It').

Douglas then enriched Durkheim's critique by showing that before we can know what people do with their many interests and for which of them they might fight, we need to understand how terms used in describing interests are classified and how the various possible kinds of thought style classifications that might be used to specify interests are actually deployed. Wildavsky (1994) showed that the concept of self-interest in rational choice theory is empty unless it is provided with content by something like Douglas' theory. For example, he was able to extend Douglas' theory to show that it made better sense than conventional economic theory could of the diversity of ways in which people do or do not tolerate externalities. Wildavsky et al. (1998) were the first to offer any schematic economic demand curves for people in each of the institutional settings, something taken further in 6 (2002a). However, to complete the argument, we then need to explain why thought styles have arisen in the first place. Interests of a kind that are sufficiently salient to people and sufficiently weighted to be the subject of what Hume (1969 [1739–40]) called the 'passions' are the very final stage of the causal process that Douglas (1986) set out in *How Institutions Think*.

Nor will pointing to 'irrationalities' provide a way forward. At best, the list makers working in the psychology of biases in decision making provide only description. Why of the many available is one psychological bias followed rather than another? Why do decision makers have one reference point against which they might determine what counts as a loss rather than another? Why do some symbols excite or disgust some people, but leave others indifferent? Psychological theories of bias, of the kind proposed by Kahneman, cannot alone answer these questions.

Many people may share an ideological belief, but few may actually go so far as to wage war for it. Often believers are quite prepared to accommodate and trim, while nevertheless insisting – in fact, quite plausibly – on the sincerity of their beliefs in 'the American way', or in the eventual victory of communism, or in European unity, or whatever it might be. Yet other apparently ideologically driven true believers will not compromise. Like the Christian fundamentalists of Münster and Mühlhausen, as described by Karl Mannheim, some are prepared to die together, claiming that they do so for their beliefs. Others, sharing more or less the same beliefs – the Mennonites, who were contemporaries of the Münster communards, for example – seek only a quiet corner where they can be left alone to apply their convictions. Beliefs alone therefore cannot be held to explain the difference between violence and peace. If we are to understand both the roots of conflict and how to contain it, we must ask not what people believe, but why they do the particular things they actually do with whatever it is they believe. For that task, Douglas argues, we need a concept of thought style and an explanation of it rooted in how people are organized.

Small group dynamics are some help. Janis' (1982 [1972]) draws attention to institutional ordering in small groups of decision makers, for example. But there are many more kinds of ordering than the 'groupthink' invoked by Janis' theory. Indeed, Janis' cases span some where people follow leaders and swallow their doubts out of apparent fear of being sanctioned and others – enclaved, in Douglas' terms – where people think collectively in ways that sustain sincerely felt commitments. Even within the category of groupthink, surely these are very different styles of thought, because there are different institutional orderings that lead people to pursue agreement above all else.

Douglas first set out her critique of these theories of too simple rationality and of far too simple irrationality when debating with the psychologists of 'risk perception' (Douglas, 1985) who took passions such as 'dread' (Slovic et al., 1981) for granted, in ways that precluded any larger explanation of how dread was caused than the numbers of deaths concentrated in any one place and time. A low level of explanatory ambition is apparent in Sjöberg's (1997) reply to Douglas' arguments about risk perception. For him, as for many psychologists, statistical goodness of fit was more important than fundamental causal explanation. What Douglas doubted was that there was any point in simply redescribing fear and dread in numerical terms. What mattered, and what was not being explained by the likes of Sjöberg, was why people were fearful in the first place, not what features could be found among the things that people fear. As her focus widened from risk conflicts in the 1990s to understanding conflict much more generally (e.g. Douglas, 1993a; Douglas and Mars, 2003) Douglas applied similar critiques to the similar claims as they reappeared in the guise of explanations of conflict.

Theories of conflict containment differ little in their fundamental conception of causation from those of conflict amplification just mentioned. For many scholars, bargaining and negotiation are required in order to address the substantive interests presumed to be really at stake (e.g. Pruitt and Carnevale, 1993). In its most ambitious version, this approach aspires to conflict 'resolution' by finding a structure of payoffs based on presumed interests around which people might be willing to settle. In effect, game theory is taken to be a guide to peace making. Bias, intransigence, small group dynamics, etc. are taken to be either obstacles to be overcome, through getting embattled parties to focus more intently on their interests, or else minor noise that need not disrupt the theory's account of what it takes to be the main stream of cases. Burton (1990) dignified these interests with the title of basic human needs and took them to remain stably ordered according to Maslow's well-known hierarchy of such needs. Indeed, declaring interests to have the status of needs is usually a way of insisting that they are to be taken for granted. Mediators therefore address them in turn. As far as other biases are concerned, in Burton's version of this theory, they can be treated as 'norms', which have to be observed as side-constraints. When people invoke claims that seem to suggest intransigence, in Burton's view, the proper response is simply to move down the hierarchy of needs to offer more security, more participation, more community, more recognition of identity, as if these things are resources to be exchanged, in order to address interests. Yet, as with interest theories of conflict amplification, this approach can say little about those who pursue conflict with little regard for their material interests or their own payoffs. In an age when suicide terrorism is once again widely used and when movements have once again emerged with only demands that cannot be negotiated or even met by surrender, short of their enemies being exterminated, the puzzle of understanding deep intransigence has become urgent. Interest-based approaches offer us little help.

For those theorists for whom people in conflict are prisoners of pre-given bias or symbol, the task for pursuing the abatement of the conflict is either to persuade them to adopt a different reference point from which to measure what they count as a loss or from which they measure what is 'available', or else to offer to be more respectful of their symbols. It is little surprise that anthropologists who have confined themselves to documenting the power of symbols have little to say about the conditions or mechanisms by which people might abate their symbolic fury. Those conflict management scholars who argue for rich and detailed descriptive secondary 'interpretation' by mediators to reconstruct accounts of the primary 'interpretations' of the parties to the conflict, as a way of supplementing work on interests (Ross, 1993), are in effect trying simply to add bias and symbol to an interest-based account. Their hope is that a sympathetic descriptive understanding of beliefs and ideas will lubricate a process of substantive talks about demands. Douglas was not at all persuaded that sending for the anthropologist bearing a can of symbolic oil to lubricate the more difficult areas of negotiation would have any positive effect whatsoever, for this is to elevate symbols as cogs in the machine rather than seeing them, as Durkheim had done, as outcomes of ritual action. This critique points to a general difficulty with symbolic approaches. Theorists who see conflicts as clashes of ideas either have to wait for believers to exhaust themselves or else for anomalies to clog up a worldview to the point where it is evident to all but the most intransigent that the choice of some other ideology might offer a clearer view of things (cf. Hall, 1993).

Across the social sciences, perhaps the most influential perspectives on how conflicts might be contained are offered by institutionalist theories. In international relations, for example, institutionalists suggest that conflicts can be contained only by the creation of, for the most part, formal and explicit institutions such as treaties, international agencies and common economic zones, and procedures for agreeing standards such as human rights, but not excluding some more informal institutions, such as the conventions of diplomacy that range from the genres of diplomatic note writing to status rules for embassies. Many of these institutions are defined by their strong regulation and already strong integration. In Douglas' terms, therefore, they have strong elements of hierarchy. Trajectories of drift, layering, displacement or conversion have been identified through which institutions, having once been created, might be maintained or grow or be substituted by other institutions (Mahoney and Thelen, 2010). The puzzle is how to get such strong integration going and then institutionalized across the divided parties in the first place, from an initial position of conflict. On this key point, institutional theory has less to say. Typically, scholars point to individuals who fill the gap by becoming 'institutional entrepreneurs' (Lawrence et al., 2009) or 'policy entrepreneurs' (Kingdon, 1995 [1984]). But where, in a conflict zone, are they to be found or grown? The vocabulary of entrepreneurship is redolent of individualism, with its capacities for individual brokering. Most institutional theories of conflict containment simply assume that these capacities will be available and that, when they are available, the 'entrepreneurs' will use them to build peaceful institutions. But in deep conflict, especially where rival enclaves dominate the available space, they may well not be available or, worse, they may be unreliable.

One reason that Douglas concentrated research during several periods of her career on enclaves (especially Douglas, 1993a; but see also Douglas and Wildavsky, 1982; Douglas and Mars, 2003) was precisely that she recognized that a theory of conflict with nothing to say about the causes of intransigence will also have little convincing to say about how intransigence might be abated. In her 2003 study with Mars, she showed just why leaders in enclaves find it so difficult to play the role of 'institutional entrepreneurs' for conflict containment without placing their leadership in jeopardy (Richards, 1999). When in her final years she turned back to the basis of hierarchical institutions, using cases from ancient Israel, she was, in effect, trying to work out how to fill the gap in the institutionalist literatures without simply using individual 'entrepreneurs' as a kind of theoretical *deus ex machina*. Moreover, her late work on conflict containment in ancient Israel contains a clear, if implicit critique of the notion that peace making is fundamentally achieved by formal institutions or forums in which substantive claims are traded up and down a hierarchy of needs or interests presumed to be given. What mattered was the informal institutional work, and this could only be done performatively and ritually, well before any possibility of formal negotiation. We glimpse it in action in the evening dances after the end of each session at the Congress of Vienna, especially when formal talks had broken down. We also glimpse it in the actions of a North London rabbi who at the height of the Israeli bombing of Gaza in 2014 imposed upon himself the disciplines of the Muslim Ramadan fast. Ritually induced shared feelings might, he appeared to imply, one day bridge huge chasms of institutional misunderstanding.

Douglas' arguments about conflict matter today, then, for several reasons. First, where each of the main approaches in social science theories falls short, her approach offers a way forward. For those frameworks that simply lack adequate variety, her explanation of the range of elementary forms allows us to recognize quite distinct forms of intransigence in, for example, enclaved groups and in structurally isolate despotic figures (6, 2011, 2014a, 2014b) and to appreciate that these are neither outliers nor noise in the data, nor yet simply noise in the data generated by groups uninterestingly deficient in rationality by comparison with those who are ready to negotiate and exchange. Second, Douglas (1999b, 2004b) emphasized the ritual basis of all reconciliation in *mise-en-scène*, in performance, and in enactment by rite of engagement. In her (1999b, 2004b) work on priestly reconciliation in ancient Israel, she conversely stressed the institutional basis in which the cultivation of ritual skills and commitment for the peace makers. This served to show that these skills might be sustained within at least one of the elementary forms. In *Leviticus as Literature*, it is hierarchy that is shown to be able to do the job. But that is only one of the options. She did not live to explore the others at all fully. Nevertheless, her argument provides a strategy for understanding causal mechanisms without having to resort to the theoretical equivalent of the well-known board game's 'get out of jail free' cards. Third, her account explains why, in some very special cases, each of the conventional approaches might initially have appeared to have had some traction. For example, in those conflicts in which rival, individualistically ordered patrons are manoeuvring for position, the game theoretic conception of identifying payoffs makes approximate sense, even though it cannot explain the emergence of actors with what, by the end of negotiations, can seem to be intractable demands. When ideas, beliefs and worldviews seem to be at stake in the manner suggested by ideational theories, Douglas forces us to ask who would wish to place such weight on grand and abstract principle, even at the expense of material interests, and perhaps even at the risk of their own destruction, and why and how might such an apparently suicidal thought style have emerged. And equally for those theories that emphasize process above all – stressing interpretation (Ross, 1993) and respect for identity, dialogue, hermeneutics and communication (Dukes, 1996; Jabri, 1996) – Douglas' theory forces us to ask who, working under what kinds of organization, would care most about process in this manner and why it would matter most to them.

Having been steeped in the Durkheimian tradition, Douglas appreciated that ritual was of central importance in conflict containment, and that above all ritual addresses itself to the performance of social time. As Hubert (1999 [1905]) had argued, all forms of social life need to be ritually 'clocked' in order to maintain or reinstate a sense of coherence and purposefulness. In her late (especially Douglas, 2004b) writings on conflict containment in ancient Israel, Douglas returned to this theme in her analysis of the role of ritually defining periods in the episode of the 'scape goat', in purification, in atonement and even in the circular structure of some key written genres. Ritual circles (often enacted as round dances) are powerful expressions of a sense of dynamic social order. Individuals come and go, but the community circles onwards. To focus on the ritual 'clocking' of time is therefore a way to approach the very basic mechanisms of institutional performance. Conflict seeks to disorient the enemy by disrupting the clocking function. Peace making is fundamentally concerned with restoring this function and providing means of coordination across groups that move to a different beat. As we shall see below, scholars who drew upon Douglas have shown that in deep conflict in enclaves, future time is foreshortened while the past is imagined to be long (Rayner, 1982), and that the other forms show their own characteristic temporal adjustment (Peck and 6, 2006, 50–77). The containment of conflict therefore rests, Douglas showed in the case of the development of the ritual calendar in conflict-ridden ancient Israel, in the accommodation of the rhythms of time sustained by the elementary forms of organization of each of the conflicting parties, as well as the timeframes of the rituals by which they are brought together. Priests and sects both get their feasts and their lamentations scheduled into the rhythm of the year. Today, to sustain the peace process, the parades commissions of Northern Ireland devote huge efforts to the preparation of agreed ritual calendars for processions in each city by which anniversaries may and may not be marked. If we are to live together in ways that will enable us to channel our conflicts into more civilized and restrained practices, Douglas implies, we need to dance our common time to each other's rhythms as well as our own.

Finally, Douglas hardly ever wrote of 'conflict management' and rarely of 'conflict resolution' precisely because these terms are the ones preferred by the theorists of interests, ideas and institutions whose arguments she found inadequate. Her theory shows that conflict is inherent in the elementary forms of human social organization and thought, but unrestrained savagery certainly is not the inevitable outcome. Ritual action for containment is possible, by which conflict can be civilized into a less chaotic dynamic tension. Sennett (2012) is perhaps the most extreme of those theorists of ritual who are romantic about its possibilities for new beginnings. Many of those who invoke Durkheim's name tend to do so in pursuit of communitarian visions in which strong social integration is emphasized (e.g. Bellah, 1985; Taylor, 2007), but without recognizing fully either the limitations of such tight integration when it leads to rejection of those outside the circle of integration or the countervailing forms of organizing that it provokes. By contrast, Douglas' argument for rites of 'reconciliation' is dry-eyed, limited and stoic. She offered a hard-headed recognition that there are organizing as well as disorganizing phases in both kinds of feedback dynamics. The possibility of organic solidarity rests, as Durkheim suspected it would have to, on human capabilities to sustain certain kinds of ritual practices, which might fix particular categories, at least for a while. But ritual cultivates thought styles of many kinds rather than, as romantics such as Sennett imagine, only strongly socially integrated and harmonious community. The implication – as her theory of positive feedback dynamics showed – is that no one form of social organization could contain conflict for long. Conflict is a neverending part of the human condition, and ritual engagement allows successive states of hard-won but temporary social coordination to be attained. In the end, there is no perfectly conflict-free society. Understanding of process is all.

Developments in Douglas' Theory of Conflict Amplification and Containment

We next examine how far Douglas' distinctive arguments about conflict amplification and containment have been used, and further developed, by those who draw upon her work. Just as in the previous section, here we begin with the amplification of conflict and then turn to its abatement.

Much work drawing upon Douglas to provide explanations of conflict has been concerned with its amplification. There are several reasons for this. One is the simplest. Douglas' most profound work on reconciliation was written late in her career. Therefore, scholars have had less time to absorb its significance. The second is the most obvious. That later work was written using biblical case studies and these have limited appeal to social scientists. The third reason is that the best known of her contributions are her early arguments in *Purity and Danger* about people responding to anomalies by debarring them. This can readily be invoked by scholars looking for concepts with which to describe conflict amplification. Her widely known fourfold typology also rather readily lends itself to explanations of why people fail to understand one another and thus come into conflict.

Douglas' (1966) invocation in *Purity and Danger* of the 'dirt as matter out of place' in her account of how and why people seek to debar anomalies through prohibition continues to be used by some scholars interested in conflict amplification. In examining the wars following the breakup of the former Yugoslavia in the 1990s, Hayden (1996) documents how classifications hardened, and how differences in 'culture' came to be treated as differences of necessity and essence. His use of Douglas is confined to offering her account of cleansing of dirt in *Purity and Danger* as one applicable to ethnic cleansing. Other writers continue to draw upon 'dirt as matter out of place' as an explanation of latent forms of oppression, for example, by class. Thus, Beall's (2006) study of Christian street sweepers in the predominantly Muslim city of Faisalabad in Pakistan argues that the 'caste-like' disdain with which many of the population treat this group of workers is an all-too-predictable consequence of the category of dirt, which supposedly reinforces beliefs about pollution and danger.

The limitation of such studies is that they select only one of the options Douglas identifies by which anomalous things might be managed. As early as the final chapter of *Purity and Danger* on the Lele manner of dealing with the puzzling pangolin and in her account of the limited variety of elementary forms in *Natural Symbols*, Douglas had shown that several other things can be done with anomalies apart from simply debarring them. Thus, it requires specific explanation why people in the Balkans or in Pakistan do not, for example, welcome anomalies as opportunities, or treat them as matters for sophisticated adjustments to achieve regulated consistency, or regard them simply as facts of life to be coped with. In addition Douglas showed consistently throughout her work that the contingency leading people into one or more of these strategies is not a contingency in the categories of 'dirt' or ethnicity or street sweeping. Ideas alone are insufficient to explain why people use ideas to justify violence or oppression. Rather, we need to explain why certain ways of using categories and styles of managing ideas come to seem to be available and intelligible to people in specific settings. The contingency on which this turns, Douglas argued, is one of social organization. If we are to understand why ethnic categories came to deployed in justification for slaughter in the Balkans in the 1990s, we need to understand the process of enclaving in the informal institutions that took over following the breakup of the state in order to see why particular usages of specific categories became available, appeared apparently intelligible or simply seemed convenient, not to mention credible as threats to certain other people. Hayden's and Beall's argument is at best a proximate explanation, which risks taking justifications for causes. They deploy, it is true, a Douglasian argument, but one from the 1960s, before she had developed the full theory of variety in the management of anomalies, conflict amplification and conflict containment.

Douglas' typology of elementary forms has been quite widely used to understand conflicts, and this literature is growing by the year, notably in political science and especially in the study of environmental politics, as well as in business and management studies, organization studies, public administration, work on consumer behaviour and other fields. We make no attempt to review this burgeoning body of work here. Instead, we pick out a handful of especially influential studies in order to briefly illustrate some of the main ways in which Douglas' typology has been used to understand conflict amplification. These instances also sometimes point to limitations in the ways in which the underlying theory has been used.

Some of the most important developments of Douglas' arguments by other scholars have been in the specification of causal mechanisms. Thus, for example, Thompson's and Wildavsky's (1986) paper on bias first worked out Douglas' own rather loosely characterized idea of 'muffled ears' in each of the forms (e.g. Douglas, 1992a) into a much more fully specified mechanism of information rejection (cf. 6, 2004). This was important for two reasons. First, much of Douglas' own work in the 1970s and early 1980s had emphasized the biases that social organization *positively* cultivates. Yet Durkheim's central insight was that institutions sustain themselves by maintaining *negative* rites, in which people perform prohibitions or avoidance. What Thompson and Wildavsky provided in the concept of information rejection was a mechanism for each of the elementary forms by which the negative rites of avoiding or prohibiting information work to shape their styles of thought. However, as each form rejects information proposed by people working under other forms, so conflict can steadily amplify. Second, Thompson's and Wildavsky's argument enriched Douglas' own argument about how the management of anomalies works in amplifying conflict. For the information that is rejected by each thought style is that which is anomalous within people's schemes of classification, whether their rejection takes the form of cramping and confining the information by adjustment into a set of rules in hierarchy, debarring it as appalling in enclaved settings or ignoring it as useless and inconvenient in individualistic ordering, or trying to work around it in isolate ordering.

Causal mechanisms have also been developed for understanding relations among and within each of the four elementary forms. For example, 6 (2014b) emphasizes the ways in which positive feedback in some forms, such as the despotic variant of isolate ordering, can serve as a mechanism of provocation for others, such as enclaved groups, resulting in a severe countervailing response.

Gross and Rayner's study *Measuring Culture* (1986) was very important in developing specific fieldwork and data analysis methods for exploring Douglas' theory in cases of conflict over environmental issues. Moreover, Gross and Rayner were scrupulous in their insistence that every effort must be made to focus on social organization among the people being studied, so that data can be collected independently on institutional ordering and on thought style. The work provided a set of algorithms for data analysis by which Douglas' theory might be examined empirically. A key contribution was to demonstrate the ways in which a sociometric network analysis of ties of acquaintanceship, friendship, collegiality and (conversely) negative ties of hostility and avoidance could be used as valid and reliable proxies for assessing dimensions of social regulation and social integration. Unfortunately, although it remains a most impressive statement of method, Gross' and Rayner's strictures are very demanding, and few studies have had the resources fully to implement every part of their approach. Moreover, there is a remarkable absence in their book. The argument that ritual provides a key causal mechanism by which social organization is performed is not as central to the theory espoused in *Measuring Culture* as Douglas herself demanded, at least from *Natural Symbols* onwards. On the few occasions on which the topic is discussed, it is treated as just one more indicator that researchers might use to code for social organization as structure. At this point in the mid 1980s, it appears that ritual was eclipsed by a focus on the *explanans* of structure. Below, we suggest that in subsequent work, it tended to be eclipsed by *explananda* of ideas, discourses, beliefs and worldviews. Either way, a central component of Douglas' own theoretical framework was missing.

Douglas acknowledged frequently in print that Thompson (especially 1979, 1982b) had first provided the dynamics for what in early formulations (Douglas, 1970a, 1982a [1978]; Douglas and Isherwood, 1979) had been a static system of comparative analysis. The point of the dynamics was, in the first instance, to provide better-specified accounts of how and by what trajectories conflicts are amplified. Thompson's first (1982a and b) formulations of the dynamics drew upon catastrophe theory and especially that tradition's use of topological representations. At this stage, shocks, jolts and surprises provided the main causal impetus for dynamism. By 1990, when the book *Cultural Theory* (Thompson et al., 1990) was published, the dynamics were rather differently specified. Now the argument drew much more on cybernetic theory and especially Ashby's (1956) concept of requisite variety. Thompson's theory of surprises, as offered in *Cultural Theory*, represented a major extension of Douglas' own arguments. Instead of surprises simply being exogenously driven shocks, Thompson et al. argued that surprises were produced by the very same process of positive feedback within and negative feedback among the elementary forms that also explained why people responded to surprises in particular ways. *Cultural Theory* also advanced the idea that cycling and instability were a central prediction of the theory; in effect, a final nail had been hammered into the coffin of structural-functionalism. Whereas *Risk and Culture* (Douglas and Wildavsky, 1982) privileged just one pairing of forms, *Cultural Theory* now explored the dynamics of formation, self-reinforcement to the point of disorganization and conflict, among all the forms of institutional hybridity that logic might suggest.

Yet in one respect, *Cultural Theory* also took a step back from Douglas' argument in *How Institutions Think*. Like a ring composition, Douglas' feedback loop does have a beginning – namely, in informal institutions of social organization. It has a primary phase, which runs from institutions to thought style. The loop running back from thought style to reinforce social organization (and thereby to undermine other elementary forms of organization) is secondary. For Thompson et al., this loop has neither a beginning nor an end. 'Culture' is, for them, a manifold, in which institutions and thought styles are inextricably mingled. Indeed, in *Cultural Theory*, Thompson et al. called them simply 'ways of life'. Douglas' own reconstruction of positive feedback had arisen from informal institutional cultivation of thought style in her *How Institutions Think* (1986). Here, her equivalent of the cybernetic machinery of feedback had been derived deductively from her Durkheimian institutional theory. But in Thompson et al.

(1990, 200–9), Douglas' insistence on the primacy of institutions over thought style and on the loop having a beginning had been dropped. In *Cultural Theory*, feedback processes between these two things play a less central role in driving the dynamics; instead, feedback is simply within and among manifolds called 'cultures'. This is the most important reason why the cybernetic concept of feedback did not play as central a role in the dynamic theory presented in *Cultural Theory* as one might expect. Only later were the relationships between the two forms of feedback presented as central to the dynamics of the theory (Douglas and Mars, 2003; 6 2003).

Nevertheless, for much of the 1980s and 1990s, the *empirical* literature drawing inspiration from Douglas' typology had maintained her commitment to the argument that institutional forms of organization explain thought style in conflict. For example, Schwarz and Thompson's major (1990) study on how conflicts over energy policy were amplified to the point of an intransigent stand-off between people organized in each of the four elementary forms argued that it was indeed the social institutions in which the advocates of positions were located that explained their incapacity to appreciate each other's potential contributions or to compromise. On the other hand, this work also showed a much closer attention to contrasting statements of belief than to the analysis either of social structure, as Gross and Rayner (1986) had called for, or to the actual patterns of behaviour manifesting themselves in relations among people, as Douglas' own ethnographic work had exemplified among the Lele.

This tendency became increasingly marked in writings of those who adopted the badge of 'cultural theory'. In 1998, Hood published his major theoretical study on public management, *The Art of the State*. In that work, the four forms do indeed appear as 'ways of organizing', which Hood traces enduring conflict within the executive arm of the state over centuries and even (in his discussion of ancient Chinese systems) over millennia. Yet much of his focus is on tropes used in justification and on normative claims about how public management should be done, rather than on observed behaviour. His chapters on each of the four forms do not distinguish *explanans* from *explanandum* within each one. However, Hood (1998, 208–19) laid out an important application of the dynamic theory to show that conflicts among approaches to organizing the state were driven by a positive feedback loop in which self-reinforcement in each way of organizing produced anomalies and disorganization; this was an argument that would be developed with comparative analysis of empirical examples of 'modernization' in public management in Margetts et al. (2010).

Also in 1998, Michael Thompson and Steve Rayner, who had both worked with Douglas since the 1970s, published an influential two-part article on environmental conflicts (Thompson and Rayner, 1998; Thompson et al., 1998). The study marked the completion of a shift away from the *explanans* of social organization and towards an almost exclusive focus in data analysis on the *explanandum* of thought, for Thompson and Rayner now argued for 'discourse analysis' and 'constructivism' to be, respectively, the method and the epistemology to be followed in examining the typological theory of conflict amplification in environmental stand-offs.

It is ironic that only a year later, Douglas published, in the prominent journal *Nature*, her review of Adam Kuper's history of anthropological theorizing on the notion of culture, in which she bluntly distanced herself from 'idealism', meaning an exclusive focus on ideas, beliefs and discourse as if they were causally fundamental.

The tendency to take Douglas' typology and to use it as an argument about conflicting beliefs and worldviews is, at least implicitly, to reject the institutional theory that underpinned it. This was by no means entirely new. The writings from the 1980s of the political scientist Aaron Wildavsky (e.g. Wildavsky, 1987) had overtly done this, even though he claimed to be following Douglas' approach. To be fair, in his final years Wildavsky showed a greater appreciation of the institutional foundations of Douglas' thought, as his 1989 and 1994 articles demonstrate. Yet by the late 1990s and early 2000s, the commonest type of application of Douglas' typology was to contrast clusters of ideas, and thereby to explain conflict amplification as the result of a process by which big ideas, measured by attitudes on general statements of worldview, explain little ideas, meaning particular judgements, decisions or actions on particular cases. Thus, for example, Shin et al. (1989) offered survey data to explain one kind of general idea – strong or weak belief in democracy – by reference to another – namely, whether people held worldviews that fell mainly into one of Douglas' four forms. Using qualitative data, Ney (2000) examined conflicts over pension policy in Europe by contrasting normative visions. On a much larger scale, Davy's (1997) study of siting conflicts over locally unwanted uses of land documented the rival moral and philosophical bases of claims to explain the acute difficulties of polarization often found in such conflicts. U.S.-based scholars working with the typology have come very largely to use it to argue that big ideas explain little ideas, as a 2011 special issue of the journal *PS: Political Science and Politics* on 'A Cultural Theory of Politics' demonstrated. For example, Ripberger et al. (2011) present survey data correlating 'cultural orientations', meaning positions held on quite general normative propositions, with specific views about nuclear weapons and terrorism. Others, such as Kahan, whose work we discussed in Chapter 2, continue to cleave to methodological individualism and therefore quite explicitly reject Douglas' theory even as they use an amended version of her typology.

In a period when many social scientists had become enamoured of ideational theories, perhaps this twisting of Douglas' arguments was not surprising. For the fetishism of cognition, as if it were the fundamental cause of everything in social life, is not confined to post-structuralists, or to discourse analysis of the kind that explains any particular thought by referring it to an underlying general one, such as a 'script', 'cultural model' (e.g. D'Andrade and Strauss, 1992) or worldview. With regard to ideology, it is also increasingly fashionable in political science (Béland and Cox, 2011), especially since the work of Peter A. Hall (e.g. 1993). One widely used answer to ideationalism, deriving from Garfinkel's (1967) arguments, is that much human activity is only rationalized with ideas after the event, as the 'sense-making' literature has shown (Weick, 1995). Explaining little or particular ideas with the claim that they are consistent with people's big or general ideas is a strategy that sacrifices too much causality for a very modest gain in goodness of fit, and rarely does it yield much useful generality. It is not always true that people approach their adversities and opportunities with heads stuffed with concepts. Institutions sustain many more intelligent ways of acting than simply following 'scripts'. Moreover, substantive ideas such as ideologies provide people with surprisingly little guidance about what to do when making specific decisions, as close analysis of histories of debates within governing party groups reminds us – hence the need to explain thought style and not just normative propositions that people believe or claim to believe. But Douglas took the argument much further. She showed that if the ideational argument were true, then conflict containment becomes very difficult to explain.

The strategy of using big ideas to explain little ideas can readily be brought to bear on polarization in order to show that contrasting specific preferences are irreconcilable because they are supposedly rooted in altogether grander and more general normative claims. For once we have made the move to claims of general principle, compromise readily comes to be seen as unprincipled and therefore, if beliefs alone determine what people are willing to do, it becomes harder to achieve. Ideational explanations, even with the benefit of a typology that allows the scholar to capture more variety, lend themselves to explaining intransigence and conflict amplification.

Yet in that case, we are entitled to ask, how is peace possible? Indeed, how is sustained human social organization possible without collapse? How, for example, did the general religious and political crisis of the seventeenth century in Europe (Parker, 2013) come to an end at all? For this kind of question, ideational explanation is much less convincing, because if the elementary forms consist, contrary to Douglas' argument, in basic but incompatible ideas of justification, then it is hard to see how humanity has sustained any degree of organization. Durkheim's point in *The Division of Labour in Society* was that, notwithstanding that we tend to classify each other in ways that might emphasize difference, there are possibilities for organization that recognize difference and dissimilarity, yet sustain varying kinds of cooperation, even if in the most minimal cases this might be only cooperation in staying out of each other's way. This is why, for instance, in the case of implacably opposed religious groups in the Netherlands in the seventeenth century, schism and temporary exile and the ritualized manner in which such detachments were attained proved to be a restrained way of handling deep ideological differences, and far more conducive to peace than the massacres and executions they displaced.

Douglas' writings such as *In the Wilderness* (1993a provide a subtler answer to the ideational account of conflict amplification described above. What would have to be the case, Douglas' argument leads us to ask, for people to cleave so firmly to the substantive claims in their statements of worldview and principle that intransigence becomes the most obvious strategy to guide their actions? After all, this is not how people use their beliefs in many contexts. It is not, for example, how people use their beliefs when they conduct trading most of the time, or how politicians in many parliaments work, even in less stable countries, or how many family members sustain their commitments to each other. If people cleave so exclusively and rigidly to the substance of beliefs as claimed by the social scientists who argue that 'big ideas explain little ideas', then we must ask what danger they could plausibly fear from any more accommodating or flexible way of handling their own and other people's beliefs. Douglas' answer is to suggest that it would be in enclaved social organization, where exchange and authority are unavailable, that resort to the assertion of principle would make most sense. The world of belief-driven action described by ideational explanation is thus a special case, and one where what is really special is not so much the fact that people hold particular worldviews as the style of thought with which they are used. That cognitively all too strongly integrated thought style that rejects influence from what it classifies as alien beliefs, Douglas argues, is best explained as the one cultivated in contexts of weak external social regulation and very strong social integration. And this is why 'power of ideas' social theories cannot achieve the general application their advocates claim for them, even when they use an ideational version of Douglas' own typology.

There have, though, been some studies of conflict amplification inspired by Douglas, which have cleaved closely to this argument about the foundational role of social organization and its ritual dynamics. Richards' (1996, 2005, 2007) study on the escalation of the conflict in the 1990s in Sierra Leone into one of the bloodiest civil wars in recent times argues that it was the ritual practices in the enclaved groups that came together to form the armed rebel organization the Revolutionary United Front (RUF), which explained the very rapid and extreme positive feedback into the most brutal sacred contagion. Richards specifically drew on Douglas' analysis of ritual practice in enclaves in *In the Wilderness* (Douglas, 1993a) to show that performance was critical to positive feedback in bringing about amplification.

However, it is significant that Richards' later work (2010, 2013) went on to show that it was a modified form of ritual performance that eventually made the climbdown from war possible. In the same way, 6's (2011) study re-examining the decision making in the U.S., Soviet and Cuban governments during the Cuban Missile Crisis argues that when the social organization of the small groups of decision makers in Washington, Moscow and Havana are analysed separately from their thought styles and when the quotidian ritual interaction order of their meetings is examined, not only does it become possible to understand how the conflict amplified but it can also be explained why the superpowers were willing at the last moment to accept the 'unprincipled' compromise that they did. In that book, it is thought style rather than ideology that does the heavy lifting with respect to the *explanandum*. It develops Douglas' arguments that we paint our thought style, and not in the first instance our ideologies, onto the faces of the people with whom we must deal, and the resulting misunderstandings explain amplification, and that the ritual capacities cultivated in each form sustain different capacities to compromise.

How then does Douglas' argument about the looping causal dynamics of performance, thought style and reorganization enable us to understand the basis for attenuation of conflict, and for its containment and channelling in more creative and civilized forms?

Two possibilities suggest themselves. One is that there might be some way of offsetting each of the forms with each of the others, so that none is absolutely dominant, perhaps so that the dependencies among them can be supported. Positive feedback within each of the forms might then be constrained and balanced by the others. As we have seen, this approach was developed principally by Thompson (1996, 2008) and Verweij (Verweij and Thompson, 2006; Verweij, 2011). The argument builds on Durkheim's insight in *The Division of Labour in Society* (1984 [1893]) that organic solidarity, or organization that recognizes, celebrates and integrates difference and dissimilarity among people, as they classify each other, must rest on creating mutual dependencies among the institutions that make for that dissimilarity. Thompson brought to this the analytical modelling resources of cybernetic theory and, in particular, the concept, taken from Ashby (1956), of 'requisite variety'. In one variant, each of the elementary forms should be sufficiently strongly articulated to offset the others. Each form on its own is a manifestation of mechanical solidarity. Mutual insistence on the dissimilarity of the others results in what the Dutch call 'pillarization', which describes a social landscape integrated through mutual insistence that differences must be maintained through separated spheres of organizational action.

From the legal scholar Schapiro (1988), Thompson (e.g. 1997a, 1997b) borrowed the term 'clumsy institution' to describe the concept of an arrangement that publicly manifested just enough of each of the elementary forms to provide the necessary offsetting. It represented a form not of consensus, but of explicit or implicit compromise. Empirically, the argument drew upon his studies of the ways in which hierarchical ordering provided services for individualistic trading, with both kept honest by moral advocacy cultivated in enclaves in communities in the Alps (Price and Thompson, 1997) and the Himalayas (Thompson et al., 1986). The precise definition of the relationship among the four forms required for clumsiness has varied. For example, Verweij et al. (2006, 20) sometimes describe clumsy institutions as ones characterized by a certain kind of outcome – namely, where none of the four forms is so underarticulated that it is excluded. Sometimes, clumsiness is seen as a certain kind of process, in which the ponderous means of arriving at an outcome is the defining feature. If the concept of clumsiness is to have a basis in Douglas' theory of institutions, then we need greater precision about the different ways in which the elementary forms might be related to each other, such that each might limit the aggrandisement of the others. First, there must be some stability, at least for a while. Not every mix is a settlement. Moreover, some settlements might be simply gridlocked, which typically offers few advantages over stand-off in conflict. Among four-way settlements that might contain or attenuate conflict and therefore might exhibit organic solidarity among the four mechanical ones, there are several possibilities. 6 (2003) distinguished four (cf. Thacher and Rein's (2004) independently developed three strategies for relating conflicts within their ideational theory). First, people might constrain conflict by arranging *separate* social zones for hierarchy, individualism, enclaved and isolate life, in which each is buffered from the others. A second possibility is that there might be some *neutral zone* in which negotiations might be sustained, but where none of the forms has a power of absolute veto or insistence. A third possibility builds on the argument in Verweij et al. (2006) about each form providing services to the others. They offer a schematic scenario in which hierarchy specifies the property rights that are traded under individualistic ordering to provide economic dynamism that is subjected to moral restraint by enclaved movements, while isolate ordering provides a space in which those disadvantaged or excluded by each of these forms can sustain a basic kind of life, at least until opportunities become available to some of them to find ways into spaces ordered by one of other forms. This kind of arrangement might be regarded as a kind of institutional *exchange*. Finally, there might be a degree of melding and blending among the four in order to allow for some *hybridity*. We can readily identify different vulnerabilities to positive feedback in each of these kinds of four-way settlements. Yet, depending on the degree to which conflicts have developed or exhausted themselves, each might have some advantages. As yet, though, few empirical studies have compared the relative resilience or robustness of each of these types of four-way settlement to different kinds of anomalies, surprises and shocks.

Nor did Verweij's and Thompson's (2006) edited volume on the concept settle the question of when, to what degree and with what vulnerability to surprises and unintended consequences four-way settlements can be deliberately planned and engineered by policy makers, particularly in situations of deep conflict when positive feedback in one or more of the forms has already erupted. If, for example, clumsy arrangements either emerge mainly without deliberate design or only in situations of fairly mild degrees of polarization, then there may be limited hope that the concept can provide a theory of *planned* conflict containment in general. Only a few of the cases examined in that volume were ones where the clumsy arrangement had resolved what had previously been a deeply violent conflict.

Nor has the performance of clumsy institutions yet been compared with other better-documented approaches for compromise, such as Lindblom's (1959, 1979) 'muddling through' and (Lindblom and

202 • *Mary Douglas*

Braybrooke, 1970 [1963]) 'disjointed incrementalism'. More fundamentally, perhaps, not all four-way settlements to conflicts need necessarily be benign. Not only moral but institutional criteria need to be
developed to avoid 'rotten' compromises (Margalit, 2010).

Perhaps equally important, much of the literature on the clumsy
institution focuses mainly on formal institutions, policies and organizations, but lacks an account of how micro-ritual engagement ensures
requisite variety. Douglas' (1972) key paper on micro-ritual processes,
'Deciphering a Meal', showed how different kinds of four-way settlement might yield viability through performance. In the feedback
models of clumsy institutions, Douglas' central insight into the crucial role played by enactment has largely been eclipsed. Thompson's
programme may show us the forms that organic solidarities might
take, but without exploring the microfoundations of the ritual order,
it is not possible to understand how those forms might be sustained.
As Durkheim (1984 [1893]) argued about the noncontractual things
on which contract rests, so too the provisional, fragile yet viable institutions of organic solidarity rest as much on ritual enactment as do
those of the ever-present mechanical solidarities.

The other possibility, apart from trying to develop particular kinds
of relations among all four elementary forms, is that there may be
some capabilities that can be cultivated within each of the forms, considered separately, for self-restraint and perhaps also for accommodation with other forms, quite apart from any restraint they might
provide upon other forms in negative feedback. This, as we have
shown in Chapter 4 above, was the strategy that Douglas decided to
pursue in her analysis of what hierarchy has to offer to the attenuation
of conflict in her later (1999b, 2004b) writings on 'the priestly work of
reconciliation'. Her concentration on hierarchy was not driven by any
claim, which would have been inconsistent with her own theory, that
hierarchy provided the optimal solution to reconciliation in any and
every context. She was very serious about her argument that her theory privileged none of the forms over any of the others. But she had
to start somewhere. She pursued the question of whether hierarchy
had its own capacities for institutional self-restraint and for reducing
appeal to other forms such as enclaving, and whether these capacities
might contribute to the more general containment or abatement of
conflict. Principally she concentrated on this task because she felt that
she had been brought up to appreciate the internal dynamics of hierarchy best and because this form had been so widely misunderstood
across the social sciences. A few of those who have drawn upon her
work have, at least implicitly, worked with the same analytic strategy,

addressing either the hierarchical ordering to which she devoted her last decade and a half or the neglected potentialities of other elementary forms.

Some of Richards' studies on the conclusions of wars in West Africa have identified, in the spirit of Douglas' (1999e) argument about the specific capacities of military hierarchies, practices of self-restraint and avoidance of provocation as a basis for ritual making of conditions for future reconciliation with defeated former enclaves. Thus, Richards (2011) shows that refraining from a final massacre at the moment of victory by diverting the emotion of collective effervescence among troops into more mundane activities of camp maintenance, and ceremonially handing over to civilian police, were vital in securing acceptance by all sides in the Nigerian civil war, when in 1970 the Biafran forces were finally overcome. In the reintegration of former RUF fighters in Sierra Leone, Richards (2010) demonstrates that key capacities within the hierarchical ordering of humanitarian organizations can be critical in opening ritual spaces, through composition of the kind defined by Douglas (2007), for the former members of enclaves to abate and attenuate their bitterness, and in which to dampen the positive feedback through which they have hitherto been moved. Nonetheless, it is an important limitation upon our aspirations for generalizing from these findings that both of these processes occurred at a point where both these conflicts had largely been fought to a standstill. These cases do not offer examples by which bloody denouement could be avoided from the midst of battle.

A small number of studies drawing upon Douglas' work have also identified capacities for self-restraint and for ritual appeal to other forms, within individualistic and enclaved ordering. In her final years, Douglas (2006a, 2006b) recognized in Gyawali's (2002) study of deep conflict in Nepal over water management issues during the 1980s a vital rebalancing to her own tendency to regard enclave as always and everywhere destructive in its tendency to sacred contagion when in deep positive feedback mode. The fact that enclaving emerged in response to (or even against) largely hierarchically and individualistically ordered business and government interests in the Nepalese conflict is no surprise. What intrigued Douglas about Gyawali's argument was that it was, of all the possible initiators, the enclaved social movement's members who were able to find ways to appeal not only to their supporters who were frustrated by the building of huge dams, but also to their opponent organizations, which were very differently ordered in ways that prevented the conflict from spiralling into catastrophic polarization. While the enclaved social movements did not achieve a negotiated compromise, the result was some articulation of concerns among rural populations, while avoiding outright violent disaster. This case perhaps suggests a combination of the first strategy, relying on Thompson's concept of a clumsy institution as a mixed arrangement (although in the Nepalese case, without a designer deliberately planning it as such) and the second strategy of both assertion and self-restraint in each form, considered separately.

Douglas (2006a, 2006b) argued that – controversially – many of the fundamentalist enclaved groups in contemporary Israel (albeit with the obvious exceptions of some violent settler groups) have sustained a degree of mildness in their relations with the Israeli state, business interests and others in the country, partly because the state has nurtured and funded them in ways that have drawn them into conversation and compromise, but also partly because they have resources within their own enclaved insistence on sacred status that have restrained what might otherwise have been tendencies toward much deeper positive feedback. Interestingly, a few scholars have found some empirical evidence that partially supports, but also qualifies, her argument. Hakak's (2009, 2011; Hakak and Rapoport, 2011) studies on the Haredi community in Israel argue that it has achieved a degree of stabilization in a comparatively mild degree of positive feedback, and that this self-restraint in accommodating both spiritual and earthly rewards within a capitalist economy is, Hakak argues, largely to be explained by capacities cultivated within the enclave.

There are fewer studies specifically devoted to individualistic ordering, and fewer still that examine its ritual interaction order when in deep conflict. Verweij (1999) argued that individualistic ordering in the management of the River Rhine in Northern Europe had enabled pragmatic agreement among partners, successfully avoiding the kinds of conflict that had dogged previous attempts to secure joint working among the several nations through which the river runs. 6 (2016a) examines the deep conflicts among the individualistically ordered rival patrons who were leading cabinet ministers in British Prime Minister Harold Wilson's second administration in the 1960s. The article shows that the very same ritual interaction order that cultivated individual squaring off and recrimination exhibiting all the hallmarks of an individualistic form of collective effervescence comprised the very same ritual practices which later sustaining a capability to strike deals both within the cabinet and with the leadership of a trades union movement under growing pressure from its enclaved shop stewards. Part of the point here is that the capacity to recognize, develop and reach for fallback options and 'reserve preferences' (things one can find worth wanting in whatever one eventually has to settle for) is a particular feature of the thought style cultivated in weakly socially integrated, weakly socially regulated settings, which enable compromise, even among hierarchically ordered and enclaved interlocutors (see, for instance, 6 (2011) on the Kennedy administration's late but rapid development of the concept of a 'trade' during the Cuban Missile Crisis).

Finally, there is one scholar, Gerald Mars, who has developed a very distinctive way of using Douglas' legacy to understand processes that turn out to be very important in conflict attenuation and abatement, although conflict was not the principal empirical subject of most of his work at all. When considered for its contribution to understanding conflict dynamics, Mars' argument appears orthogonal to both clumsy institutions and to the approach of finding capacities for self-restraint and appeal to other forms. His argument works with either of these strategies, but perhaps somewhat subversively.

Mars made his best-known contributions to social science in the field of industrial anthropology, especially his 1982 book *Cheats at Work: An Anthropology of Workplace Crime*. This developed what was perhaps the most scandalous of Durkheim's arguments – that crime is a 'normal' and 'necessary' social phenomenon (Durkheim, 1982 [1895], 97–104). Part of his argument was that crime sustained sufficient outrage among the law-abiding population to help maintain morality and solidarity (cf. Durkheim, 1984 [1893], 57–64). This claim long remained problematic among scholars because it could never be reconciled with the structural-functionalism that Talcott Parsons sought to foist retrospectively on Durkheim. For structural-functionalism, in both Radcliffe-Brown's and Parsons' formulations, rested principally on the thesis that it is the internalizing and following of norms that is somehow functional for the whole 'society', not the *violation* of those norms. Another part of Durkheim's argument was that what gets classified as crime can be seen in retrospect by people who operate under different institutions as creative. A third argument made rather briefly was that: 'Far from there being cause for congratulation when [crime] drops too noticeably below the normal level, this apparent progress assuredly coincides with and is linked to some social disturbance' (Durkheim, 1982 [1895], 102).

Mars took Durkheim's argument seriously. His detailed ethnographic analyses of crime within organizations demonstrated that very often, cheating and fiddling were quietly tolerated by managers in part to avoid latent discontent or to dampen actual conflict, either between management and workers or, just as often, between sets (not necessarily groups) of workers. Crime, Mars found, often provided the safety valve by which peace was kept, or else kept a lid kept on outright conflict (see especially Mars, 2015). Conversely, some of his studies of outright and amplifying conflict between managers and workers trace their origins to efforts to control workplace crime in ways that were not regarded as sufficiently legitimate (e.g. Mars, 2009). Efforts to crack down on fiddling, if they did not simply provoke enclave countermobilization and deepen conflict, usually had the effect, Mars (2013) showed – both for capitalist systems and for the Soviet Union – of displacing crime into other areas of the informal economy, which might operate under different institutions. The rewards from fiddles not only diverted energies but, mostly importantly, cemented each of the four forms of social organization distinguished by Douglas in crucially different ways. How was this possible? In part, Mars shows, it was achieved because crime turns out to be as much or as little an institutionalized activity channelled by weak and strong social regulation and integration as is activity that is recognized and classified as legitimate. Moreover, Mars' oeuvre (especially Mars, 2013, 2015) is replete with detailed quotations from and examination of the significance of particular strips of everyday conversation between workers, their peers and their managers, in which he attends closely to the quotidian ritual interaction order by which, performatively, quiet permission is given for crime, or through which permission is limited in various ways.

Methodologically, the breaking of rules is a case of an anomaly and, indeed, its use as a key diagnostic in Mars' work is much the same as that of the anomalous classification in Douglas' own ethnographic work. When following rule-breaking behaviour and showing the 'rules' (institutions of informal organization) it nevertheless follows, Mars is able to explain how organizations dampen conflict. Whereas Thompson argues that clumsy institutions sacrifice efficiency for the legitimacy and resilience from requisite variety and redundancy, Mars' work offers a subtler analysis. He shows that the conditions under which particular kinds of informally tolerated criminal activity themselves actually contribute to sustaining efficiency. Far from workplace crime being evidence of slack that is competed away in competitively efficient markets, Mars demonstrates that in every case, from plundering in the highest financial services to coarse fiddling in seaside town catering and amusement services, the motivations for efficient working and the specifications of the rewards required by each of Douglas' four elementary forms can be sustained in ways that dampen conflict only to the point that crime is not fully eliminated.

Mars' argument was presumably intended to be as scandalous as Durkheim's, and for the same reason. The attenuation of conflict cannot be presumed to be possible only by noble means. Mars' work suggests that a degree of acceptance of 'fiddles' is often a permanent condition for constraining conflict within organizations.

In the future, a more fully specified theory of conflict containment may emerge, combining the mechanisms of offsetting mix among the four forms, capacities for both self-restraint and an altogether less noble tolerance of a degree of corruption. Such a synthesis has yet to be attained. Even so, Douglas' legacy has been developed, extended and refined in a number of significant ways. Those who have drawn upon her work have added dynamics, modelling techniques, analytic methods, a host of specific empirical measures of social relations and thought style for both qualitative and quantitative studies, theoretical concepts such as that of the clumsy institution, and richer and more precisely specified causal mechanisms of blinkering, information rejection and provocation. The body of empirical studies using the typology is also impressive. There is every reason to celebrate these advances.

Yet it is also true that the body of work using Douglas' theory has achieved more in understanding the amplification of conflicts than in their containment and abatement. Moreover, a gulf has widened between those whose interest in her work lies mainly in her typology and those convinced by her causal theory that the performative business of everyday, mundane ritual interaction is what drives confrontation and compromise, not argumentation over ideas. It will be clear to the reader that the present authors belong to the second camp and believe that if the full promise of Douglas' arguments is to be fulfilled, the underlying Durkheimian causal engine with its institutional, anomaly-driven, performative and ritual machinery will have to be better articulated in future research.

Douglas' Theory and Douglasian Studies of Thought and Conflict

Many of those who have drawn upon Douglas' approach have presented their work as explorations of 'cultural theory' and, as we have seen, by the end of the 1980s, Douglas herself was willing to adopt the label. Critical as she could be in private of arguments put to her by scholars seeking to use to her work, rarely did she distance her own position from theirs in print. But how closely aligned were the arguments that are most central and fundamental in her thought to those developed by the scholars who sought to use her typology to explain conflict amplification? Because Douglas continued to cite her followers' work supportively even in her final years, when her own arguments were becoming more defined, the issue is less straightforward than the question historians of ideas sometimes ask, such as: 'Was Keynes a Keynesian?' Nevertheless, her writings show a marked reserve about some of the approaches taken by those seeking to apply her theory, and although in print she only hinted obliquely at differences, our reconstruction of her core argument serves to highlight some key ones.

Although in the early 1980s in her work with Hampton (1982), Douglas was interested to see what might be done to explore the theory using survey methods, in later years she grew more cautious. This stemmed not from any general objection to surveys, which have had a long and important place in the development of anthropology; rather, it was driven by a number of specific considerations.

The first was the difficulty in moving from analysis at the level of the unit of observation, the individual respondent, to the level of analysis required by her theory, namely the institutional context. Rejecting methodological individualism as Douglas did, the form of social organization in any setting, whether it is the workplace or the household or the industry or a governing executive, is not simply the aggregate sum of any aspect of individual life. The researcher cannot (for example) infer from summing up what interviewees tell her or him about their attitudes to authority that the context is a hierarchical one. We need additional information about behaviour – specifically, in respect of who holds whom accountable for what and how those being held accountable respond. Thompson et al. (1990) also pointed out that the institutions shaping behaviour may differ from those shaping answers to surveys; this they called the problem of 'stolen' or 'borrowed rhetoric'. Much depends on what the interviewee supposes the background to the survey to be. Many will assume they are answering to 'government' rather than 'science', whatever assurances to the contrary the survey interviewer may give.

More fundamentally still, Douglas regarded much of the work of justification (as in answers to questions about why we behave as we do) to be ex post facto sense making (cf. Garfinkel, 1967; Weick, 1995). People do not typically begin with a fully specified general worldview and then proceed to act in ways that implement those beliefs; rather, they make sense of what they are doing or have done by appealing to available beliefs, which they deploy in more or less coherent ways.

Explaining participation in, for instance, a massacre after the event in terms of available beliefs in ethnicity may be quite at variance with the actual performative drivers of participation. Like looters and rioters, people who kill may be caught up in the excitement of what Durkheim termed 'sacred contagion', which rests as much on bonds to fellow rioters or ethnic avengers and on styles of thought and feeling as it does on particular prior normative beliefs.

Second, by the time she wrote *How Institutions Think*, Douglas was clear that the theory explained thought style, or the manner in which people deployed whatever beliefs they might have had or used. Most surveys developed around her typology focused on substantive claims rather than on the style of thought. If social organization shapes thought, then we need data separately on each of these things. One of Douglas' concerns about survey work was that too often, the instruments asked only about thought, in the form of general attitudes, worldviews and specific judgements. Dake's and Wildavsky's (1990) scales, for example, were mainly about ideas. Too rarely did survey designers seek to ask respondents about behaviour from which accountability pressures might be inferred, or even to note the form in which particular manifestations of social relations took place, or the modalities of involvement in, or the relationships invoked by, particular quotidian ritual interactions considered as performances.

Third, many of us must move between household, workplace, wider family, friendship, leisure, voluntary associational and perhaps also worship contexts, each of which may be ordered by very different informal institutions of weak or strong social regulation and social integration. Rayner (1992) pointed out that this makes it very difficult to be sure what context to draw inferences about from responses to general attitudes and worldviews and specific preferences or judgements, unless surveys are designed very specifically to direct respondents only to think about one context, and if the survey is physically administered in a contextually relevant locale, such as at home or in an office or church. Douglas herself thought that typically people would seek and perhaps find some individual-level consistency, but admitted that this would vary markedly. However, too many surveys were designed on the assumption that the individual held fixed and given views independent of context, which is precisely what Douglas' theory fundamentally denied.

In the years since Douglas' death, these issues have been worried over in greater detail. Notably, Olli (2012) set out a sophisticated argument about the various ways in which individual units of observation might be related to institutional units of analysis. But his solution for survey work continued to focus on worldview and measuring bias in judgements rather than on efforts to capture social relations. So far, there has been only limited work on the Maussian approach advocated by Douglas of trying to capture the institution through mapping its networks of ceremonial exchanges and quotidian ritual transactions, independently of the ideas and interpretations entertained by its members.

Although these three considerations were clearest with respect to survey design, Douglas had similar concerns about qualitative work. Talk of natural persons as, for example, 'individualists', 'hierarchists' or 'enclavists' turned her theory into one focused on reconstructing people's ideas. Indeed, she was often scathing about interpretivism and constructivism, the approaches most often invoked by qualitative researchers to justify confining efforts to reconstructing informants' beliefs, classifications, worldviews, assumptions, etc. (cf. 6 and Bellamy, 2016). This recapitulated the mistake of the methodological individualists, who used surveys to measure attitudes. Both approaches are ideational, not institutional. Neither engages with explaining how people think by reference to how they are organized. Both mistake the measurement of the extent of disagreement in ideas for an explanation of the depth of conflict. Nor were qualitative researchers less vulnerable to becoming prisoners of cross-sectional data, because very often qualitative studies also collect data only at a point in time, leaving us unable to tell from an observed degree of divergence in ideas whether the gulf is widening or narrowing.

These issues are fundamentally theoretical. They are not simply disagreements about method. They have to do with the basis of Douglas' explanation that in particular contexts, the informal institutions of social organization cultivate and shape styles of thought rather than the worldview as much through retrospective sense making as through prior belief.

Was Douglas, then, a 'cultural theorist' about the amplification of conflict? She used the label 'culture' to persuade those in those social sciences who had taken a cultural 'turn' in the 1980s of her arguments about thought styles, but in many cases, she did not succeed. Many remained committed to methodological individualism or at least to Wildavsky's (1987) theory that worldviews explain particular judgements. The debates about survey design were not fundamentally about method or the design of questions. They were really about whether 'cultural theory' would become the Durkheimian, causally looping, institutionalist, performative theory Douglas wanted it to be, or whether it would become a typology of worldviews underpinned either by a psychological theory of pre-given individual dispositions (as Kahan argues) or by a constructivist, interpretivist theory of a limited number of available political frameworks held to be matters of belief and driving particular judgements. If 'cultural theory' has by now become a label for a theory of individual dispositions or a typology of worldviews, then it follows that Douglas' explanation of conflict amplification was not at all that of a 'cultural theorist'. Equally, it implies that the work of testing Douglas' profound theory regarding the nature of social institutions has hardly yet begun.

Douglas' Legacy and the Durkheimian Programme in the Social Sciences

For the social sciences, Douglas' intellectual legacy matters because it represents the most ambitious attempt made in recent decades to demonstrate the explanatory potential of the Durkheimian programme.

Now that there is growing disillusion even within the heartlands of economics with purely methodologically individualistic rational choice models, and now that the high tides of postmodernism and interpretivism have passed, so that the notion that human thought can float free of the ways in which people are organized no longer seems plausible to many scholars, there is growing interest across anthropology, sociology, political science, development studies, business and management studies, and history in a return to causally explanatory, realist approaches that accept the central importance of social relations and social institutions in shaping bias, decision, action and response.

But more than methodology and epistemology is at stake. We have argued that Douglas provided one of the most profound understandings yet achieved in the social sciences of the roots of human conflict in human thought, but also went on to offer an account of how conflict can be contained and channelled into more civil forms of tension.

Douglas' mature argument is that to understand the viability and resilience of institutions and strategies, the analyst needs to take account of the full range of ways of organizing and disorganizing, and not just whatever organizational forms happen to be, at any one point, pre-eminent in the markets or among political leaders or voters. To apprehend that full range, Douglas built on Durkheim's two analytic dimensions of social regulation and social integration (1951 [1897]), or to use his later (1961 [1925]) and simpler, but perhaps too psychological terms, 'discipline' and 'attachment'. These analytic parameters have been refined but hardly improved upon in more than a century. Taking off from this analytic standpoint, Douglas showed how the ways in which we are organized lead us to make assumptions about our interlocutors, our problems and our opportunities, and that in turn this yields a social dynamic that assumes patterned form amidst instability and fluidity. Her neo-Durkheimian emphasis on substantive styles of agency in performed ritual interaction is both an impressive achievement and also an agenda with much potential for empirical social research on institutions and conflict.

Douglas has been much misunderstood as a structuralist, as a functionalist (Spickard, 1991), as a symbolist believing that cultural ideas drive social relations (Wuthnow et al., 1984, 77–132), as a believer in 'group minds', as a cultural relativist (Spiro, 1968; Skorupski, 1979a, 1979b), as a determinist turning people into 'cultural dopes' (Boholm, 1996), as a crude typologist without a theory (Marsh et al., 2001), as a static comparativist without a theory of dynamics (Bellaby, 1990). In this book, we have tried to clear away much of this misunderstanding as serving only to obscure the importance of her central message about institutions and conflict. These misunderstandings are not dissimilar to those that once plagued the reception of Durkheim's work. Recent scholarship has made clear that Durkheim never did make a turn towards idealism and symbolism, but remained committed to a performative explanation, in which practices explain thought (Rawls, 2004). His theory was not structural-functionalism *avant la lettre*, requires no mystical group minds and took agency so seriously that it sought to explain its forms (Alexander and Smith, 2005). It also provided a rich body of causal mechanisms for explaining historical change without crude progressive evolutionism (Emirbayer, 1996). Douglas' arguments are Durkheimian in precisely these ways. There is a performative dynamic running through the works of both these theorists.

Douglas' social theory, as a body of rigorously argued explanatory theory, is neither saturnine nor sanguine about the prospects for organic solidarity, by which we mean a series of shifting and provisional settlements among the conflicting yet mutually dependent elementary forms of human social organization. Being entirely free of Marxist dualism, Douglas saw few good arguments for separating pessimism of the intellect from optimism of the will, to use Gramsci's phrase. She argued that social science should undertake the most dry-eyed explanations of conflict and breakdown, and avoid bringing moral preferences into the analysis of the merits and demerits of each of the rival elementary forms, as each brings its own disorganization, and even, as Mars demonstrated, its own peculiar modes of corruption. Her central insight that to explain human thought is to explain human conflict heavily qualifies the hopes of other kinds of 'realism' for a 'critical' (Bhaskar, 1993) or 'emancipatory' social science (Habermas 1972, [1968]). No epistemological basis for social science will deliver us from injustice. Douglas' theory is a sober one, insisting on tradeoffs, compromise and the inevitability of anomaly and of countervailing responses to the claims of each of the elementary forms. This is no simple claim of 'value-neutrality'. The fierce moral commitment of her late (2004a) piece on 'traditional culture' and poverty should convince any sceptic that she understood more clearly than most scholars the difference between neutrality *in* explanation and neutrality *of* explanation.

Douglas' argument for constant attention to the rites of reconciliation is based on a theory about why there is no coming era of perpetual peace. Her own brand of realism requires us to address an endemically conflicted social world, though manifestly she felt there were better and worse ways of living with what we have, and that anthropological insight never came amiss. Bombing embittered enclaved groups into oblivion will not succeed and will only provoke more countermobilization, as she told the British political magazine *The Spectator* in 2007, in one of her last public utterances a few days before she died.

In sum, then, Douglas' legacy offers the social sciences a rigorous body of theory of astonishing range, profundity, distinctiveness and philosophical merit to overcome problems that bedevil the major frameworks dominating social scientific debate. Perhaps as important, from her own perspective, is a point we have tried to emphasize throughout this book. Douglas offered her theory not in support of ideals or of vested interests, but in support of the only kind of society she thought possible – complex, messy, endlessly conflictual, but less chaotic, violent and suicidal than it might otherwise have been. This is society that achieves recurrent, temporary settlement between its varied and competing institutional forms. In short, it is – up to a point or, more exactly, up to four elementary points – society that works.

Coda

The first author of this book saw Douglas for the last time shortly before she moved from her Highgate home. Shedding possessions, she gave him her copy in the original French of Durkheim's *Lettres à tous les Français (Letters to the whole French people)* (Durkheim and Lavisse, 1916), which were among the very last of his writings before his untimely death in 1917. The letters are entirely concerned, as we should expect, with the Great War. Durkheim regarded the war as an analytic problem for social science, even though he had moral as well as intellectual reasons for selecting it for attention.

It is with the last words of the opening letter that we will conclude (Durkheim and Lavisse, 1916, 31–32). Although we do not know exactly when it was drafted, Durkheim published the letter after hearing on 10 January 1916 that his son, André, was missing in the melée of the retreat from Serbia, and perhaps after April, when he received the confirmation of André's death.

His words serve well to summarize the challenge that Douglas's work presents to social scientists today trying to develop accounts of the ways in which complex dynamics in different kinds of institutions can cultivate styles of human thought that sustain conflict amplification and disorganization, but can also contribute to the attenuation and channelling of conflict:

> Thus the watchwords which we have adopted are self-explanatory: patience, determination, trust. In themselves, these themes provide no novel reassurance. But it appears to us that it is useful to present in the clearest terms, free from all external considerations, a kind of chart and also the principal facts which that chart explains. Having constructed that chart, it can serve us as a stable counterweight for the changing emotions which the vicissitudes of conflict elicit in us. In these difficult times, we can use it for honest description. We can even find in it some reliable reasons for hope. And indeed at any time, it will recall in us the need for the greatest, the most energetic and persistent commitment.

In responding to this, his final ambition, Douglas was not merely Durkheim's faithful disciple, but the author of a profound and creative scheme of her own for assessing the vicissitudes of conflict in our tightly packed world of competing institutional loyalties.

References

Cited Works by Mary Douglas

Douglas, M. 1951. 'A Form of Polyandry among the Lele of the Kasai', *Africa* 21(1): 1–12.

Douglas, M. 1955. 'Social and Religious Symbolism of the Lele of Kasai', *Zaire* 9(4): 385–402.

Douglas, M. 1957. 'Animals in Lele Religious Symbolism', *Africa* 27(1): 46–58.

Douglas, M. 1958. 'Raffia Cloth Distribution in the Lele Economy', *Africa* 28(2): 109–22.

Douglas, M. 1960. 'Blood Debts and Clientship among the Lele', *Journal of the Royal Anthropological Institute* 90(1): 1–28.

Douglas, M. 1962. 'Lele Economy Compared with the Bushong: A Study of Economic Backwardness', in P. Bohannan and G. Dalton (eds), *Markets in Africa*. Evanston: Northwestern University Press, 211–233.

Douglas, M. 1964. 'Matriliny and Pawnship in Central Africa', *Africa* 34(4): 301–13.

Douglas, M. 1966. *Purity and Danger: An Analysis of Concepts of Pollution and Taboo.* London: Routledge.

Douglas, M. 1969. 'Is Matriliny Doomed in Africa?', in M. Douglas and P. Kaberry (eds), *Man in Africa*. London: Tavistock, pp. 123–37.

Douglas, M. 1970a. *Natural Symbols: Explorations in Cosmology.* London: Routledge.

Douglas, M. 1970b. 'Introduction: Thirty Years after *Witchcraft, Oracles and Magic*', in M. Douglas (ed.), *Witchcraft Confessions and Accusations*. London: Tavistock, pp. xiii–xxxviii.

Douglas, M. 1972. 'Deciphering a Meal', *Daedalus* 101(1): 61–82, reprinted in M. Douglas, *Implicit Meanings: Selected Essays in Anthropology*, 2nd edn. London: Routledge, 1999. pp. 231–51.

Douglas, M. (ed.). 1973a. *Rules and Meanings: The Anthropology of Everyday Knowledge – Selected Readings.* Harmondsworth: Penguin.

Douglas, M. 1973b. 'Techniques of Sorcery Control in Central Africa', in *Implicit Meanings: Selected Essays in Anthropology*, 2nd edn. London: Routledge, 1999, pp. 63–76.

Douglas M (ed.). 1973c. *Food in the Social Order: Studies of Food and Festivities in Three American Communities*. London: Routledge.

Douglas, M. 1975a. *Implicit Meanings: Selected Essays in Anthropology*. London: Routledge.

Douglas, M. 1975b. 'In the Nature of Things', in *Implicit Meanings: Selected Essays in Anthropology*. London: Routledge, pp. 276–318.

Douglas, M. 1977 [1963]. *The Lele of the Kasai*, 2nd edn. Oxford: Oxford University Press for the International African Institute.

Douglas, M. 1979. 'World View and the Core', in S.C. Brown (ed.), *Philosophical Disputes in the Social Sciences*. Brighton: Harvester Press, pp. 177–87.

Douglas, M. 1980. *Evans-Pritchard*. Brighton: Harvester Press.

Douglas, M. 1982a [1978]. 'Cultural Bias', in *In the Active Voice*. London: Routledge & Kegan Paul, pp. 183–254.

Douglas, M. (ed.) 1982b. *Essays in the Sociology of Perception*. London: Routledge & Kegan Paul.

Douglas, M. 1982c. *In the Active Voice*. London: Routledge & Kegan Paul.

Douglas, M. 1982d. 'Passive Voice Theories in Religious Sociology', in *In the Active Voice*. London: Routledge & Kegan Paul, pp. 1–15.

Douglas, M. 1985. *Risk Acceptability According to the Social Sciences*. London: Routledge & Kegan Paul.

Douglas, M. 1986. *How Institutions Think*. London: Routledge & Kegan Paul.

Douglas, M. 1987. *Constructive Drinking: Perspectives on Drink from Anthropology*. Cambridge: Cambridge University Press.

Douglas, M. 1989a. 'The Hotel Kwilu – A Model of Models', *American Anthropologist* 91(4): 855–65, reprinted in M. Douglas, *Risk and Blame: Essays in Cultural Theory*. London: Routledge, 1992. pp. 295–313.

Douglas, M. 1989b. 'The Background of the Grid Dimension: A Comment [Reply to Spickard, 1989]', *Sociological Analysis* 50(2): 171–76.

Douglas, M. 1990. 'Foreword: No Free Gifts', in M. Mauss, *The Gift: The Form and Reason for Exchange in Archaic Societies*. trans. W.D. Halls. New York: W.W. Norton & Co., pp. vii–xviii.

Douglas, M. 1992a. *Risk and Blame: Essays in Cultural Theory*. London: Routledge.

Douglas, M. 1992b. 'Rightness of Categories', in M. Douglas and D. Hull (eds), *How Classification Works: Nelson Goodman among the Social Sciences*. Edinburgh: Edinburgh University Press, 239–271.

Douglas, M. 1992c. 'Comment on Van Beek (1992)', *Current Anthropology* 32(2): 161–62.

Douglas, M. 1993a. *In the Wilderness: The Doctrine of Defilement in the Book of Numbers*. Oxford: Oxford University Press.

Douglas, M. 1993b. 'Emotion and Culture in Theories of Justice', *Economy and Society* 22(4): 501–15.

Douglas, M. 1996a. 'Sacred Contagion', in J.F.A. Sawyer (ed.), *Reading Leviticus: Responses to Mary Douglas*. Sheffield, MA: Sheffield Academic Press, pp. 86–106.

Douglas, M. 1996b. *Thought Styles: Critical Essays on Good Taste*. London: Sage.

Douglas, M. 1997. 'Knowing the Code', *Demos Collection 12*, London: Demos, 13–14, reprinted in R. Fardon, 2013b, *Mary Douglas: A Very Personal Method – Anthropological Writings Drawn from Life*. London: Sage, pp. 211–15.

Douglas, M. 1999a [1975]. *Implicit Meanings: Selected Essays in Anthropology*, 2nd edn. London: Routledge.

Douglas, M. 1999b. *Leviticus as Literature*. Oxford: Oxford University Press.

Douglas, M. 1999c. 'Sorcery Accusations Unleashed: The Lele Revisited, 1987', *Africa* 69(2): 177–93, reprinted in M. Douglas, *Implicit Meanings: Selected Essays in Anthropology*, 2nd edn. London: Routledge, 1999. pp. 77–94.

Douglas, M. 1999d. 'Culture Clash in American Anthropology' (Review of Kuper, A. 1998. *Culture: The Anthropologists' Account*: Cambridge, MA: Harvard University Press), *Nature* 400: 631.

Douglas, M. 1999e. 'Four Cultures: The Evolution of a Parsimonious Model', *GeoJournal* 47: 411–15.

Douglas, M. 2000. 'Deep Thoughts on the Forbidden: Review of Valeri [2000]', *Science* 289(5488): 2288–90.

Douglas, M. 2004a. 'Traditional Culture: Let's Hear No More about it', in V. Rao and M. Walton (eds), *Culture and Public Action*. Stanford: Stanford University Press, pp. 85–108.

Douglas, M. 2004b. *Jacob's Tears: The Priestly Work of Reconciliation*. Oxford: Oxford University Press.

Douglas, M. 2004c. 'Reply by Mary Douglas, Book Review Forum on Mary Douglas's *Leviticus as Literature*', *Journal of Ritual Studies* 18(2): 152–91.

Douglas, M. 2005. 'A Feeling for Hierarchy', in J.L. Heft (ed.), *Believing Scholars: Ten Catholic Intellectuals*. New York: Fordham University Press, pp. 94–120.

Douglas, M. 2006a. 'A History of Grid and Group Cultural Theory', published at http://projects.chass.utoronto.ca/semiotics/cyber/douglas1.pdf

Douglas, M. 2006b. 'Seeing Everything in Black and White', published at http://projects.chass.utoronto.ca/semiotics/cyber/douglas2.pdf

Douglas, M. 2007. *Thinking in Circles: An Essay on Ring Composition*. New Haven: Yale University Press.

Douglas, M. 2010. 'Preface', in *Purity and Danger: An Analysis of the Concepts of Pollution and Taboo*, Hebrew edition, tr. Sela Y, Tel Aviv: Resling Publishing, pp. 7–15.

Douglas, M. and Hull, D. (eds) 1992. *How Classification Words: Nelson Goodman among the Social Sciences*. Edinburgh: Edinburgh University Press.

Douglas, M. and Isherwood, B. 1979. *The World of Goods: Towards an Anthropology of Consumption*. London: Routledge.

Douglas, M. and Mars, G. 2003. 'Terrorism: A Positive Feedback Game', *Human Relations* 56(7): 763–86.

Douglas, M. and Ney, S. 1998. *Missing Persons: A Critique of Personhood in the Social Sciences*. Berkeley and New York: University of California Press and Russell Sage Foundation.

Douglas, M. and Wildavsky, A. 1982. *Risk and Culture: An Essay on the Selection of Technological and Environmental Dangers*. Berkeley: University of California Press.

Fardon, R. 2013a. *Mary Douglas: Cultures and Crises – Understanding Risk and Resolution*. London: Sage.
Fardon, R. 2013b. *Mary Douglas: A Very Personal Method – Anthropological Writings Drawn from Life*. London: Sage.

Other Works Cited in the Text

6, P. 2002a. 'Who Wants Privacy Protection, and What Do They Want?', *Journal of Consumer Behaviour* 2(1): 80–100.
6, P. 2002b. 'What is There to Feel? A Neo-Durkheimian Theory of the Emotions', *European Journal of Psychotherapy, Counselling and Health* 5(3): 263–90.
6, P. 2003. 'Institutional Viability: A Neo-Durkheimian Theory', *Innovation: The European Journal of Social Science Research* 16(4): 395–416.
6, P. 2004. *E-governance: Styles of Political Judgement in the Information Age Polity*. Basingstoke: Palgrave Macmillan.
6, P. 2006. 'Viable Institutions and the Scope for Incoherence', in L. Daston and C. Engel (eds), *Is There Value in Inconsistency?* Baden-Baden: Nomos, pp. 299–354.
6, P. 2007. 'Mary Douglas', in J. Scott (ed.), *Fifty Key Sociologists: The Contemporary Theorists*. London: Routledge, pp. 63–69.
6, P. 2011. *Explaining Political Judgement*. Cambridge: Cambridge University Press.
6, P. 2014a. 'Explaining Decision Making in Government: The Neo-Durkheimian Institutional Framework', *Public Administration* 92(1): 87–103.
6, P. 2014b. 'Explaining Unintended and Unexpected Consequences of Policy Decisions: Comparing Three British Governments, 1959–74', *Public Administration* 92(3): 673–91.
6, P. 2014c. 'Elementary Forms and Their Dynamics: Revisiting Mary Douglas', *Anthropological Forum* 24(3): 287–307.
6, P. 2015a. 'If Governance is Everything, Maybe it's Nothing', in A. Massey and K. Johnston (eds), *The International Handbook of Public Administration and Governance*. Cheltenham: Edward Elgar, pp. 56–80.
6, P. 2015b. 'Explaining Styles of Political Judgement in British Government: Comparing Isolation Dynamics 1959–74', *Journal of Public Policy* 36(2), 219–250.
6, P. 2015c. 'Quiet Unintended Transitions? A Neo-Durkheimian Explanation of Puzzling Institutional Change', *Journal of Organisational Change Management* 28(5): 770–90.
6, P. 2016a. 'How "Natives" Work: Political Judgement and Cohesion through Ritual Interaction among Ministers', *Public Administration* 94(4), 1005–1022.
6, P. 2016b. 'Opportunistic Decision-Making in Government: Concept Formation, Variety and Explanation', *International Review of Administrative Sciences*, doi: 10.1177/0020852315595279.
6, P., and Bellamy, C. 2012. *Principles of Methodology: Research Design in Social Science*. London: Sage.

6, P., and Bellamy, C. 2016. 'The Inadequacy of Interpretivism: Accounting for Britain's Failure to "Number the People"', in N. Turnbull (ed.), *Interpreting Governance, High Politics, and Public Policy Essays Commemorating Interpreting British Governance*. London: Routledge, pp. 151–71.

6, P., Bellamy, C., Raab, C.D., Warren, A. and Heeney, C. 2007. 'Institutional Shaping of Inter-agency Working: Managing Tensions between Collaborative Working and Client Confidentiality', *Journal of Public Administration Research and Theory* 17(3): 405–34.

6, P. Goodwin, N., Peck, E. and Freeman, T. 2006. *Managing Networks of Twenty-First Century Organizations*. Basingstoke: Palgrave Macmillan.

6, P., and Mars, G. (eds). 2008. *The Institutional Dynamics of Culture: The New Durkheimians*, vols I and II. Farnham: Ashgate.

Alexander, J., Giesen, B., Munch, R. and Smelser, N. (eds). 1987. *The Micro-Macro Link*. Berkeley: University of California Press.

Alexander, J.C., and Smith, P. 1996. 'Social Science and Salvation: Risk Society as Mythical Discourse', *Zeitschrift für Soziologie* 25(4): 251–62.

Alexander, J.C., and Smith, P. (eds). 2005. *The Cambridge Companion to Durkheim*. Cambridge: Cambridge University Press.

Allison, G.T. 1971. *Essence of Decision: Explaining the Cuban Missile Crisis*, Boston, MA: Little, Brown.

Allison, G.T., and Zelikow, P. 1999 [1971]. *Essence of Decision: Explaining the Cuban Missile Crisis*, 2nd edn. New York: Addison Wesley Longman.

Almond, G., and Verba, S. 1963. *The Civic Culture: Political Attitudes and Democracy in Five Nations*. Boston, MA: Little, Brown & Co.

Archer, M. 2000. *Being Human: The Problems of Agency*. Cambridge: Cambridge University Press.

Archibald, S. and Richards, P. 2002. 'Converts to Human Rights? Popular Debate about War and Justice in Rural Central Sierra Leone'. *Africa* 72(3), 339–367.

Ashby, W.R. 1956. *An Introduction to Cybernetics*. London: Chapman & Hall, now available online. Retrieved 20 November 2016 from http://pespmc1.vub.ac.be/books/IntroCyb.pdf.

Bale, T. 1999. *Sacred Cows and Common Sense: The Symbolic Statecraft and Political Culture of the British Labour Party*. Aldershot: Ashgate.

Banfield, E.C. with Fasano Banfield, L. 1958. *The Moral Basis of a Backward Society*. New York: Free Press.

Barnes, R.H. 1985. 'Hierarchy without Caste', in R.H. Barnes, D. de Coppet and R.J. Parkin (eds), *Contexts and Levels: Anthropological Essays on Hierarchy*, JASO Occasional Paper No 4. Oxford: *Journal of the Anthropological Society of Oxford*, pp. 8–20.

Baumgarten, A. 1985. 'The Torah as a Public Document in Judaism', *Studies in Religion* 14: 17–24.

Baumgarten, A. 2016. 'Sacred Scriptures Defile the Hands', *Journal of Jewish Studies* 67(1): 46–67.

Baumgarten, A. Forthcoming. *Dame Mary Douglas (1921–2007): An Appreciation*.

Beall, J. 2006. 'Dealing with Dirt and the Disorder of Development: Managing Rubbish in Urban Pakistan', *Oxford Development Studies* 34(1): 81–97.

Béland, D., and Cox, R.H. (eds). 2011. *Ideas and Politics in Social Science Research*. Oxford: Oxford University Press.

Bell, C. 1992. *Ritual Theory, Ritual Practice*. Oxford: Oxford University Press.

Bell, D. 1976. *The Cultural Contradictions of Capitalism*. New York: Basic Books.

Bellaby, P. 1990. 'To Risk or Not to Risk? Uses and Limitations of Mary Douglas on Risk-Acceptability for Understanding Health and Safety at Work and Road Accidents', *Sociological Review* 38: 465–83.

Bellah, R.N. 1985. *Habits of the Heart: Individualism and Commitment in American Life*. Berkeley: University of California Press.

Bellamy, C.A., 6, P., Raab, C.D., Warren, A. and Heeney, C. 2008. 'Information-Sharing and Confidentiality in Social Policy: Regulating Multi-agency Working', *Public Administration* 86(3): 737–59.

Bernstein, B. 1971. *Class, Codes and Control, Vol 1: Theoretical Studies Towards a Sociology of Language*. London: Routledge & Kegan Paul.

Bernstein, B. 1975 [1966]. *Class, Codes and Control, Vol 3: Towards a Theory of Educational Transmissions*, 2nd edn. London: Routledge & Kegan Paul.

Bernstein, P.L. 1996. *Against the Gods: The Remarkable Story of Risk*. New York: John Wiley & Sons.

Bhaskar, R. 1993. *Dialectic: The Pulse of Freedom*. London: Verso.

Bloor, D. 1991 [1976]. *Knowledge and Social Imagery*, 2nd edn. Chicago: University of Chicago Press.

Blyth, M. 1997. '"Any More Bright Ideas?" The Ideational Turn in Comparative Political Economy', *Comparative Politics* 29(1): 229–50.

Boholm, A. 1996. 'Risk Perception and Social Anthropology', *Ethnos* 61(1–2): 64–84.

Bueno de Mesquita, B. 2009. *Predictioneer: One Who Uses Maths, Science and the Logic of Brazen Self-Interest to See and Shape the Future*. London: Bodley Head.

Bulmer, R. 1967. 'Why is the Cassowary Not a Bird? A Problem of Zoological Taxonomy among the Karam of the New Guinea Highlands', *Man* (NS) 2: 5–25.

Burton, J. (ed.). 1990. *Conflict: Human Needs Theory*. London: Macmillan.

Byrne, D. 1998. *Complexity Theory and the Social Sciences*. London: Routledge.

Calvert, R.L. 1995. 'Rational Actors, Equilibrium and Social Institutions', in J. Knight and I. Sened (eds), *Explaining Social Institutions*. Ann Arbor: University of Michigan Press, pp. 57–94.

Cherkaoui, M. 2008. *Durkheim and the Puzzle of Social Complexity*. Oxford: Bardwell Press.

Cohen, S. 2002 [1972]. *Folk Devils and Moral Panics: The Creation of the Mods and Rockers*, 3rd edn. London: Routledge.

Collier, P., and Hoeffler, A. 2000. *Greed and Grievance in Civil War*. World Bank Policy Research Working Paper 2355. Washington DC: World Bank.

Collins, R. 1986. *Weberian Sociological Theory*. Cambridge: Cambridge University Press.

Collins, R. 1999. *Macrohistory: Essays in the Sociology of the Long Run*. Stanford: Stanford University Press.

Collins, R. 2004. *Interaction Ritual Chains*, Princeton: Princeton University Press.

Corbin, A. 1998. *Village Bells: Sound and Meaning in the Nineteenth Century French Countryside*, trans. M. Thom. New York: Columbia University Press.

Coughlin, R.M., and Lockhart, C. 1998. 'Grid-Group Theory and Political Ideology: A Consideration of Their Relative Strengths and Weaknesses for Explaining the Structure of Mass Belief Systems', *Journal of Theoretical Politics* 10(1): 33–58.

Coyle, D.J. 1994a. '"This Land is Your Land, This Land is My Land": Cultural Conflict in Environmental and Land-Use Regulation', in D.J. Coyle and R.J. Ellis (eds), *Politics, Policy and Culture*, Boulder: Westview Press, 33–50.

Coyle, D.J. 1994b. 'The Theory that Would Be King', in D.J. Coyle and R.J. Ellis (eds), *Politics, Policy and Culture*, Boulder: Westview Press, pp. 219–39.

Coyle, D.J., and Ellis, R.J. (eds). 1994. *Politics, Policy and Culture*. Boulder: Westview Press.

Cross I, 2003. 'Music and Biocultural Evolution', in M. Clayton, T. Herbert and R. Middleton (eds), *The Cultural Study of Music: A Critical Introduction*. London: Routledge, pp. 19–30.

D'Andrade, R. and Strauss, C. (eds). 1992. *Human Motives and Cultural Models*. Cambridge: Cambridge University Press.

Dake, K. and Wildavsky, A. 1990. 'Theories of Risk Perception: Who Fears What and Why?', *Daedalus* 119(3): 41–60.

Davy, B. 1997. *Essential Injustice: When Legal Institutions Cannot Resolve Environmental and Land Use Disputes*. Vienna: Springer.

Dukes, E.F. 1996. *Resolving Public Conflict: Transforming Community and Governance*. Manchester: Manchester University Press.

Dumont, L. 1980 [1966]. *Homo Hierarchicus: The Caste System and its Implications*. Chicago: University of Chicago Press.

Dunn, D.J. 2004. *From Power Politics to Conflict Resolution: The Work of John W. Burton*. Basingstoke: Palgrave Macmillan.

Durkheim, É. 1915, *'Germany above all': German Mentality and War*, trans. 'JS'. Paris: Armand Colin.

Durkheim, É. 1951 [1897]. *Suicide: A Study in Sociology*, trans. J.A. Spaulding and G. Simpson. London: Routledge & Kegan Paul.

Durkheim, É. 1961 [1925]. *Moral Education: A Study in the Theory and Application of the Sociology of Education*, trans. E.K. Wilson and H. Schnurer. New York: Free Press.

Durkheim, É. 1973. 'Individualism and the Intellectuals', in R.N. Bellah (ed.), *Émile Durkheim on Morality and Society*. Chicago: University of Chicago Press, pp. 43–57.

Durkheim, É. 1977 [1938]. *The Evolution of Educational Thought: Lectures on the Formation and Development of Secondary Education in France*, trans. P. Collins. London: Routledge & Kegan Paul.

Durkheim, É. 1982 [1895]. *'The Rules of the Sociological Method' and Selected Texts on Sociology and its Method*, trans. W.D. Halls. London: Macmillan.

Durkheim, É. 1984 [1893]. *The Division of Labour in Society*, trans. W.D. Halls. London: Macmillan.

Durkheim, É. 1995 [1912]. *The Elementary Forms of Religious Life*, trans. K. Fields. New York: Free Press.

Durkheim, É., and Lavisse, E. 1916. *Lettres à tous les Français*. Paris: Armand Colin.

Durkheim, É., and Mauss, M. 1963 [1902–3]. *Primitive Classification*, trans. Needham R. Chicago: University of Chicago Press.

Edelman, M. 1985 [1967]. *The Symbolic Uses of Politics*, 2nd edn. Urbana: University of Illinois Press.

Elster, J. 1983. *Explaining Technical Change: A Case Study in the Philosophy of Science*. Cambridge: Cambridge University Press.

Emirbayer, M. 1996. 'Durkheim's Contribution to the Sociological Analysis of History', *Sociological Forum* 11(2): 263–84.

Eriksson, L. 2011. *Rational Choice Theory: Potential and Limits*. Basingstoke: Palgrave Macmillan.

Evans-Pritchard, E. 1940, *The Nuer*. Oxford: Oxford University Press.

Evans-Pritchard, E. 1965, *Theories of Primitive Religion*. Oxford: Clarendon Press.

Fardon, R. 1987. 'The Faithful Disciple: On Mary Douglas and Durkheim', *Anthropology Today* 3(5): 4–6.

Fardon, R. 1999. *Mary Douglas: An Intellectual Biography*. London: Routledge.

Fardon, R. 2010. 'Margaret Mary Douglas, 1921–2007', *Proceedings of the British Academy* 166: 135–58.

Fardon, R. 2013c. 'Citations out of Place or Lord Palmerston Goes Viral in the Nineteenth Century But Gets Lost in the Twentieth', *Anthropology Today* 29(1): 25–26.

Finnegan, R. 2012 [1970]. *Oral Literature in Africa*. Cambridge: Open Book Publishers.

Fiske, A.P. 1990. 'Relativity within Moose ("Mossi") Culture: Four Incommensurable Models for Social Relationships', *Ethos* 18(2) 180–204.

Fiske, A.P. 1991. *Structures of Social Life: The Four Elementary Forms of Human Relations*. New York: Free Press.

Fiske, A.P. 1992. 'The Four Elementary Forms of Sociality: Framework for a Unified Theory of Social Relations', *Psychological Review* 99(4): 689–723.

Flanagan, J.G., and Rayner, S. (eds). 1988. *Rules, Decisions and Inequality in Egalitarian Societies*. Aldershot: Avebury.

Fleck, L. 1979 [1935]. *Genesis and Development of a Scientific Fact*, trans. F. Bradley and T.J. Trenn. Chicago: University of Chicago Press.

Fraenkel, E. 1941. *The Dual State: A Contribution to the Theory of Dictatorship*, trans. E.A. Shils with E. Lowenstein and K. Knorr. Oxford: Oxford University Press.

Freud, S. 1917. 'The Taboo of Virginity', in *Collected Works: Standard Edition*. London: Hogarth Press , pp. 191–208.

Frevel, C., and Nihan, C. 2013. 'Introduction', in C. Frevel and C. Nihan (eds), *Purity and the Forming of Religious Traditions in the Ancient Mediterranean World and Ancient Judaism*. Leiden: Brill, pp. 1–46.

Fuchs, S. 2001. *Against Essentialism: A Theory of Culture and Society*. Cambridge, MA: Harvard University Press.

Garfinkel, H. 1967. *Studies in Ethnomethodology*. Englewood Cliffs, NJ: Prentice Hall.

Gauvain, R. 2005. 'Ritual Rewards: A Consideration of Three Recent Approaches to Sunni Purity Law', *Islamic Law and Society* 12(3): 333–93.

Geertz, G. 1973. *The Interpretation of Cultures*. London: HarperCollins.

Girard, R., and Smith, J. 1987. *Violent Origins*. Stanford: Stanford University Press.

Gluckman, M. 1955. *Custom and Conflict in Africa*. Oxford: Blackwell.

Goffman, E. 1959, *The Presentation of Self in Everyday Life*. Harmondsworth: Penguin.

Goffman, E. 1967a. *Interaction Ritual: Essays on Face-to-Face Behaviour*. New York: Pantheon.

Goffman, E. 1967b [1956]. 'The Nature of Deference and Demeanour, in *Interaction Ritual: Essays on Face-to-Face Behaviour*. New York, Pantheon, pp. 47–96.

Goodman, N. 1970. 'Seven Strictures against Similarity', in L. Foster and J. Swanson (eds), *Experience and Theory*. Boston, MA: University of Massachusetts Press.

Goodman, N. 1978. *Ways of Worldmaking*. Indianapolis: Hackett Publishing.

Goody, J. 2010. *Myth, Ritual and the Oral*. Cambridge: Cambridge University Press.

Grendstad, G., and Sundback, S. 2003. 'Socio-demographic Effects on Cultural Biases: A Nordic Study of Grid-Group Theory', *Acta Sociologica* 46(4): 289–306.

Grendstad, G. 2000. 'Grid-Group Theory and Political Orientations: Effects of Cultural Biases in Norway in the 1990s', *Scandinavian Political Studies* 23(3): 217–44.

Grendstad, G. 2001. 'Nordic Cultural Baselines: Accounting for Domestic Convergence and Foreign Policy Divergence', *Journal of Comparative Policy Analysis* 3(1): 5–29.

Grendstad, G. 2003a. 'Reconsidering Nordic Party Space', *Scandinavian Political Studies* 26(3): 193–217.

Grendstad, G. 2003b. 'Comparing Political Orientations: Grid-Group Theory versus the Left–Right Dimension in the Five Nordic Countries', *European Journal of Political Research* 42(1): 1–21.

Grijspaarde, H., Voors, M., Bulte, E., and Richards, P. 2013. 'Who Believes in Witches? Institutional Flux in Sierra Leone'. *African Affairs* 112/446: 22–47.

Gross, J.L., and Rayner, S. 1986. *Measuring Culture: A Paradigm for the Analysis of Social Organization*. New York: Columbia University Press.

Guyer, J.I. 2004. *Marginal Gains: Monetary Transactions in Atlantic Africa*. Chicago: University of Chicago Press.

Gyawali, D. 2002. *Water in Nepal*. Kathmandu: Himal Books.

Habermas, J. 1972 [1968]. *Knowledge and Human Interests*. London: Heinemann.

Hakak, Y., and Rapoport, T. 2011. 'Equality or Excellence in the Name of God? The Case of Ultra-orthodox Enclave Education in Israel', *Journal of Religion* 92(2): 251–76.

Hakak, Y. 2009. 'Holy Amnesia: Remembering Religious Sages as Super Humans or as Simply Human', *Contemporary Jewry* 29(3): 215–40.

Hakak, Y. 2011. 'Egalitarian Fundamentalism: Preventing Defection in the Israeli Haredi Community', *Journal of Contemporary Religion* 26(2): 291–310.

Hall, P.A. 1993. 'Policy Paradigms, Social Learning and the State: The Case of Economic Policymaking in Britain', *Comparative Politics* 25(3): 275–96.

Halperin, M., and Clapp, P.A. with Kanter, A. 2006 [1974]. *Bureaucratic Politics and Foreign Policy*, 2nd edn. Washington DC: Brookings Institution Press.

Hampton, J. 1982. 'Giving the Grid / Group Dimensions an Operational Definition', in M. Douglas (ed.), *Essays in the Sociology of Perception*. London: Routledge and Kegan Paul, pp. 64–82.

Hargreaves Heap, S., and Ross, A. (eds). 1992. *Understanding the Enterprise Culture*. Edinburgh: University of Edinburgh Press.

Harris, E.L. 2006. 'Mary Douglas's Typology of Grid and Group', in V.A. Anfara and N.T. Mertz (eds), *Theoretical Frameworks in Qualitative Research*. Thousand Oaks: Sage, 129–54.

Harris, M. 2001 [1979]. *Cultural Materialism: The Struggle for a Science of Culture*. Walnut Creek: Altamira.

Hay, C. 2002. *Political Analysis: A Critical Introduction*. Basingstoke: Macmillan.

Hay, C. 2009. 'King Canute and the "Problem" of Structure and Agency: On Times, Tides and Heresthetics', *Political Studies* 57(2): 260–79.

Hayden, R.M. 1996. 'Imagined Communities and Real Victims: Self-Determination and Ethnic Cleansing in Yugoslavia', *American Ethnologist* 23(4): 783–801.

Hayes, C. 2002. *Gentile Impurities and Jewish Identities*. Oxford: Oxford University Press.

Heald, S., Grabbe, L.L., Handelman, D., Segal, A.F. and Hendel, R.S. 2004. 'Book Review Forum on Mary Douglas's *Leviticus as Literature*', *Journal of Ritual Studies* 18(2): 152–91.

Hebdige, D. 1979. *Subculture: The Meaning of Style*. London: Routledge.

Heclo, H., and Wildavsky, A. 1974. *The Private Government of Public Money: Community and Policy inside British Politics*. London: Macmillan.

Hendriks, F. 2010. *Vital Democracy: A Theory of Democracy in Action*. Oxford: Oxford University Press.

Hirsch, F. 1976. *The Social Limits to Growth*: Cambridge, MA: Harvard University Press.

Hood, C.C. 1998. *The Art of the State: Culture, Rhetoric and Public Management*. Oxford: Oxford University Press.

Horton, R. 1967. 'African Traditional Thought and Western Science', *Africa* 37(2): 155–187.

Hubert, H. 1999 [1905]. *Essay on Time: A Brief Study of the Representation of Time in Religion and Magic*, trans. R. Parkin and J. Redding. Oxford: Durkheim Press.

Hume, D. 1969 [1739–40]. *A Treatise of Human Nature*, ed. E.C. Mossner. Harmondsworth: Penguin.

Huntington, S.P. 1996. *The Clash of Civilizations*. New York: Simon and Schuster.

Ingram, D., Tayler, P. and Thompson, M. 2012. 'Surprise, Surprise from Neoclassical Economics to E-life', *ASTIN Bulletin: Journal of the International Actuarial Association* 42(2): 389–411.

Jabri, V. 1996. *Discourses on Violence: Conflict Analysis Reconsidered*. Manchester: Manchester University Press.

Janis, I.L. 1982 [1972]. *Groupthink: Psychological Studies of Policy Decisions and Fiascos*, 2nd edn. Boston, MA: Houghton Mifflin.

Jervis, R. 1997. *System Effects: Complexity in Political and Social Life*. Princeton: Princeton University Press.

Jones, R.A. 1999. *The Development of Durkheim's Social Realism*. Cambridge: Cambridge University Press.

Kahan, D., Jenkins-Smith, H. and Braman, D. 2011. 'Cultural Cognition of Scientific Consensus', *Journal of Risk Research* 14(2): 147–74.

Kahan, D., Slovic, P., Braman, D. and Gastil, J. 2006. 'Fear of Democracy: A Cultural Critique of Sunstein on Risk', *Harvard Law Review* 119: 1071–109.

Kahneman, D. 2011. *Thinking, Fast and Slow*. Harmondsworth: Penguin.

Kahneman, D., Slovic, P. and Tversky, A. (eds). 1982. *Judgement under Uncertainty: Heuristics and Biases*. Cambridge: Cambridge University Press.

Kahneman, D., and Tversky, A. (eds). 2000. *Choices, Values and Frames*. Cambridge: Cambridge University Press.

Kincaid, H. 1990. 'Assessing Functional Explanations in the Social Sciences', *PSA: Proceedings of the Biennial Meeting of the Philosophy of Science Association* I: 341–54.

Kincaid, H. 1996. *Philosophical Foundations of the Social Sciences: Analysing Controversies in Social Research*. Cambridge: Cambridge University Press.

Kingdon, J. 1995 [1984]. *Agendas, Alternatives and PublicPpolicies*, 2nd edn. New York: HarperCollins.

Klawans, J. 2001. 'Pure Violence: Sacrifice and Defilement in Ancient Israel', *Harvard theological Review* 94(2): 133–55.

Klawans, J. 2003. 'Rethinking Leviticus and Rereading *Purity and Danger*', *Association for Jewish Studies Review* 27(1): 89–101.

Knight, F. 1921. *Risk, Uncertainty and Profit*. Boston, MA: Hart, Schaffner & Marx; Houghton Mifflin.

Kristeva, J. 1982 [1980]. *The Powers of Horror: An Essay on Abjection*, trans. L.S. Roudiez. New York: Columbia University Press.

Larsen, T. 2014. *The Slain God: Anthropologists and the Christian Faith*. Oxford: Oxford University Press.

Latham, A.J.H. 1998. *Rice: The Primary Commodity*. London: Routledge.

Lawrence, T.B., Suddaby, R. and Leca, B. (eds). 2009. *Institutional Work: Actors and Agency in Institutional Studies of Organizations*. Cambridge: Cambridge University Press.

Leach, E. 1954, *Political Systems of Highland Burma*. London: Athlone Press.

Lemos, T.M. 2009. 'The Universal and the Particular: Mary Douglas and the Politics of impurity', *Journal of Religion* 89(2): 236–51.

Levitsky, S. 1998. 'Institutionalization and Peronism: The Concept, the Case, and the Case for Unpacking the Concept', *Party Politics* 4(1): 77–92.

Lewis, I. 1991. 'The Spider and the Pangolin', *Man* (NS) 26(3): 513–25.

Lienhardt, R.G. 1961. *Divinity and Experience: The Religion of the Dinka*. Oxford: Oxford University Press.

Lindblom, C.E. 1959. 'The Science of "Muddling through"', *Public Administration* 19(2): 78–88.

Lindblom, C.E. 1979. 'Still Muddling, Not Yet through', *Public Administration* 39(4):517–26.

Lindblom, C.E., and Braybrooke, D.E. 1970 [1963]. *A Strategy of Decision: Policy Evaluation as a Social Process*. New York: Free Press.

Lipsky, M. 1980. *Street-Level Bureaucracy: Dilemmas of the Individual in Public Services*. New York: Russell Sage Foundation.

Little, D. 1998. *Microfoundations, Methods, and Causation: On the Philosophy of the Social Sciences*. New Brunswick: Transaction Publishers.

Lockhart, C. 1999. 'Cultural Contributions to Explaining Institutional Form, Political Change and Rational Decisions', *Comparative Political Studies* 32: 862–93.

MacMillan, M. 2001. *Peacemakers: The Paris Conference of 1919 and its Attempt to End War*. London: John Murray.

Mahoney, J., and Thelen, K (eds). 2010. *Explaining Institutional Change: Ambiguity, Agency and Power*. Cambridge: Cambridge University Press.

Mannheim, K. 1936, *Ideology and Utopia: An Introduction to the Sociology of Knowledge*, trans. L. Wirth L and E. Shils. San Diego: Harcourt Brace & Co.

Margalit, A. 2010. *On Compromise and Rotten Compromises*. Princeton: Princeton University Press.

Margetts, H., 6, P. and Hood, C.C. (eds). 2010. *Paradoxes of Modernization: Unintended Consequences of Public Policy Reform*. Oxford: Oxford University Press.

Marris, C., Langford, I.H. and O'Riordan, T. 1998. 'A Quantitative Test of the Cultural Theory of Risk Perceptions: Comparison with the Psychometric Paradigm', *Risk Analysis* 18: 635–47.

Mars, G. 1982. *Cheats at Work: An Anthropology of Workplace Crime*. Aldershot: Dartmouth.

Mars, G. 2009. 'East End Warehouse: A Case Study of "Organizational Capture" and Cultural Conflicts', *Culture and Organization* 15(3–4): 237–56.

Mars, G. 2013. *Locating Deviance: Crime, Change and Organizations*. Aldershot: Ashgate.

Mars, G. 2015. *Becoming an Anthropologist: A Memoir and a Guide to Anthropology*. Newcastle upon Tyne: Cambridge Scholars Publishing.

Marsh, D., Richards, D. and Smith, M.J. 2001. *Changing Patterns of Governance in the United Kingdom: Reinventing Whitehall*. Basingstoke: Palgrave Macmillan.

Martin, P.J. and Dennis, A. (eds). 2010. *Human Agents and Social Structures*. Manchester: Manchester University Press.

Mauss, M. 1990 [1950]. *The Gift: The Form and Reason for Exchange in Archaic Societies*, trans. W.D. Halls. New York: W.W. Norton & Co.

Mauss, M., with Beuchat, H. 1979 [1904–5]. *Seasonal Variations of the Eskimo: A Study in Social Morphology*, trans. J.J. Fox. London: Routledge & Kegan Paul.

McClymond, K. 2008. *Beyond Sacred Violence: A Comparative Study of Sacrifice*. Baltimore: Johns Hopkins University Press.

McDermott, R. 1998. *Risk Taking in International Politics: Prospect Theory in American Foreign Policy*. Ann Arbor: University of Michigan Press.

Montefiore, S.S. 2003. *Stalin: The Court of the Red Tsar*. London: Weidenfeld & Nicolson.

Moore, J.D. 1997. *Visions of Culture: An Introduction to Anthropological Theories and Theorists*. Walnut Creek: Altamira.

Moran, M. 2003. *The British Regulatory State: High Modernism and Hyper-Innovation*. Oxford: Oxford University Press.

Nelkin, D. 1982. 'Blunders in the Business of Risk', *Nature* 298: 775–76.

Netting, R. 1993. *Smallholders, Householders: Farm Families and the Ecology of Intensive, Sustainable Agriculture*. Stanford: Stanford University Press.

Ney, S. 2000. 'Are You Sitting Comfortably? … Then We'll Begin: Three Gripping Policy Stories about Pension Reform', *Innovation* 13(4): 341–71.

North, D.C. 1990. *Institutions, Institutional Change and Economic Performance*. Cambridge: Cambridge University Press.

Ohnuki-Tiernay, E. 1981. 'Phases in Human Perception/Conception/Symbolization Processes: Cognitive Anthropology and Symbolic Classification', *American Ethnologist* 8(3): 451–67.

Olli, E. 2012. 'Rejected Cultural Biases Shape Our Political Views: A Migrant Household Study and Two Large-Scale Surveys', Ph.D. dissertation. Bergen: University of Bergen, Norway. Retrieved 20 November 2016 from http://www.eero.no/publ/olli_2012_thesis_rejected_cultural_biases_shape_our_political_views.pdf.

Ostrander, D. 1982. 'One- and Two-Dimensional Models of the Distribution of Beliefs', in M. Douglas (ed.), *Essays in the Sociology of Perception*. London: Routledge & Kegan Paul, pp. 14–30.

Ouchi, W.G. 1980. 'Markets, Bureaucracies and Clans', *Administrative Sciences Quarterly* 25: 129–41.

Parker, G. 2013. *Global Crisis: War, Climate Change and Catastrophe in the Seventeenth Century*. New Haven: Yale University Press.

Peck, E., and 6, P. 2006. *Beyond Delivery: Policy Implementation as Sense-Making and Settlement*. Basingstoke: Palgrave Macmillan.

Peck, E., 6, P., Gulliver, P. and Towell, D. 2004. 'Why Do We Go on Meeting Like This? The Board as Ritual in Health and Social Care', *Health Services Management Research* 17: 100–9.

Pettit, P. 2000. 'Rational Choice, Functional Selection and Empty Black Boxes', *Journal of Economic Methodology* 7(1): 33–57.

Pierson, P. 2004. *Politics in Time: History, Institutions and Social Analysis*. Princeton, NJ: Princeton University Press.

Price, M. and Thompson, M. 1997. 'The Complex Life: Human Land Uses in Mountain Eco-systems', *Global Ecology and Biogeography Letters* 6: 77–90.

Pronyk, P., Rogers, B., Lee, S., Bhatnagar, A., Wolman, Y., Monasch, R., Hipgrave, D., Salama, P., Kucharski, A. Chopra, M. and on behalf of the UNICEF Sierra Leone Ebola Response Team. 2016. 'The Effect of Community-Based Prevention and Care on Ebola Transmission in Sierra Leone', *American Journal of Public Health* 106(4): 727–32.

Pruitt, D.G., and Carnevale, P.J. 1993. *Negotiation in Social Conflict*. Buckingham: Open University Press.

Przeworski, A., and Teune, H. 1970. *The Logic of Comparative Social Inquiry*. New York: Wiley.

Putnam, R.E. 2015. *Our Kids: The American Dream in Crisis*. New York: Simon & Schuster.

Quine, W.V.O. 1960. *Word and Object*. Cambridge, MA: Massachusetts Institute of Technology Press.

Radano, R. 2003. *Lying up a Nation: Race and Black Music*. Chicago: University of Chicago Press.

Rai, T., and Fiske, A.P. 2011. 'Moral Psychology is Relationship Regulation: Moral Motives for Unity, Hierarchy, Equality and Proportionality', *Psychological Review* 118(1): 57–75.

Rappaport, R.A. 1999. *Ritual and Religion in the Making of Humanity*. Cambridge: Cambridge University Press.

Rawls, A.W. 2004. *Epistemology and Practice: Durkheim's 'The Elementary Forms of Religious Life'*. Cambridge: Cambridge University Press.

Rayner, S. 1982. 'The Perception of Time and Space in Egalitarian Sects: A Millenarian Cosmology', in M. Douglas (ed.), *Essays in the Sociology of Perception*. London: Routledge and Kegan Paul, pp. 247–274.

Rayner, S. 1986a. 'Management of Radiation Hazards in Hospitals: Plural Rationalities in a Single Institution', *Social Studies of Science* 16: 573–91.

Rayner, S. 1986b, 'The Politics of Schism: Routinization and Social Control in the International Socialists/Socialist Workers' Party', in J. Law (ed.), *Power, Action and Belief: A New Sociology of Knowledge?* London: Routledge & Kegan Paul, pp. 46–67.

Rayner, S. 1988. 'The Rules That Keep Us Equal: Complexity and the Costs of Egalitarian Organization', in J.G. Flanagan and S. Rayner (eds), *Rules, Decisions and Inequality in Egalitarian Societies*. Aldershot: Avebury, pp. 20–42.

Rayner, S. 1992. 'Cultural Theory and Risk Analysis', in S. Krimsky and D. Golding (eds), *Social Theories of Risk*. Westport: Praeger, pp. 83–116.

Renn, O. 1992. 'Concepts of Risk: A Clarification', in S. Krimsky and D. Golding (eds), *Social Theories of Risk*. Westport: Praeger, pp. 53–79.

Richards, P. 1996. *Fighting for the Rain Forest: War, Youth and Resources in Sierra Leone*. Oxford: James Currey.

Richards, P. 1999. 'New Political Violence in Africa: Secular Sectarianism in Sierra Leone', *GeoJournal* 47: 433–42.

Richards, P. 2005. 'War as Smoke and Mirrors: Sierra Leone 1991–2, 1994–5, 1995–6', *Anthropological Quarterly* 78(2): 377–402.

Richards, P. 2007. 'The Emotions at War: A Musicological Approach to Understanding Atrocity in Sierra Leone', in P. 6, S. Radstone, C. Squire and A. Treacher (eds), *Public Emotions*. Basingstoke: Palgrave Macmillan, pp. 62–84.

Richards, P. 2009. 'Against Ethnicity: Ring Composition and Conflict Resolution (In Memoriam Dame Mary Douglas, 1921–2007)', *Focaal* 54: 3–15.

Richards, P. 2010. 'Ritual Dynamics in Humanitarian Assistance', *Disasters* 34(S2): S138–S146.

Richards, P. 2011. 'Sacred Contagion: Cults of War in Nigeria and Sierra Leone Compared', in E. Jul-Larsen, P.-J. Laurent P.-Y. Le Meur and E. Léonard (eds), *Une anthropologie entre pouvoirs et histoire: conversations autour de l'oeuvre de Jean-Pierre Chaveau*. Paris: APAD-IRD-Karthala, pp. 535–551.

Richards, P. 2012. 'Mining and the Messiah: War and the Masterless Classes in Sierra Leone', in K. Werthmann and T. Graetz (eds), *Mining Frontiers in Africa: Anthropological and Historical Perspectives*. Cologne: Rüdiger Köppe Verlag, pp. 55–72.

Richards, P. 2013. 'Elementary Forms of War: Performative Aspects of Youth Militia in Sierra Leone', in S. Hausner (ed.), *Durkheim in Dialogue: A Centenary Celebration of 'The Elementary Forms of Religious Life'*. New York: Berghahn Books, pp. 67–85.

Richards, P. 2016. *Ebola: How a People's Science Helped End an Epidemic*. London: Zed Books.

Richman, M.H. 2002. *Sacred Revolutions: Durkheim and the Collège de Sociologie*. Minneapolis: University of Minnesota Press.

Riesman, D., with Glazer, N. and Denney R. 1961. *The Lonely Crowd: A Study of the Changing American Character*. New Haven, CT: Yale University Press.

Ripberger, J.T., Jenkins-Smith, H.C. and Herron, K.G. 2011. 'How Cultural Orientations Create Shifting National Security Coalitions on Nuclear Weapons and Terrorist Threats in the American Public', *PS* 44(4): 715–19.

Room, G. 2011. *Complexity, Institutions and Public Policy: Agile Decision-Making in a Turbulent World*. Cheltenham: Edward Elgar.

Rosenthal, J.-L. 1998. 'The Political Economy of Absolutism Reconsidered', in R.H. Bates, A. Greif, M. Levi, J.-L. Rosenthal and B.R. Weingast (eds), *Analytic Narratives*. Princeton: Princeton University Press, pp. 64–108.

Ross, M.H. 1993. *The Management of Conflict: Interpretations and Interests in Comparative Perspective*. New Haven: Yale University Press.

Sahlins, M. 1976. *Culture and Practical Reason*. Chicago: University of Chicago Press.

Sahlins, M. 2003 [1972]. *Stone Age Economics*. London: Tavistock.

Sawyer, J.F.A. (ed.). 1996. *Reading Leviticus: Responses to Mary Douglas*. Sheffield, MA: Sheffield Academic Press.

Schapiro, M. 1988. 'Judicial Selection and the Design of Clumsy Institutions', *Southern California Law Review* 61: 1555–69.

Schatzki, T. 1996. *Social Practices: A Wittgensteinian Approach to Human Activity and the Social*. Cambridge: Cambridge University Press.

Schluchter, W. 1981 [1979]. *The Rise of Western Rationalism: Max Weber's Developmental History*, trans. G. Roth. Berkeley: University of California Press.

Schmitt, R. 2008. 'The Problem of Magic and Monotheism in the Book of Leviticus', *Journal of Hebrew Scriptures* 8, doi: 10.5508/jhs.2008.v8,a11.

Schmutzer, M., and Bandler, W. 1980. 'Hi and Low – in and out: Approaches to Social Status', *Journal of Cybernetics* 10: 283–99.

Schwarz, M., and Thompson, M. 1990. *Divided We Stand: Redefining Politics, Technology and Social Choice*. Philadelphia: University of Pennsylvania Press.

Scott, W.R. 1995. *Institutions and Organizations*. Thousand Oaks: Sage.

Scruton, R. 2012. *Green Philosophy: How to Think Seriously about the Planet*. London: Atlantic.

Sennett, R. 2012. *Together: The Rituals, Pleasures and Politics of Cooperation*. New Haven: Yale University Press.

Shin, D.C., Chey, M. and Kim, K.-W. 1989. 'Cultural Origins of Public Support for Democracy in Korea: An Empirical Test of the Douglas-Wildavsky Theory of Culture', *Comparative Political Studies* 22(2): 217–38.

Shove, E., Panzar, M. and Watson, M. 2012. *The Dynamics of Social Practice: Everyday Life and How it Changes*. London: Sage.

Simon, H. 1983. *Reason in Human Affairs*. Stanford: Stanford University Press.

Simon, H. 1996. *Sciences of the Artificial*, 3rd edn: Cambridge, MA: Massachusetts Institute of Technology Press.

Sjöberg, L. 1997. 'Explaining Risk Perception: An Empirical and Quantitative Evaluation of Cultural Theory', *Risk, Decision and Policy* 2: 113–30.

Sjöberg, L. 2003. 'Distal Factors in Risk Perception', *Journal of Risk Research* 3: 187–211.

Skorupski, J. 1979a. 'Pangolin Power', in S.C. Brown (ed.), *Philosophical Disputes in the Social Sciences*. Brighton: Harvester Press, pp. 151–76.

Skorupski, J. 1979b. 'Our Philosopher Replies', in S.C. Brown (ed.), *Disputes in the Social Sciences*. Brighton: Harvester Press, pp. 188–94.

Slovic, P., Fischhoff, B., Lichtenstein, S. and Roe, F.J.C. 1981. 'Perceived Risk: Psychological Factors and Social Implications (and Discussion)'. *Royal Society Proceedings A: Mathematical and Physical Sciences* 376(1764): 17–34.

Smith, J.Z. 1987. *To Take Place: Toward Theory in Ritual*. Chicago: University of Chicago Press.

Smith, M. 1952, 'The Common Theology of the Ancient Near East', *Journal of Biblical Literature* 71(3): 135–47.

Spickard, J.V. 1989. 'A Guide to Mary Douglas's Three Versions of Grid/Group Theory', *Sociological Analysis* 50(2): 150–70.

Spickard, J.V. 1991. 'A Revised Functionalism in the Sociology of Religion: Mary Douglas's Recent Work', *Religion* 21(2): 141–64.

Spiro, M., 1968, Religion and Myth: Review of M. Douglas, 1966, *Purity and Danger: An Analysis of Concepts of Pollution and Taboo*, New York: Praeger, *American Anthropologist*, 70(2) 391–393.

Staal, F. 1990. *Rules without Meaning*. Toronto Studies in Religion, 4. San Francisco: Peter Land.

Stern, J.P. 1984 [1975]. *Hitler: The Führer and the People*. London: Fontana.

Stinchcombe, A.L. 1986. 'Rationality and Social Structure: An Introduction', in *Stratification and Organization: Selected Papers*. Cambridge: Cambridge University Press, pp. 1–29.

Stinchcombe, A.L. 1990. *Information and Organizations*. Berkeley, CA: University of California Press.

Strenski, I. 2006. 'Durkheim Sings: Teaching the "New Durkheim" on Religion', in *The New Durkheim*. New Brunswick: Rutgers University Press, pp. 229–48.

Tambiah, S.J. 1969. 'Animals are Good to Think and Good to Prohibit', *Ethnology* 7: 423–59.

Taylor, C. 2007. *A Secular Age*. Cambridge, MA: Harvard University Press.

Thacher, D., and Rein, M. 2004. 'Managing Value Conflict in Public Policy', *Governance* 17(4): 457–86.

Thompson, M. 1979. *Rubbish Theory: The Creation and Destruction of Value*. Oxford: Oxford University Press.

Thompson, M. 1982a. 'A Three-Dimensional Model', in M. Douglas (ed.), *Essays in the Sociology of Perception*. London: Routledge & Kegan Paul, pp. 31–63.

Thompson, M. 1982b. 'The Problem of the Centre: An Autonomous Cosmology', in M. Douglas (ed.), *Essays in the Sociology of Perception*. London: Routledge & Kegan Paul, pp. 302–28.

Thompson, M. 1992. 'The Dynamics of Cultural Theory and Their Implications for the Enterprise Culture', in S. Hargreaves Heap and A. Ross (eds), *Understanding the Enterprise Culture: Themes in the Work of Mary Douglas*. Edinburgh; Edinburgh University Press, pp. 182–202.

Thompson, M. 1996. *Inherent Relationality: An Anti-dualist Approach to Institutions*. Bergen: LOS Senteret, University of Bergen.

Thompson, M. 1997a. 'Rewriting the Precepts of Policy Analysis', in R.J. Ellis and M. Thompson (eds), *Culture Matters: Essays in Honour of Aaron Wildavsky*. Boulder: Westview Press, pp. 203–16.

Thompson, M. 1997b. 'Cultural Theory and Integrated Assessment', *Environmental Modelling and Assessment* 2: 139–50.

Thompson, M. 2008. *Organising and Disorganising: A Dynamic and Non-linear Theory of Institutional Emergence and its Implications*. Axminster: Triarchy Press.

Thompson, M., Ellis, R.J. and Wildavsky, A. 1990. *Cultural Theory*. Boulder: Westview Press.

Thompson, M., and Rayner, S. 1998. 'Risk and Governance, Part I: The Discourses of Climate Change', *Government and Opposition* 33: 139–66.

Thompson, M., Rayner, S. and Ney, S. 1998. 'Risk and Governance, Part II: Policy in a Complex and Plurally Perceived World', *Government and Opposition* 33: 330–54.

Thompson, M., Warburton, M. and Hatley, T. 2007 [1986]. *Uncertainty on a Himalayan Scale*. Kathmandu: Himal Books.

Thompson, M., and Wildavsky, A. 1986. 'A Cultural Theory of Information Bias in Organizations', *Journal of Management Studies* 23(3): 273–86.

Thucydides, 1954. *History of the Peloponnesian War*, trans. R. Warner. Harmondsworth: Penguin.

Turner, V. 1969. *The Ritual Process: Structure and Anti-structure*. Chicago: Aldine De Gruyter.

Valeri, V. 2000. *The Forest of Taboos: Morality, Hunting and Identity among the Huaulu of the Moluccas*. Madison: University of Wisconsin Press.

Van Beek, W. 1992. 'Dogon Revisited: A Field Evaluation of the Work of Marcel Griaule [and Comments and Replies]'. *Current Anthropology* 32(2): 139–67.

Vansina, J. 1979 [1969]. 'The Bushong Poison Ordeal', in M. Douglas and P.M. Kaberry (eds), *Man in Africa*. New York: Anchor Books, pp. 245–61.

Vansina, J. 1990. *Paths in the Rainforests: Toward a History of Political Tradition in Equatorial Africa*. London: James Currey.

Verweij, M., and Thompson, M. (eds). 2006. *Clumsy Solutions for a Complex World: Governance, Politics and Plural Perceptions*. Basingstoke: Palgrave Macmillan.

Verweij, M. 1999. 'A Watershed on the Rhine: Changing Approaches to International Environmental Cooperation', *GeoJournal* 47(3): 453–61.

Verweij, M. 2011. *Clumsy Solutions for a Wicked World: How to Improve Global Governance*. Basingstoke: Palgrave Macmillan.

Verweij, M., Douglas, M., Ellis, R., Engel, C., Hendriks, F., Lohmann, S., Ney, S., Rayner, S. and Thompson, M. 2006. 'Clumsy Solutions for a Complex World: The Case of Climate Change', *Public Administration* 84(4): 817–43.

Vick, B.E. 2014. *The Congress of Vienna: Power and Politics after Napoleon*. Cambridge, MA: Harvard University Press.

Wallace-Hadrill, A. (ed.). 1989. *Patronage in Ancient Society*. London: Routledge.

Weber, M. 1978, *Economy and Society: An Outline of Interpretive Sociology*, 2 vols, trans. G. Roth and C. Wittich. Berkeley: University of California Press.

Weick, K.E. 1995. *Sensemaking in Organizations*. London: Sage.

Wildavsky, A. 1964, *The Politics of the Public Budgetary Process*. Boston, MA: Little, Brown & Co.

Wildavsky, A. 1979. *Speaking Truth to Power: The Art and Craft of Policy Analysis*. Boston, MA: Little, Brown & Co.

Wildavsky, A. 1987. 'A Cultural Theory of Responsibility', in Lane, J-E. (ed), *Bureaucracy and Public Choice*. London: Sage, pp. 283–293.

Wildavsky, A. 1989. 'If Institutions Have Consequences, Why Don't We Hear about Them from Moral Philosophers?', *American Political Science Review* 84(4): 1343–50.

Wildavsky, A. 1994. 'Why Self-Interest Means Less Outside of a Social Context: Cultural Contributions to a Theory of Rational Choices', *Journal of Theoretical Politics* 6: 131–59.

Wildavsky, A. 1998. *Culture and Social Theory*, ed. S.-K. Chai and B. Swedlow. New Brunswick: Transaction Publishers.

Wildavsky, A. Fogerty, D. and Jeanrenaud, C. 1998. 'At Once Ubiquitous and Elusive, the Concept of Externalities Is Either Vacuous or Misapplied', in A. Wildavsky, *Culture and Social Theory*, ed. S.-K. Chai and B. Swedlow. New Brunswick: Transaction Publishers, pp. 55–84.

Williamson, O.E. 1985. *The Economic Institutions of Capitalism: Firms, Markets, Relational Contracting*. New York: Free Press.

Winkler, I., Háden, G., Ladinig, O., Sziller, I. and Honing, H. 2009. 'Newborn Infants Detect the Beat in Music', *Proceedings of the National Academy of Sciences* 106(H. 7): S2468–S2471.

Wuthnow, R., Hunter, J.D., Bergeson, A. and Kurzweil, E. 1984. *Cultural Analysis: The Work of Peter L. Berger, Mary Douglas, Michel Foucault and Jürgen Habermas*. London: Routledge.

Zamoyski, A. 2007. *Rites of Peace: The Fall of Napoleon and the Congress of Vienna*. London: HarperCollins.

Zuesse, E.M. 1979. *Ritual Cosmos: The Sanctification of Life in African Religion*. Athens, OH: Ohio University Press.

Index

9 781785 335617